THE TEXTUAL TRANSMISSION
OF THE NEW TESTAMENT

TEXT-CRITICAL STUDIES

Juan Hernández Jr., General Editor

Editorial Board:

Deirdre N. Fulton
Todd R. Hanneken
Roderic L. Mullen
W. Andrew Smith

Number 16

THE TEXTUAL TRANSMISSION OF THE NEW TESTAMENT

Manuscripts, Variants, and Authority

Juan Chapa

Translated by
Juan Hernández Jr.

Atlanta

Copyright © 2025 by SBL Press

All rights reserved. No part of this work may be reproduced or transmitted in any form or by any means, electronic or mechanical, including photocopying and recording, or by means of any information storage or retrieval system, except as may be expressly permitted by the 1976 Copyright Act or in writing from the publisher. Requests for permission should be addressed in writing to the Rights and Permissions Office, SBL Press, 825 Houston Mill Road, Atlanta, GA 30329 USA.

Library of Congress Control Number: 2025946704

Cover art is a reproduction of a miniature from *Avis pour faire le passage d'outre-mer*, fifteenth century (MS 9095, folio1). Image copyright © by the Royal Library of Belgium, Brussels. Used with permission.

Contents

Translator's Preface	vii
Sigla and Abbreviations	xi
Introduction	1
The Witnesses	9
Variants That Matter	45
Critical Concern to Establish the Text	71
Variants, the Living Text, and Textual Fluidity	95
Translations as a Living Text	117
Early Christian Book Production and Canon	133
The Question of the Authoritative Text	157
Conclusion: The Text in the Church	177
Bibliography	191
Biblical References Index	221
Manuscripts Index	224
Modern Authors Index	227

Translator's Preface

Producing an English translation of Juan Chapa's *La transmisión textual del Nuevo Testamento: Manuscritos, variantes, autoridad* is not a project I had ever imagined taking up. In fact, the existence of this kind of book had never even crossed my mind—that is, until a prepublished version of the study landed on my desk for peer review. It was the first time I would encounter (and deeply engage) a book-length treatment of the complexities of the New Testament's textual transmission from a Catholic perspective. That it was undertaken not only by a premier papyrologist but also by an Opus Dei priest was all the more intriguing and added an undeniable gravitas to the project. I learned more than I would have imagined from the task.

The book was not originally slated for translation. My task was simply to offer a careful review of the Spanish edition before its publication by Ediciones Sígueme. It was immediately apparent upon reading it, however, that the work merited as broad an audience as possible. Not only had several textual critics expressed an interest in an English translation, but it was also clear that Chapa's work struck a different chord from those that resonate within today's text-critical circles. The work serves to contribute a series of Catholic notes to the chorus of Protestant voices in the field. As such, it fills a lacuna in contemporary text-critical conversations. Translations rights were thus sought, and the translation work begun in earnest in March 2024. It was completed a year later.

Readers will encounter more than the "Scripture and tradition" mantra associated with Catholicism in this book. Chapa offers nuanced discussions of many of the text-critical topics that currently occupy the field: debates over the dating of New Testament papyri, the preference for the codex, the liturgical use of texts, the presence of *nomina sacra*, textual variants, establishing the New Testament text, problems with the term *original*, and the challenge of textual fluidity. The distinctives of a Catholic perspective emerge more clearly in discussions of textual authority and the relationship between the text, the canon, and the rule of faith. The Old Latin, the Vulgate, and the Neo-Vulgate are also fully integrated into the text-critical conversation. As such, the work models an approach that attempts to bypass the asymptomatic curve textual critics face in their pursuit of an elusive original. For Chapa, the original is the text read *in ecclesia* and in line with the *regula fidei*.

The original Spanish version of Chapa's work has been thoroughly revised and updated in the present translation. *The Textual Transmission of the New Testament: Manuscripts, Variants, and Authority* is, in many respects, a fully transformed work, the product of a full and extensive collaboration between author and translator. Every item subject to translation, revision, and updating was thoroughly discussed and decided on jointly. The distinctive Catholic voice and details of the work, of course, remain those of the author, while the English prose, framing, revisions, and expansions were initiated by the translator but undertaken collaboratively. The objective was to render as clearly and fairly as possible a Catholic perspective on text-critical matters and questions of textual authority for a broader audience. The fact that today readers and communities of various stripes—both ancient and modern—are readily recognized for their critical roles in shaping and understanding sacred texts makes this a propitious moment for the appearance of such a work.

The collaborative scope of this project, of course, extends well beyond the author and translator. We are indebted to a number of friends, colleagues, and textual experts who have generously offered their critical reflections, feedback, and corrections and thereby improved the work considerably. Among these are the textual critics who live and breathe the jots and tittles of the text: Elijah Hixson, Michael W. Holmes, Peter Malik, Gregory S. Paulson, and Elizabeth Schrader Polczer. We were also fortunate to have received guidance from Mark Reasoner and William M. Wright IV, two Catholic scholars who ensured the material was presented faithfully and accurately, as well as from Robert von Thaden Jr., friend, trusted colleague, and careful reader, who improves whatever he sets his eyes on. Finally, a word of thanks to Maya Phillips and Johanna Johnson, two exceptionally bright students who somehow manage to spot what seasoned scholars may miss.

None of this, of course, would have been possible without long stretches of time to undertake the arduous task of translation. Hours of uninterrupted duration are required nearly daily for successful execution. My greatest debt of gratitude on this score is therefore reserved for

Brannin and Tanya Pitre, who, along with Doris and Terry Looper, have generously invested in my scholarship over the years and have facilitated (yet again) the production of a project with their unfailing support. The community of laborers therefore extends well beyond those who work a project at various levels to those who provide the space and the means for its production. Such achievements are impossible without them.

Ad maiorem Dei gloriam
Juan Hernández Jr.

Sigla and Abbreviations

*	indicates the original reading when a correction has been made
1 Apol.	Justin, *Apologia i*
ℵ	01, Codex Sinaiticus
A	02, Codex Alexandrinus
AAG	Aramaeo-Arabica et Graeca
ABD	Freedman, David Noel, ed. *Anchor Bible Dictionary*. 6 vols. Doubleday, 1992.
AJP	*American Journal of Philology*
ANTF	Arbeiten zur neutestamentlichen Textforschung
arm	Armenian
ASBT	Acadia Studies in Bible and Theology
ASE	*Annali di Storia dell'Esegesi*
ASP	American Studies in Papyrology
B	03. Codex Vaticanus
BA	Bibliothèque Augustinienne
Bapt.	Tertullian, *De baptismo*
BDF	Blass, Friedrich, Albert Debrunner, and Robert W. Funk. *A Greek Grammar of the New Testament and Other Early Christian Literature*. University of Chicago Press, 1961.
BETL	Bibliotheca Ephemeridum Theologicarum Lovaniensium
Bib	*Biblica*
BICSSup	Bulletin of the Institute of Classical Studies Supplements
bo	Bohairic
BT	*The Bible Translator*
BTB	*Biblical Theology Bulletin*
BTS	Biblical Tools and Studies
BZNW	Beihefte zur Zeitschrift für die neutestamentliche Wissenschaft
C	04, Ephraemi Rescriptus

CBQ	*Catholic Biblical Quarterly*
CCSB	Corso completo di studi biblici
CCSL	Corpus Christianorum Series Latina
CHB	The Cambridge History of the Bible
CHC	The Cambridge History of Christianity
ch(s).	chapter(s)
Civ.	Augustine, *De civitate Dei*
Cl	Clement
cm	centimeter(s)
Comm. Jo.	Cyril of Alexandria, *Commentarii in evangelium Joannis*
Comm. Jo.	Origen, *Commentarii in evangelium Joannis*
Comm. Matt.	Origen, *Commentarium in evangelium Matthaei*
cop	Coptic
CRBR	*Critical Review of Books in Religion*
CSEL	Corpus Scriptorum Ecclesiasticorum Latinorum
CTeo	*Cuestiones teológicas*
D	05, Codex Bezae
DH	Denzinger, Heinrich, and Peter Hünermann, eds. *Compendium of Creeds, Definitions, and Declarations on Matters of Faith and Morals*. 43rd ed. Ignatius Press, 2012.
Diatess[Ephrem]	Ephrem, *Diatessaron*
Did.	Didache
DJD	Discoveries in the Judaean Desert
Doctr. chr.	Augustine, *De doctrina christiana*
DOP	*Dumbarton Oaks Papers*
EC	Early Christianity
ECM	Editio Critica Maior
EnchB.	*Enchiridion Biblicum: Documenta ecclesiastica Sacram Scripturam spectantia*. 4th ed. Librariam Vaticanam, 1927.
EncJud	Skolnik, Fred, and Michael Berenbaum, eds. *Encyclopedia Judaica*. 2nd ed. 22 vols. Macmillan Reference USA, 2007.
Ep.	*Epistula(e)*
Ep. Carp.	Eusebius, *Eusebii epistola ad Carpianum et canones*
EstBib	Estudios bíblicos
EstBib	*Estudios bíblicos*
ETL	Ephemerides Theologicae Lovanienses
Exc.	Clement of Alexandria, *Excerpta ex Theodoto*
Exp. Matt.	Christianus Druthmarus, *Expositio in Matthaeum evangelistam*

ExpTim	*Expository Times*
GCS	Die griechischen christlichen Schriftsteller der ersten [drei] Jahrhunderte
geo	Georgian
GNT	Greek New Testament
GR	*Greece and Rome*
Haer.	Irenaeus, *Adversus haereses*
Hier	Jerome
Hipp	Hippolytus
Hist. eccl.	Eusebius, *Historia ecclesiastica*
Hom. Ezech.	Gregory the Great, *Homiliae in Ezechielem*
Hom. Jo.	John Chrysostom, *Homiliae in Joannem*
Hom. sup.	Bernard of Clairvaux, *Homilia super missus est*
HTR	*Harvard Theological Review*
IGNTP	International Greek New Testament Project
In. Ps.	Hilary of Poitiers, *In Psalmum*
Inst.	Quintilian, *Institutio oratoria*
INTF	Institut für Neutestamentliche Textforschung
Ir^{lat}	Irenaeus, Latin translation
it	Itala (i.e., Old Latin)
JBL	*Journal of Biblical Literature*
JECS	*Journal of Early Christian Studies*
JETS	*Journal of the Evangelical Theological Society*
Jov.	Jerome, *Adversus Jovinianum libri II*
JRASup	Journal of Roman Archaeology Supplementary Series
JSNT	*Journal for the Study of the New Testament*
JSNTSup	Journal for the Study of the New Testament Supplement Series
JSOT	*Journal for the Study of the Old Testament*
JSRC	Jerusalem Studies in Religion and Culture
JTS	*Journal of Theological Studies*
km	kilometer(s)
l	a lectionary with a text of the gospels of the Byzantine Church tradition
Lat.	Latin
LCSB	Lagos: Corso di studi biblici
LFHCC	A Library of Fathers of the Holy Catholic Church
LNTS	The Library of New Testament Studies
LSTS	The Library of Second Temple Studies

LXX	Septuagint
m.	Mishnah
M.p.th.f.67	gospel manuscript, Universitätsbibliothek, Würzburg.
MB	Manuscripta Biblica
MH	*Museum Helveticum*
MS(S)	manuscript(s)
NA^{26}	*Novum Testamentum Graece*, Nestle-Aland, 26th ed.
NA^{27}	*Novum Testamentum Graece*, Nestle-Aland, 27th ed.
NA^{28}	*Novum Testamentum Graece*, Nestle-Aland, 28th ed.
NewDocs	Horsley, Greg H. R., and Stephen Llewelyn, eds. *New Documents Illustrating Early Christianity*. The Ancient History Documentary Research Centre, Macquarie University, 1981–.
NHC	Nag Hammadi codices
NHC VI 3	Authoritative Discourse
NovT	*Novum Testamentum*
NovTSup	Supplements to Novum Testamentum
NPNF	Schaff, Philip, and Henry Wace, eds. *A Select Library of Nicene and Post-Nicene Fathers of the Christian Church*. 28 vols. in 2 series. 1886–1889.
NRSVue	New Revised Standard Version Updated Edition
NTGF	The New Testament in the Greek Fathers
NTS	New Testament Studies
NTTS	New Testament Tools and Studies
NTTSD	New Testament Tools, Studies, and Documents
Odes Sol.	Odes of Solomon
Or	Origen
P.Ant.	*The Antinoopolis Papyri*. 3 vols. London, 1950–1967.
P.Bad.	*Veröffentlichungen aus den badischen Papyrus-Sammlungen*. 6 vols. Heidelberg, 1923–1938.
P.Beatty	Kenyon, F. G., ed. *Chester Beatty Biblical Papyri*. London, 1933–1941.
P.Bodm.	*Papyrus Bodmer*. 52 vols. Bibliotheca Bodmeriana, 1954–1998
P.Egerton	Bell, H. I., and T. C. Skeat, eds. *Fragments of an Unknown Gospel and Other Early Christian Papyri*. London, 1935.
P.Laur.	*Dai Papiri della Biblioteca Medicea Laurenziana*. 5 vols. Florence, 1976–1984.
P.Mich.	*Michigan Papyri*. 21 vols. 1931–2018.

P.Oxy.	Grenfell, Bernard P., et al., eds. *The Oxyrhynchus Papyri*. Egypt Exploration Fund, 1898–.
Pamm.	Jerome, *Ad Pammachium*
Parm. Donat.	Optatus, *Contra Parmenianum Donatistam*
pc	*pauci* (a few manuscripts)
PF	Papyrologica Florentina
PG	Patrologia Graeca [= *Patrologiae Cursus Completus: Series Graeca*]. Edited by Jacques-Paul Migne. 161 vols. Migne, 1857–1886.
PL	Patrologia Latina [= *Patrologiae Cursus Completus: Series Latina*]. Edited by Jacques-Paul Migne. 217 vols. Paris, 1844–1864.
Praescr.	Tertullian, *De praescriptione haereticorum*
Prax.	Tertullian, *Adversus Praxean*
Quaest. ev.	Eusebius, *Quaestiones evangelicae*
RB	*Revue biblique*
RBS	Resources for Biblical Study
RFC	*Revista de filología clásica*
sa	Sahidic
Sat.	Horace, *Satirae*
SBLSBS	Society of Biblical Literature Sources for Biblical Study
SC	Sources chrétiennes
SCJ	Studies in Christianity and Judaism
ScrTh	*Scripta Theologica*
SHGR	Studies in the History of Greece and Rome
SJOT	*Scandinavian Journal of the Old Testament*
SJT	*Scottish Journal of Theology*
Soll. an.	Plutarch, *De sollertia animalium*
STDJ	Studies on the Texts of the Desert of Judah
STP	Studi e Testi di Papirologia
StPatr	Studia Patristica
StTe	*Studii Teologice*
sy	all the Syriac versions extant for a given passage
sy^c	Syrus Curetonianus
sy^h	Harklensis
sy^{hmg}	marginal reading of the Harklensis
sy^p	Peshitta
TBN	Themes in Biblical Narrative
TC	*TC: A Journal of Biblical Criticism*

TCS	Texts from Cuneiform Sources
TENTS	Texts and Editions for New Testament Study
Tert	Tertullian
Text	*Text: An Interdisciplinary Annual of Textual Studies*
Tract. Ps.	Jerome, *Tractatus in Psalmos*
TS	*Theological Studies*
TUGAL	Texte und Untersuchungen zur Geschichte der altchristlichen Literatur
TynBul	*Tyndale Bulletin*
UBS	*The Greek New Testament*, United Bible Societies
VC	*Vigiliae Christianae*
vg	Vulgata
vid	videtur
Virg.	Tertullian, *De virginibus velandis*
VL	Vetus Latina
VT	*Vetus Testamentum*
WTJ	*Westminster Theological Journal*
WUNT	Wissenschaftliche Untersuchungen zum Neuen Testament
Yad.	Yadayim
ZNW	*Zeitschrift für die neutestamentliche Wissenschaft und die Kunde der älteren Kirche*
ZPE	*Zeitschrift für Papyrologie und Epigraphik*

Introduction

Embedded within the author's personal instructions at the end of the Second Letter to Timothy, we encounter the following request: "When you come, bring the cloak that I left with Carpus at Troas, also the books [τὰ βιβλία], and above all the parchments [μάλιστα τὰς μεμβράνας]" (2 Tim 4:13 NRSVue). Scholars debate over the exact meaning of these words and how to understand τὰ βιβλία and μεμβράνας. The terms point to books in roll format (βιβλία) and notebooks on parchment (μεμβράνας), although some maintain that μεμβράνας may also include books in codex format.[1] Regardless of the semantic range of the terms and the letter's reputed pseudepigraphic status, the statement reveals an undeniable fact: Paul was associated with an interest in written documents. The instructions coincide with Paul's own words about his activity. We know that he wrote numerous letters, some of which are lost, and that his detractors seized on his writings to question his teaching (2 Cor 10:9–10). We also know that these letters were venerated and read in various communities (1 Thess 5:27, Col 4:16). We encounter a tireless preacher whose ministry is inextricably linked to the letters he wrote.

But Paul is not the only one to make use of the written word. John's Apocalypse displays a similar interest in texts. In this case, however, the

---

1. See Larry W. Hurtado, *The Earliest Christian Artifacts: Manuscripts and Christian Origins* (Eerdmans, 2006), 76–77. The word μεμβράνα is a Latin borrowing that was normally used for a parchment notebook. Theodore C. Skeat understood μάλιστα in an explanatory sense, as "I mean," so that the author of the letter would be alluding only to a group of writings, specifically to some parchment notebooks. See Theodore C. Skeat, "Especially the Parchments: A Note on 2 Timothy IV.13," *JTS* 30 (1979): 173–77. However, most authors think that βιβλία refers to books in roll format and μεμβράνας to writings in another format. See also Harry Y. Gamble, *Books and Readers in the Early Church: A History of Early Christian Texts* (Yale University Press, 1997), 64–65; Graham N. Stanton, *Jesus and the Gospel* (Cambridge University Press, 2004), 177–78.

text is to be heard in liturgical settings.² The Seer writes a book to seven churches that should be read and observed as a prophetic text. The work's beginning and end clearly indicate this: "Blessed is the one who keeps the words of the prophecy of this book" (Rev 22:7 NRSVue; cf. 1:3). The gospels also share this same interest in texts, as Luke affirms in his prologue as he sets out to compose an account on the basis of what others have compiled (Luke 1:1–3). This is also clear in John 20:30–31 (the so-called first conclusion of John's Gospel), which discloses the book's purpose, and John 21:25 (the second conclusion), which states that the world could not possibly contain all the books that could be written about what Jesus did.³

These passages are only a handful of samples that illustrate the importance of writings at the dawn of the early Christian movement. Moreover, their significance is inseparable from the fact that, for the first followers of Jesus, there were also received texts that founded, confirmed, and nourished their faith: the sacred books of Israel. Christians of the first generation understood that God had sealed a new covenant with humankind through Jesus's death and resurrection, as had been prophesied (see Jer 31:31–34) and recorded in the sacred books of the Jews. The Scriptures of Israel, therefore, remained the Scriptures for Christians.

Although Jesus left nothing in writing, his followers did, composing stories that recalled their Master's life and teachings in order to shape the faith, praxis, and liturgical life of the early Christian communities. Community life, which was nourished by oral traditions, especially at the beginning, eventually supplemented these traditions with texts. These texts complemented Jesus's teachings and explained and sustained the faith.⁴ In this way, nascent Christianity grew so inseparably linked to particular older texts (the Scriptures of Israel) and other newer texts that accompa-

---

2. On the liturgical character of Revelation, see Ugo Vanni, *Apocalisse: Una assemblea liturgica interpreta la storia*, 12th ed. (Queriniana, 2003); Vanni, "Liturgical Dialogue as a Literary Form in the Book of Revelation," *NTS* 37 (1991): 348–72.

3. It is fairly widely held that the main part of the gospel concludes in John 20:30–31 and that John 21:24–25 is the conclusion of the epilogue of ch. 21. See, e.g., Colin Roberts, "John 20:30–31 and 21:24–25," *JTS* 38 (1987): 409–10; Chris Keith, *The Gospel as Manuscript: An Early History of the Jesus Tradition as Material Artifact* (Oxford University Press, 2020), 131–36.

4. This would also include collections of *testimonia*. See Gamble, *Books and Readers*, 24–28, 65; Margaret M. Mitchell, "The Emergence of the Written Record," in *Origins to Constantine*, ed. Mitchell and Frances M. Young, CHC 1 (Cambridge University Press, 2006), 178–79.

nied the apostolic kerygma (letters, accounts of Jesus's teaching and life, apocalyptic prophecies) that we can call the early Christian movement a "textual community."[5]

However, even if these new texts played a decisive role, we do not know to what extent they were binding or when they had acquired the necessary degree of authority and venerability to explain their eventual inclusion in the canon. Questions abound: How did they come to be considered texts to set apart? When did they receive special treatment? Were there texts that mattered more than others? And which ones were they? Did they have a normative value? What authority did they enjoy?

Clear answers to all these questions are elusive. In the pages that follow, we will turn to what we can gather about the materiality of the earliest Christian writings and their transmission. In this sense, our approach is an initial inquiry. It is an attempt to investigate to what extent the following assumption is legitimate, namely that if these texts were regarded as somehow special and became normative at a given point, it is reasonable to imagine that this status would find expression in their formal aspect (perhaps through signs or particular characteristics) or in their manner of transcription and transmission. After all, if a religion finds its support in certain texts, we may expect that their material appearance or the manner of their transmission could disclose whether they were gradually treated differently from books that played no relevant role in the life of that religious group. This is what appears to happen in rabbinic Judaism, in which the expression "texts that defile the hands" suggests a perception of the book that, if not sacred, is at least special.[6] In other words, if no formal aspects distinguish early Christian

---

5. See the considerations of Harry Y. Gamble, "Literacy, Liturgy, and the Shaping of the New Testament Canon," in *The Earliest Gospels: The Origins and Transmission of the Earliest Christian Gospels; The Contributions of the Chester Beatty Codex P45*, JSNTSup 258 (T&T Clark, 2004), 27–29. Gamble states, "Early Christianity was manifestly a 'textual community,' whose communal life was recognizably oriented around books" (29). Guy G. Stroumsa prefers to call them "reading communities." See Guy G. Stroumsa, "Reading Practices in Early Christianity and the Individualization Process," in *Reflections on Religious Individuality: Greco-Roman and Judeo-Christian Texts and Practices*, ed. Jörg Rüpke and Wolfgang Spickermann (De Gruyter, 2012), 186. See also Mitchell, "Emergence of the Written Record," 194; and more recently Keith, *Gospel as Manuscript*, 18–26.

6. On this principle of m. Yad. 3.5, see, e.g., Martin Goodman, "Sacred Scripture and 'Defiling the Hands,'" *JTS* 41 (1990): 99–107; John Barton, *The Spirit and*

texts from other writings (once the new faith had spread over a wide geographical area), we may suspect that these texts played no formative role in the emergence of the new religion. We may then attribute the normative character they acquired over time to circumstances of convenience unrelated to the particular character of these books. In this case, their authority could be questioned or at least defined in light of other considerations. Certainly, the data are scarce, but this uncertainty supports an examination of the materiality of our oldest New Testament manuscripts. Such an examination is even more justified when the manuscripts provide valuable clues to understand their eventual inclusion in the canon.

We must not lose sight of one important detail, however: materiality is but one feature. Although Christianity can be defined as a textual community, strictly speaking it is not a "religion of the book." The latter claim, of course, is a theologically informed statement and operates as such in the present work. More than a religion of the book, it is a religion of the Word. Books are fundamental, but they are so because the Christian faith confesses that the eternal Word of the Father has become incarnate in Jesus. Books proclaim that Word, bearing witness to it in writing.[7] This is how a number of Christians of the first generations appeared to understand it.

Christian texts were intended to bear witness rather than to preserve a deposit of what was to be believed: they were intended to be a word uttered, a word to be heard as it was first proclaimed. This is an aspect we should not lose sight of in our analysis. Texts cannot be separated from the living faith community that reads them. In this sense, the present work is not limited to textual and historical questions. The approach is also theo-

---

the Letter (SPCK, 1997), 108–21; Timothy H. Lim, "The Defilement of the Hands as a Principle Determining the Holiness of Scripture," *JTS* 61 (2010): 501–15; Lee M. McDonald, *The Old Testament: Its Authority and Canonicity*, vol. 1 of *The Formation of the Biblical Canon* (Bloomsbury, 2017), 41–44.

7. As such, primacy is given to the Word of God (i.e., the Second Person of the Trinity), the revelation of which is mediated through Scripture and tradition. See *The Catechism of the Catholic Church* §108 and Benedict XVI, *Apostolic Exhortation Verbum Domini*, September 30, 2010, n. 7, https://tinyurl.com/SBL7016a. "While in the Church we greatly venerate the sacred Scriptures, the Christian faith is not a 'religion of the book': Christianity is the 'religion of the word of God,' not of 'a written and mute word, but of the incarnate and living Word.' Consequently the Scripture is to be proclaimed, heard, read, received and experienced as the word of God, in the stream of the apostolic Tradition from which it is inseparable."

logically informed, as the final two chapters disclose. The work is intended as a reflection on the authority of the biblical text in the church informed by this author's Catholic perspective.

The book's agenda is simple. First, we will examine the materiality of our oldest extant documents—documents that would eventually form part of the New Testament canon. We will discuss their number, the problems they pose, their format, their subordinate character vis-à-vis orality, and so on. As their content will disclose, none of these texts is identical to any other. A brief review of the textual diversity among manuscripts allows us to describe the degree to which scribes introduced changes during transcription. Having established that, we will survey text-critical attempts to recover the text closest to the one that gave rise to these manuscripts. The history of the discipline, of course, demonstrates the difficulties of the task. Accordingly, new approaches have emerged to secure a text that is in itself unattainable; a process that has prompted growing interest in the value of its textual variants for what they disclose about the world of the scribes who produced them. The variants, as it were, tell stories that are interesting in their own right and showcase a living text that resists final fossilization. Moreover, the first translations of the New Testament into other languages reveal a text that eludes attempts at a definitive stabilization. Even so, the writings that would form part of the canon did not arrive at this port by independent streams. From the start, they were transmitted alongside other books that would also end up becoming part of the same canon. The codex format used for these writings contributed significantly to the determination of which books would (or would not) be considered authoritative.

Our journey, which spans the appearance of the first written witnesses of an apparently normative character to the formation of a canon, will demonstrate that purely material analyses and the use of certain texts over others do not provide sufficient warrants to confer authoritative status on the text. This observation offers an opportunity for theological reflection on the question of where the authority of the text lies and an exploration of the role of the biblical text in the church. The writings are part of a tradition that is not solely textual. It begins with the Christ-event and is partially attested in texts that are inseparable from the faith community that produced, proclaimed, and transmitted them.

The chapters that comprise the present work have their origin in various publications of the last few years. They offer an opportunity to reflect on the authority that the text of the New Testament has in the church, beginning with the material and formal features of the earliest New Testament witnesses and the dynamics of their transmission.

Obviously, many of the issues discussed here are open to debate. As noted, the present book serves to offer a series of theological reflections on the question of scriptural authority from the perspective of our oldest extant New Testament witnesses. In any case—and independent of the reception of the ideas articulated in the present work—I trust the book can serve to deepen interest in the fascinating world of New Testament manuscripts, encourage reflection on the implications of a discipline that lacks original autographs, and lead readers to rediscover the complex processes behind the formation of the New Testament canon.

The present work, of course, would never have seen the light of day without the support and encouragement of a number of people. I therefore wish to express my gratitude first of all to Santiago Guijarro Oporto, professor of New Testament at the Pontifical University of Salamanca (Spain), who encouraged me to bring together some of my articles for publication in monograph form. Oporto's sound guidance and editorial expertise were critical to the project's successful execution.

A very special acknowledgment is also due to Juan Hernández Jr., professor of biblical studies (New Testament) at Bethel University (Minnesota), whom I first met in Athens at the General Meeting of the Society for New Testament Studies in the summer of 2018. A couple of years after our initial meeting—during the 2020 pandemic, in fact—I sent him a draft version of *La transmisión textual del nuevo testamento*. Knowing of Hernández's text-critical pursuits and passion for reading Spanish literature, I thought the material might be of interest to him. More than expressing a willingness to engage the draft, Hernández's collaboration proved invaluable and went beyond a careful review of the manuscript. He further felt that the book's approach might be of interest to an English-speaking audience unfamiliar with how a Catholic biblical scholar handles text-critical issues related to the Greek New Testament. Although the original work was not conceived with the expressed intention of reflecting (or promoting) a confessional stance, it did represent the modest result of a study on the transmission of the New Testament text, carried out from a Catholic perspective—my own—of the Word of God, that very Word of God to which Scripture has borne witness and that has been transmitted in the church. Hernández's enthusiasm, dedication, narrative mastery, and tenacity have contributed significantly to the improvement of the original

Spanish edition. I therefore reserve my deepest expression of gratitude to my distinguished colleague and friend.

I am, of course, also grateful to every additional reader (mentioned in the translator's preface) who contributed to the improvement of this work, including Ignacio Carbajosa and Vicente Balaguer, who reviewed the first edition of the manuscript in Spanish and offered valuable suggestions. I am indebted to all of them.

Naturally, I am solely responsible for any remaining errors and debatable claims. My hope is that this book will contribute, albeit very modestly, to making the words of Christ a reality among his followers: "That they may all be one" (John 17:21). For, as the Second Vatican Council teaches in its decree on ecumenism, "Sacred Scriptures provide for the work of dialogue an instrument of the highest value in the mighty hand of God for the attainment of that unity which the Saviour holds out to all" (*Unitatis redintegratio*, n. 21).

The Witnesses

The task of determining which early Christian texts carried some authority is not simple. The difficulties and limitations of our available sources mean that such a study raises more questions than it answers. The fragile material on which they were copied, the ravages of time, and the circumstances of their discovery set limits on the knowledge we can have of the data provided by the documents. Numerous obstacles stand in the way of clear conclusions. Methodologically speaking, it is best to begin by considering the kind of documents that are extant and the challenges they present.

1. The Oldest Papyri of the New Testament

The circumstances surrounding the writing of the original documents that eventually constituted the New Testament collection are unknown to us. Neither have any of the originals survived. The oldest extant manuscripts are papyrus fragments with partial texts of some New Testament books copied perhaps at the end of the second or the beginning of the third century. Their fragmentary state is unsurprising, since the material on which they were copied, papyrus sheets, is plant matter susceptible to the ravages of time unless deposited in an extremely dry environment. Although the number of papyrus witnesses increases in the third century and remains stable in the fourth, only a rise in parchment use (a material much more resilient in harsh climates) accounts for the steady decrease of papyrus witnesses and the concomitant increase of parchment copies.

Despite their mostly fragmentary character and the fact that papyri constitute only 2 percent of the total number of extant Greek New Testament manuscripts, recent decades have seen a growing recognition of the importance of the papyri for establishing the New Testament text (although they often attest a known text) and for learning about the communities where the papyri were copied and transmitted. This is due to the fact that most of the oldest New Testament manuscripts are papyri and predate the large parchment codices of the mid-fourth and fifth centuries, which preserve the Bible, and thus the New Testament, almost in its entirety.[1] Not everyone agrees on how to understand the value or importance of the papyri vis-à-vis the rest of the manuscripts. Sometimes they are afforded too much importance.[2] Even so, the papyri have played a fundamental role in the reconstruction of the New Testament text, at least in terms of three functions: (1) isolating the oldest text types that can be defined, that is, whether Alexandrian, Western, or Byzantine (the labels are, of course, disputed today); (2) tracing the New Testament text's earliest history; and (3) helping to redefine the principles of textual criticism, that is, the criteria for judging which variants are most important. Papyri allow us to distinguish the earliest stages of textual transmission with concrete examples of how scribes carried out their transcriptions and therefore the kinds of errors and changes they could introduce in their copies.[3] However, we must also recognize that the papyri do not offer a rich supply of new readings.[4] They

---

1. As is known, the other categories of witnesses into which the New Testament manuscripts are grouped are uncial or majuscule manuscripts, minuscule manuscripts, and lectionaries. Ostraca and amulets with New Testament texts are not included in the total count but as an appendix.

2. See the timely remarks of Brent Nongbri, *God's Library: The Archeology of the Earliest Christian Manuscripts* (Yale University Press, 2018), 18–19.

3. Eldon J. Epp, "The New Testament Papyrus Manuscripts in Historical Perspective," in *To Touch the Text: Biblical and Related Studies in Honor of Joseph A. Fitzmyer, S.J.*, ed. Maurya P. Horgan and Paul J. Kobelski (Crossroad, 1989), 288. See also Epp, "The Papyrus Manuscripts of the New Testament," in *The Text of the New Testament in Contemporary Research*, 2nd rev. ed., ed. Bart D. Ehrman and Michael W. Holmes, NTTSD 42 (Brill, 2013): "This impact is clearest in the extraordinary importance of the papyri as textual witnesses, for they furnish both confirmative readings and numerous fresh variants that challenge the text critic's ingenuity in ascertaining the earliest attainable [New Testament] text" (24). In any case, the quest to isolate the oldest text types corresponds more to mid-twentieth century concerns than those of this century, when scholars are moving away from the text-type label. See the short piece by Klaus Wachtel, "Notes on the Text of Mark," in *The Synoptic Gospels, Part 2: The Gospel of Mark*, vol. 1 of *Novum Testamentum Graecum: Editio Critica Maior*, ed. Holger Strutwolf et al. (German Bible Society, 2021), 1–7.

4. "The New Testament papyri contribute virtually no new substantial variants." Eldon J. Epp, "The Significance of the Papyri for Determining the Nature of the New Testament Text in the Second Century: A Dynamic View of Textual Transmission," in *The Gospel Traditions in the Second Century*, ed. William L. Petersen (University of Notre Dame Press, 1989), 101.

usually provide additional support for known readings. There is no doubt, however, that the study of scribal habits offers valuable insights for assessing the weight of a particular variant.[5] We will return to this point later.

1.1. Available Material

So far, of the 141 cataloged New Testament papyri, 135 have been published or are available for consulting.[6] This is not many, but it is not an insignificant number and, fortunately, we have papyri witnesses for each of the twenty-seven books that make up the New Testament (except for 2 Timothy).[7] It

---

5. Ernest C. Colwell, "Method in Evaluating Scribal Habits: A Study of P45, P66, P75," in *Studies in Methodology in Textual Criticism of the New Testament*, NTTS 9 (Eerdmans, 1969), 106–24; James R. Royse, "Scribal Tendencies in the Transmission of the Text of the New Testament," in Ehrman and Holmes, *Text of the New Testament*, 475.

6. 141 numbers have been assigned in the papyri category, but some have been eliminated or combined. See Katie Leggett and Greg Paulson, "How Many Greek New Testament Manuscripts Are There REALLY? The Latest Numbers," *INTF Blog*, 29 September 2023. It should also be noted that we are not entirely certain that all the texts included in the papyri category are from continuous texts due to the fragmentary state of the witnesses. When they are identified as noncontinuous texts, such as P99 (excerpts from Paul's letters) and P78 and P105 (amulets with quotations from the New Testament), they are excluded from the official list of papyri.

7. Of these 141 cataloged papyri, the pairs of papyri P11+P14, P33+P58, P64+P67, and perhaps P77+P103 contain parts of text from the same manuscript, although they have been published separately. It is also likely that P15 (1 Corinthians) and P16 (Philippians) come from the same codex. In addition, scholars disagree over whether P4 is also part of the same codex as P64+P67. Head, Charlesworth, and Wasserman think that all three are the work of the same scribe but do not belong to the same codex. See Peter M. Head, "Is P4, P64, and P67 the Oldest Manuscript of the Four Gospels? A Response to T. C. Skeat," *NTS* 51 (2005): 450–57; Scott D. Charlesworth, "T. C. Skeat, P64, P67 and P4, and the Problem of Fibre Orientation in Codicological Reconstruction," *NTS* 53 (2007): 582–604; Tommy Wasserman, "A Comparative Textual Analysis of P4 and P64+67," *TC* 15 (2010): 1–27. However, Hill considers all three papyri to come from the same codex. See Charles E. Hill, "Intersections of Jewish and Christian Scribal Culture," in *Among Jews, Gentiles, and Christians in Antiquity and the Middle Ages: Studies in Honour of Professor Oskar Skarsaune on His Sixty-Fifth Birthday* (Tapir Academic, 2011), 75–91. See also Simon Gathercole, "The Earliest Manuscript Title of Matthew's Gospel (BnF Suppl. gr. 1120 ii 3 / P4)," *NovT* 54 (2012): 209–35. Although P49 and P65 have been considered part of the same third-century codex attesting some verses of Ephesians and 1 Thessalonians, they appear to come from two different codices. Of the 141 papyri, more than 50 come from one place, Oxyrhynchus. At the

is true, of course, that the period they cover is very broad, ranging from the end of the second to the eighth/ninth century. Of particular interest are manuscripts assumed to have been copied in the second, third, or early fourth centuries, that is, prior to the most important majuscule codices on parchment, such as Codex Sinaiticus (01) and Codex Vaticanus (03), from the mid-fourth century, and the fifth-century codices Alexandrinus (02), Bezae (05), and Washingtonianus (032) (see table 1.1a).

Most of these papyrus manuscripts are fragmentary. In many cases they preserve no more than a few lines corresponding to a single codex leaf. Only the six codices listed below preserve a noteworthy amount of text and accordingly deserve special attention.[8] They belong to the Bodmer and Chester Beatty collections:

- P45: Thirty-one leaves of a codex of the four gospels and Acts of the Apostles. The codex originally had about 110 leaves (220 pages) from 55 quires (55 folded bifolia). Scholars date it to the third century, fluctuating between the first and second half of that century.
- P46: Eighty-six leaves of a codex that originally had 104; this is a single-quire codex of 52 folded bifolia (208 pages); it preserves the Pauline letters in the following order: Romans, Hebrews, 1 Corinthians, 2 Corinthians, Ephesians, Galatians, Philippians, Colossians, and 1 Thessalonians. The original is thought to also have included 2 Thessalonians and Philemon. Scholars disagree, however, over whether the Pastoral Epistles were part of the collection, although it is probable that they were not.[9] P46 is usually dated to the first half of the third century.
- P47: Ten leaves of a codex that originally had about thirty-two leaves (16 bifolia, 64 pages) and preserved the entire book of Rev-

---

time of writing (July 2024), four papyri already cataloged (P129, P130, P131, P135) have not yet been published.

8. These manuscripts probably have an Egyptian origin, given the orthographic peculiarities they present, conforming to known trends among papyri found in Egypt and often revealing Coptic influence. They were copied at a crucial period, before 300 (for some, even before 200), which is when most variants emerge. For an analysis see Nongbri, *God's Library*, 116–215, and the thorough study by James R. Royse, *Scribal Habits in Early Greek New Testament Papyri*, NTTSD 36 (Brill, 2008).

9. Brent Nongbri, "The Construction and Contents of the Beatty-Michigan Pauline Epistles Codex (P46)," *NovT* 64 (2022): 388–407.

elation. The manuscript is usually dated between the end of the third and beginning of the fourth century.
- P66: Seventy-five leaves of a codex that was originally made up of thirty-nine bifolia arranged in eight quires (78 leaves, 156 pages); it transmits almost the entire first fifteen chapters of John's Gospel and fragments of the rest of it. P66 is commonly dated between 200 and 250 CE, although later dates have also been proposed (Nongbri and Orsini place it in the third–fourth centuries).
- P72: Eighty-five leaves of a miscellaneous codex, the work of four or five scribes, that originally had 87 leaves (174 pages) and preserves 1 and 2 Peter and Jude. Additionally, P72's collection of texts includes the Nativity of Mary; the apocryphal correspondence between Paul and the Corinthians; Odes Sol. 11; Jude; Melito of Sardis, *On the Passover*; and a fragment of a hymn. P72 is usually dated to the fourth century.[10]
- P75: Fifty-one leaves of a single-quire codex with sections of the Gospels of Luke and John (parts of Luke 3–5, all of chs. 6–17, half of ch. 18, and almost all of chs. 22–24; almost all of John 1–12 and part of chs. 13–15). It is thought that it was originally composed of thirty-six bifolia (144 pages). Scholars generally date it between 200 and 250 CE, although recently it has been pushed back to late third or early fourth century (Orsini) or fourth century (Nongbri; see below).

To these we may add P6 (John), with remains of fourteen leaves; P115 (Revelation), with small fragments from nine leaves; P127 (Acts), in eight leaves of considerable size, P4 (Luke and Matthew), with remains of six leaves; and P70 (Matthew) with texts corresponding to three or four leaves. The rest are fragments of one or two leaves.[11] However, there are

---

10. It was thought that the Apology of Phileas (P.Bodm. 20) and Ps 33:2–34, 16 (LXX; P.Bodm. 19) also belonged to the same codex, but it is more likely that they were not part of it. See Brent Nongbri, "P.Bodmer XX+IX and the Bodmer Composite Codex," *Variant Readings* (blog), 31 March 2018, https://tinyurl.com/SBL7016c.

11. Specifically, 104 papyri correspond to text portions of one or two leaves of a codex. For other details on the number of pages they attest and the books to which they correspond, see Eldon J. Epp, "Are Early New Testament Manuscripts Truly Abundant?," in *Israel's God and Rebecca's Children: Christology and Community in Early Judaism and Christianity; Essays in Honor of Larry W. Hurtado and Alan F. Segal*, ed. David B. Capes et al. (Baylor University Press, 2007), 94–102. This work discusses

also less extensive papyri that are valuable for their antiquity and the text they transmit, such as P38, P52, P90, P98, and P104.

Although most of these witnesses are severely damaged and fragmentary, they offer valuable information for ascertaining the text closest to that written by the New Testament authors. This fact should not be overlooked, considering that many centuries separate the composition of the vast majority of Greco-Roman writings of antiquity and the most ancient witnesses of those works. Even so, the temporal proximity to the original writings does not mean that the earliest New Testament witnesses facilitate a textual reconstruction closer to the original. They present many problems, starting with the difficulty of ascertaining the date when they were copied.

1.2. Dating Problems

It is clear that, in order to establish which New Testament text is closest to the original, it is important to know when manuscripts that have come down to us were copied and thus which ones have special value for their antiquity. But dating these manuscripts and determining which are the oldest or earliest is not an easy task. Several caveats are in order. As we know, the dating of the vast majority of New Testament papyri, including those considered most ancient, is at best an educated guess. In fact, it is not uncommon to encounter conflicting dates in different studies. This is due to the fact that the criteria for dating manuscripts are not exact, and often the historical or theological assumptions of editors or textual scholars influence the proposed dating.

In most cases the date assigned to a manuscript is probable or quite probable, but only in rare cases will we have certainty about the transcription of a particular manuscript.[12] This is because none of our most ancient Christian manuscripts have dates.[13] Further, in the vast majority of cases,

---

papyri to the publication of P127 in Epp, "Papyrus Manuscripts on the New Testament," 4 n. 11. After P127, eleven more papyri have been published, with remains of one or two pages.

12. For an approach to the problem of paleographic dating, see Nongbri, *God's Library*, 56–72, esp. 63–64. See also, though with a different perspective, Elijah Hixson, "Dating Myths 1: How We Determine the Ages of Manuscripts," in *Myths and Mistakes in New Testament Textual Criticism*, ed. Hixson and Peter Gurry (IVP Academic, 2019), 90–109.

13. It is only from the eighth–ninth centuries that colophons begin to appear, sometimes with the date indicated.

dates are allocated according to paleographic criteria, that is, according to the characteristics of the script, which involves placing the document approximately in a period when that script was used and comparing it with manuscripts whose dating is known. The proposed dates, therefore, have a wide margin of error since a literary text's paleographic dating is not an exact science.[14] The paleographic dating of a particular manuscript, then, may be more or less accurate and may even enjoy a consensus, but we should remember that, in the best of cases and when there is no other data to determine an *ante quem* or *post quem* date for the copying of a manuscript, the assigned dating should be offered as a wide range.[15] In fact, experienced paleographers are reluctant to establish precise dates for manuscripts that cannot be dated by means other than paleographic criteria and instead date them according to a broad time period. Brent Nongbri's words are therefore timely:

> Although paleography, when practiced in a disciplined manner involving close comparison with securely dated examples of handwriting, can establish a range of possible dates for an undated literary manuscript, it

---

14. Paleographers traditionally assume a fifty-year margin of error for literary writing. See Eric G. Turner, *Greek Manuscripts of the Ancient World*, 2nd rev. ed., rev. and enl. Peter J. Parsons, BICSSup 46 (University of London Press, 1987), 20: "For book hands a period of 50 years is the least acceptable spread of time." See also Don C. Barker, "The Dating of New Testament Papyri," NTS 57 (2011): 582. For a different perspective, see Stanley E. Porter, "Recent Efforts to Reconstruct Early Christianity," in *Christian Origins and Greco-Roman Culture: Social and Literary Contexts for the New Testament*, ed. Stanley E. Porter and Andrew W. Pitts, TENTS 9 (Brill, 2013), 71–84.

15. We know very little about the career of a scribe. It has been said that it could be between twenty-five and thirty years (Nongbri, *God's Library*, 64). What is certain is that there is a clear degeneration of the writing after forty years of office. See, e.g., Robert W. Daniel, "Palaeography and Gerontology: The Subscriptions of Hermas Son of Ptolemaios," *ZPE* 167 (2008): 151–52. On the other hand, it seems that fashions had an influence. There are cases where sons are observed to write in a style different from their fathers and similar to others of their time. See Jennifer Cromwell, "Following in Father's Footsteps: The Question of Father-Son Training in Eighth Century Thebes," in *Actes du 26e Congrès international de papyrologie. Genève, 16–21 août 2010*, ed. Paul Schubert (University of Geneva Press, 2012), 156. And yet the reverse was also true, as in the obvious similarity between a mother's writing and that of her daughter. See Raffaella Cribiore, *Writing, Teachers, and Students in Graeco-Roman Egypt*, ASP 36 (Scholars Press, 1996), 15. In any case, it is always possible that a scribe imitated his teacher's handwriting and copied a manuscript in a style that was already out of fashion at the time.

can never be conclusive. Paleographic comparison is by its very nature a subjective undertaking, and oftentimes, especially when early Christian manuscripts are concerned, paleographic dating can devolve into little more than an exercise in wishful thinking.[16]

Despite the precautions, it is not uncommon to find that the dates proposed by the publisher of a papyrus or by other paleographers are (apparently) assumed to be definitive and are used to make claims that ignore the tentative nature of manuscript dating. Recent studies have shown this to be a real problem. Roger Bagnall, for example, notes that there has been a general tendency to date biblical manuscripts to very early dates, whereas we have much less evidence than is usually mentioned to prove the existence of Christian books prior to the second century.[17] Along the same lines, Pasquale Orsini and Willy Clarysse, in reviewing the dating of the oldest New Testament manuscripts, have assigned slightly later dates than those usually accepted in some cases (P9, P15, P16, P22, P24, P28, P39, P48, P53, P70, P77, P98, P103, 0188, 0220), in other cases later (P25, P35), and in one particular case much later (P80). However, for other manuscripts they propose dates earlier than those that are currently assigned in the literature (e.g., P4, P18, P23, P30, P64, P116, 0171, 0188, 0308). Orsini and Clarysse nonetheless agree with Bagnall in reducing the number of manuscripts datable to the second century to three (P52, P90, P104) and those dated between the end of the second century and the beginning of the third century to five (P4, P30, P64, 0171, 0212).[18] Orsini, however, has subsequently modified some of the dating of the Bodmer papyri. P66

---

16. Nongbri, *God's Library*, 72.
17. Roger S. Bagnall, *Early Christian Books in Egypt* (Princeton University Press, 2009), 24. See also Christoph Markschies, "The Canon of the New Testament in Antiquity: Some New Horizons for Future Research," in *Homer, the Bible, and Beyond: Literary and Religious Canons in the Ancient World*, ed. Margalit Finkelberg and Guy G. Stroumsa, JSRC 2 (Brill, 2003), 175. Markschies argues that of all the Christian literature of the second century of which we have knowledge from our sources, we have only 14 percent preserved.
18. Pasquale Orsini and Willy Clarysse, "Early New Testament Manuscripts and Their Dates: A Critique of Theological Palaeography," *ETL* 88 (2012): 443–74. The study covers up to and including P118. Since then twenty more have been published. The authors share Bagnall's view that there is an apologetic interest in some theological attempts to date New Testament papyri early. This is probably true of the proposals of Carsten Peter Thiede, Philip Wesley Comfort and David P. Barrett, or Karl Jaroš but cannot be extended to the whole community of exegetes and theologians.

and P75, which were dated as 200–250 in the Orsini-Clarysse list, are now assigned between the mid-third and mid-fourth centuries and between the late third and early fourth centuries, respectively.[19] Similarly, Nongbri, upon reviewing the dating of New Testament papyri, suggests new dates for a handful of important witnesses. For example, he argues that the dating range of P52, commonly assigned to the middle of the second century, should be extended to the first third of the third century. He also considers it preferable to date P66 to the fourth century on the basis of paleographical and codicological characteristics as well as circumstances related to its discovery, and he believes that P75 fits better in the fourth century.[20] The implications of his proposal for P75 are not minor, given the codex's importance for New Testament textual criticism. If the new dating were to be adopted, the widely held assertions that P75, given its similarity to Codex Vaticanus (03), reflects a text type that predates this codex by more than a hundred years would have to be revised.

The proposals, of course, are not definitive, but they offer a glimpse of the tricky terrain we face. So, considering the ease with which paleographic dating is often accepted, the new proposals remind us of the fragility of the available data for reconstructing the New Testament text. The risk does not warrant a wholesale dismissal of the dating of these manuscripts. Unless there are strong arguments to the contrary, one can continue to work within the broad range of dates assigned to particular manuscripts (provided they have not been specifically revised). In any case, we must be aware of the limits of paleographic dating. There is always the risk that ideas about the supposedly canonical or apocryphal character of some books of the first Christian generations will be made to depend on the date assigned to a particular extant manuscript witness and unduly affect our understanding of the development and formation of the canon.

---

19. See table 2 in Pasquale Orsini, "I papiri Bodmer: scritture e libri," *Adamantius* 21 (2015): 77.

20. Brent Nongbri, "The Use and Abuse of P52: Papyrological Pitfalls in the Dating of the Fourth Gospel," *HTR* 98 (2005): 23–48. Orsini and Clarysse do not deviate too much from the traditional dating of P52 (Nestle-Aland, 100–150 CE), although they date it a little later (125–175 CE; see "Early New Testament Manuscripts," 470). On the dating of P66 and P75, see Brent Nongbri, "The Limits of Palaeographic Dating of Literary Papyri: Some Observations on the Date and Provenance of P.Bodmer II (P66)," *MH* 71 (2014): 1–35; Nongbri, "Reconsidering the Place of P.Bodmer XIV–XV (P75) in the Textual Criticism of the New Testament," *JBL* 135 (2016): 405–37.

In sum, as paleographic criteria cannot guarantee the date when a given manuscript was copied, statements made on the basis of the dating of a particular papyrus must be tempered by uncertainty about the actual date of transcription, accepting with reservations its dating within a century (keeping a margin of about fifty years before and after a document dated at the beginning or end of a century) and allowing for the possibility that the margin may be even wider.

Considering the above and the dating proposed by Orsini-Clarysse and Nongbri, the distribution of the oldest papyri by centuries is as follows: Of the 135 New Testament papyri published so far, eighty-two are from the first four centuries (provided that one considers that P4 belongs to the same codex as P64+P67 and that P103 is part of the same codex as P77). Of these there are only three assigned to the second century, three to the late second or early third century, thirty-eight to the third century (of which five are usually dated to the beginning of that century), thirteen to the late third or early fourth century, and twenty-seven to the fourth century (although some of these may be later). A total of eleven rolls are preserved from these centuries, which have been dated as follows: two from the late second or early third century, one from the third century, eight from the fourth century. For specific data, see table 1.2a.

1.3. Other Limitations

In addition to dating difficulties, the extant papyri are subject to other limitations. Geographical limitations are at the top of these other limitations. Almost all our extant Greek New Testament papyri come from Egypt, and from only one place, Oxyrhynchus, a city located about 200 km south of Cairo, the third largest in Egypt in Greco-Roman times, famous in Christian times for its churches and monasteries.[21] The largest percentage of the oldest biblical texts come from there, although the best-preserved manuscripts (those in the Chester-Beatty and Bodmer collections) come from other areas.[22] In any case, for none of these papyri do we have reliable

---

21. On the various aspects of the city, see Alan K. Bowman et al., eds., *Oxyrhynchus: A City and Its Texts* (Egyptian Exploration Society, 2007); Peter J. Parsons, *The City of the Sharp-Nosed Fish: Greek Lives in Roman Egypt* (Weidenfeld & Nicolson, 2007).

22. For the biblical, Christian, and Jewish texts found at Oxyrhynchus, see Eldon J. Epp, "The New Testament Papyri at Oxyrhynchus in Their Social and Intellectual Context," in *Sayings of Jesus: Canonical and Non-canonical*, ed. William L. Petersen et

data about where they were copied, as it is likely that their recovery site is not the place of their origin. At the very least, the textual variants of these papyri appear to point to various provenances.[23] It is, further, not possible to know the degree to which copying practices in Egypt resembled those of other parts of the empire. And we do not know whether what we can deduce from texts recovered from archaeological digs of ancient cities is applicable to texts from rural areas. It is quite likely that the circumstances in the *chora* (in the countryside) differed from those in the capitals of the *nomoi* (provinces) or in other more or less large towns.[24]

We should also keep in mind the random nature of the excavations. The publication of our extant manuscripts, and therefore our knowledge of the New Testament text, depends on accidental findings (i.e., what has come to light may not be representative of what the reality was) and editorial decisions (which involve judgment calls).[25] A new archaeological

---

al., NovTSup 89 (Brill, 1997), 47–68; Epp, "The Codex and Literacy in Early Christianity and at Oxyrhynchus: Issues Raised by Harry Y. Gamble's *Books and Readers in the Early Church*," *CRBR* 11 (1998): 15–37; Epp, "The Oxyrhynchus New Testament Papyri: 'Not without Honor except in Their Hometown'?" *JBL* 123 (2004): 5–55; Nongbri, *God's Library*, 216–46. See also Lincoln H. Blumell and Thomas A. Wayment, eds., *Christian Oxyrhynchus: Texts, Documents, and Sources* (Baylor University Press, 2015); AnneMarie Luijendijk, *Greetings in the Lord: Early Christians and the Oxyrhynchus Papyri*, HTS 60 (Harvard University Press, 2008); Parsons, *City of the Sharp-Nosed Fish*, 193–210. Aphroditopolis has been proposed for the Chester Beatty papyri and the Dishna region for the Bodmer. On the difficulties with these proposals, see Nongbri, *God's Library*, 122–30 (Chester-Beatty) and 159–68 (Bodmer).

23. The rapid circulation of texts within the Roman Empire accounts for the varied provenances. See Eldon J. Epp, "New Testament Papyrus Manuscripts and Letter-Carrying in Greco-Roman Times," in *The Future of Early Christianity: Essays in Honor of Helmut Koester*, ed. Birger A. Pearson (Fortress, 1991), 35–56. Epp also believes that the types of manuscript texts found in Egypt are probably representative of the types of texts of all manuscripts of their time (see Epp, "Significance of the Papyri," 90). In any case, we have no evidence one way or the other. Turner believes that manuscripts testifying to a routine writing style would have been copied where they were found, while those of higher quality may have been imported. Since most of the oldest manuscripts that have come down to us were written in routine fashion, it could be inferred (with many caveats) that they had a local origin. See Eric G. Turner, *The Typology of the Early Codex* (University of Pennsylvania Press, 1977), 40–41.

24. Bagnall, *Early Christian Books*, 7–9.

25. Judgment calls include how many and which papyri to publish. Such decisions are often guided by several factors, especially economic considerations by the researchers and publishers.

site is likely, at least in theory, to redefine the current data. Additionally, a large part of the New Testament papyri have been found in trash heaps, likely due to the fact that they had become worn through use.[26] We do not know the degree to which these extant papyri are characteristic of all the manuscripts of their time. Perhaps many others, with different features, were destroyed or lost in other ways.[27]

Finally, an additional problem is the apparently poor quality of the script of these codices. In principle, the literary works of the time were copied by professional scribes. The oldest New Testament manuscripts, however, are not characterized by particularly calligraphic handwriting. They are copied by a hand that has been called "reformed documentary," which refers to a type of calligraphy for daily use that lies between literary and documentary writing.[28] Scholars dispute whether the copyists were professional scribes or private individuals who made copies

---

26. See AnneMarie Luijendijk, "Sacred Scriptures as Trash: Biblical Papyri from Oxyrhynchus," *VC* 64 (2010): 217–54. The author draws out some of the implications that arise from the fact that the Oxyrhynchus manuscripts were found in the ancient city's rubbish dumps.

27. Of course, we hardly have any Jewish LXX manuscripts, perhaps because those who possessed them disposed of them by other means. It is likely that the scarcity of Jewish texts contemporary to the Christian texts is due to the veneration the Jews showed their sacred texts, a posture incompatible with getting rid of them by throwing them away. See below and Juan Chapa, "The 'Jewish' LXX Papyri from Oxyrhynchus: Witnesses of Ways That Did Not Part?," *SJOT* 35 (2021): 207–29.

28. On this type of writing, see Colin H. Roberts, *Manuscript, Society and Belief in Early Christian Egypt* (British Academy and Oxford University Press, 1979), 12–15. Turner comments on the codices of the second and third centuries: "Their handwriting is in fact often of an informal and workaday type, fairly quickly written, serviceable rather than beautiful, of value to a man interested in the content of what he is reading rather than its presentation" (*Typology of the Early Codex*, 37; see also 86). See also Kim Haines-Eitzen, *Guardians of Letters: Literacy, Power, and the Transmitters of Early Christian Literature* (Oxford University Press, 2000), 53–75, esp. 64–65. In any case, even though many of these texts present this type of writing, there are also many others copied with a more calligraphic writing, close to that of literary works. On the link between manuscripts with book hand or documentary hand in relation to the professionalism of the scribes, see Alan Mugridge, "Writing and Writers in Antiquity: Two 'Spectra' in Greek Handwriting," in *Proceedings of the Twenty Fifth International Congress of Papyrology, Ann Arbor*, ed. Traianos Gagos (American Studies in Papyrology, 2007), 573–80. Mugridge develops this theme at length in his *Copying Early Christian Texts: A Study of Scribal Practice*, WUNT 362 (Mohr Siebeck, 2016).

for private use.²⁹ Moreover, we do not know for whom they were written or who their immediate and/or remote readers were. Presumably, the immediate recipients were Christians, but it is also worth inquiring whether these books were popular among non-Christian readers, who could read, especially the gospels, as escapist literature in the style of other works at the time.³⁰

All these limitations (chronological, geographical, conservational, narrative, transcriptional, etc.) condition the study of the oldest Christian manuscripts, including their presumed status as special texts, and ought to discourage unwarranted assumptions of any kind. Despite these challenges, there are three elements that surface or are systematically associated with Christian biblical manuscripts and can shed some light on the consideration users gave these writings and their value as witnesses to the New Testament text. These include the preference for the codex, the use of *nomina sacra*, and the presence of reading aids.

2. Preference for the Codex

The oldest extant witness of the New Testament writings are codices, that is, notebooks made up of papyrus (or parchment) sheets folded in half and later sewn and bound.³¹ They were written on both sides of the sheets.

---

29. From the analysis of the type of writing, it has been proposed that the oldest manuscripts were copied by individuals, giving rise to a network of manuscript copying among the various Christian communities (this is the thesis of Haines-Eitzen, *Guardians of Letters*). But there is no clear evidence for this. On the other hand, the manuscripts present corrections, which indicate a concern for the careful transmission of the copied text. And just as it is unlikely that there were scriptoria as we know them in later times, it does not seem entirely convincing that the texts were on the whole copied privately and without any control. At least in the third century, there is evidence to suggest that in Oxyrhynchus Bishop Sotas was concerned with producing texts for the formation of his communities, seeing to their quality (Luijendijk, *Greetings in the Lord*, 144–51, esp. 150).

30. See Peter J. Parsons, "A People of the Book?," in *I papiri letterari cristiani: Atti del convegno internazionale di studi in memoria di Mario Naldini, Firenze, 10–11 giugno 2010*, ed. Guido Bastianini and Angelo Casanova, STP NS 13 (Istituto Papirologico "G. Vitelli," 2011), 48–49.

31. The literature on this subject is extensive. In addition to the classic work of Colin H. Roberts and Theodore C. Skeat, Turner, *Typology of the Early Codex*, is fundamental, to which we should add the pages devoted to the subject by Nongbri, *God's Library*, 21–46. See Roberts and Skeat, *The Birth of the Codex* (British Academy and

Put this way, this statement is unremarkable. But if one considers that the format of literary works in Greco-Roman antiquity until practically the end of the third century was the roll (i.e., a long strip of papyrus sheets glued one after the other, inside of which the text was written in columns and then rolled up), the fact that the books that became part of the New Testament are codices is striking. In contrast to the roll, which was dominant and continued to be so for the sacred writings of the Jews and for Greek and Latin literary works until the third century CE, the oldest surviving New Testament papyri are codices.

Despite the preference for this new format, the codex was not Christianity's invention. Its existence preceded the rise of the early Christian movement. In fact, there is practically no formal difference between pagan and Christian codices.[32] Neither did Christians use it exclusively. They also used the roll for their writings, especially for theological treatises and other texts, both liturgical and for study or personal devotion.[33] And yet, despite the fact that Christians did not invent the codex, it is quite possible they contributed to the popularization of its use. Indeed, we can say that such an association was established between the content of Christian books and the writing format that it is possible speak of a synergy between Christianity and the use of the codex.[34]

Oxford University Press, 1983). See also Alain Blanchard, ed., *Les débuts du codex* (Brepols, 1989); Stephen R. Llewelyn, "The Development of the Codex," *NewDocs* 7:249–56; Eldon J. Epp, "The Codex and Literacy in Early Christianity and at Oxyrhynchus: Issues Raised by Harry Y. Gamble's *Books and Readers in the Early Church*," *CRBR* 11 (1998): 15–37. See a synthesis in William A. Johnson, "The Ancient Book," in *The Oxford Handbook of Papyrology*, ed. Roger S. Bagnall (Oxford University Press, 2009), 265–67.

32. On this point I basically follow Bagnall, *Early Christian Books*, 71–79. For Bagnall, the data fail to show that the codex was a specifically Christian book form or that the transition from roll to codex in the Roman world occurred hand in hand with Christianity.

33. See Bagnall, *Early Christian Books*, 76–79; see also Hurtado, *Earliest Christian Artifacts*, 57–58; Hurtado, "Manuscripts and the Sociology of Early Christian Reading," in *The Early Text of the New Testament*, ed. Charles E. Hill and Michael J. Kruger (Oxford University Press, 2012), 55–56; Gamble, *Books and Readers*, 80–81.

34. See Claire Clivaz, "The New Testament in the Time of the Egyptian Papyri: Reflections Based on P12, P75 and P126 (P.Amh. 3B, P.Bod. XIV–XV and PSI 1497)," in *Reading the New Testament Papyri in Context: Lire les papyrus du Nouveau Testament dans leur context*, BETL 242 (Peeters, 2011), 27. On the Christian preference for the codex over the roll, see Hurtado, *Earliest Christian Artifacts*, 43–93; Bagnall,

2.1. First Witnesses

The codex had its precursor in tablets joined with strings by the left margin that, as would happen with codices of papyrus or parchment sheets, were used as notebooks. It is easy to suppose that these notebooks in papyrus or parchment were used for writings that did not rank as high literature but that had to be consulted frequently.[35] Examples include para-literary works, selections of texts, recipe books (to which Galen alludes), astronomy books in which the consultation of tables of diverse types is facilitated, and so on.[36]

The fact of the matter is that, because the codex began to be used more widely, there is a greater proportion of Christian works in this format than of works by non-Christian authors, so much so that about a third of all extant codices of the first centuries are Christian.[37] More-

---

Early Christian Books, 70–90; Stanley E. Porter, "What Do We Know and How Do We Know It? Reconstructing Early Christianity from Its Manuscripts," in Porter and Pitts, *Christian Origins and Greco-Roman Culture*, 41–70; Stanton, *Jesus and the Gospel*, 249–87; Stephen Emmel, "The Christian Book in Egypt: Innovation and the Coptic Tradition," in *The Bible as Book: The Manuscript Tradition*, ed. John L. Sharpe and Kimberly van Kampen (British Library and Oak Knoll, 1998), 35–43. See also Guy G. Stroumsa, "On the Status of Books in Early Christianity," in *Being Christian in Late Antiquity: A Festschrift for Gillian Clark*, ed. Carol Harrison, Caroline Humfress, and Isabella Sandwell (Oxford University Press, 2014), 57–73.

35. Pliny the Younger says that his uncle left him "one hundred and sixty notes of selected fragments [*volumina ... electorumque commentarios*], written by the way on both sides [*opisthographos*] and in very small handwriting" (*Ep.* 3.5.17). On notebooks, see also John C. Poirier, "The Roll, the Codex, the Wax Tablet and the Synoptic Problem," *JSNT* 35 (2012): 18–24. On the use of codices for practical texts in late antiquity, such as ritual formulas, medical manuals, agricultural guides, and astronomical tables, which were used in a variety of situations, such as reading aloud, following instructions to perform a ritual, preparing medicine, or designing a horoscope tailored for nonlinear access, see Jeremiah Coogan, "Gospel as Recipe Book: Nonlinear Reading and Practical Texts in Late Antiquity," *EC* 12 (2021): 45–50.

36. Alexander Jones, *Astronomical Papyri from Oxyrhynchus (P.Oxy. 4133–4300a)* (American Philosophical Society, 1999), 1:60–61. A work by Galen, Περὶ Ἀλυπίας, was published in 2010, in which he refers to how some "medical recipes were preserved with the utmost care in two parchment codices" (33). See Matthew Nicholls, "Parchment Codices in a New Text of Galen," *GR* 57 (2010): 378–86. See also Clare K. Rothschild and Trevor W. Thompson, "Galen: Περὶ ἀλυπησίας ('On the Avoidance of Grief')," *EC* 2 (2011): 110–29.

37. See Nongbri, *God's Library*, 22. Practically no codices are preserved from the

over, it is more than likely that a greater number of Christian books were written in codex rather than roll format in these early centuries.[38] In the case of biblical manuscripts, almost 100 percent of them are codices. On the other hand, there are more or less the same number of codices as rolls for other Christian writings.[39] There are also biblical manuscripts that are "opisthographs," that is, manuscripts in which the biblical text has been copied on the back of an ancient document (although, apparently, a strictly opisthographic work is one in which the text continues to be written on the back of the roll).[40] In this sense, it is striking that most of the oldest witnesses (prior to the fourth century, as the codex's use is practically universal subsequently) of the writings that would later be labeled apocryphal come from rolls, while those that would become canonical come from codices. Take, for example, the case of Oxyrhynchus.[41] The thirty-four witnesses of texts that would later become canonical are in codex format, except for P22, which is a fragment of John's Gospel that appears to come from a roll.[42] Of the eleven witnesses of texts that would not make it into the canon, four are rolls (two of the Gospel of Thomas, one of the Gospel of Mary, and one of an unknown gospel, which could also be a codex), and seven are codices. Of these last codices, six belong to writings of an unknown gospel type and one to the Gospel of Thomas.

---

first century. Of the second century, about 2 percent of the books that have come down to us are codices; of the third century, about 24 percent; of the fourth century, about 79 percent; and of the fifth century, about 96 percent.

38. Bagnall, *Early Christian Books*, 74. In the second century, when codices begin to appear, the rolls constitute 90 percent of the books that have come down to us. In the fourth century, codices constitute 80 percent of the total. In the sixth century, the passage from roll to codex is complete (see Johnson, "Ancient Book," 266).

39. Juan Chapa, "La materialidad de la Palabra," *EstBib* 69 (2011): 18–25.

40. Of the oldest New Testament papyri, P13, P18, and P98 are written on the back of previously used rolls (textual scholars disagree over whether P18 is a codex with Exodus and Revelation; see below). Textual scholars also disagree over whether P22 is a roll (see n. 42). On the concept of the "opisthograph," see Nongbri, *God's Library*, 25 n. 15.

41. The data here is drawn from Nongbri, *God's Library*, 237, 274–75.

42. P22 has the text written on one side only (against the direction of the fibers). It is possible that it was written on the back of a previously used roll. For a recent study, see Larry W. Hurtado, "A Fresh Analysis of P.Oxyrhynchus 1228 (P22) as Artefact," in *Studies on the Text of the New Testament and Early Christianity: Studies in Honour of Michael W. Holmes*, ed. Daniel Gurtner, Juan Hernández Jr., and Paul Foster, NTTSD 50 (Brill, 2015), 206–16.

Something similar happens with the Shepherd of Hermas. The fragments that have been found in Oxyrhynchus appear to reflect doubts about its normative character. Of the extant witnesses, eight are codices and two rolls.[43]

Therefore, with due caution, we can conclude with Bagnall that, when Christians of the early communities copied a text for private use, they did as everyone else: they used the blank back of a used papyrus. On the other hand, when they copied biblical texts intended for public use, they probably copied them in codices (allowing for possible exceptions). And when they copied homilies and works of religious but not scriptural content, they generally used the roll in the style of non-Christian literary works.[44]

All this leads us to conclude that the codex was not adopted universally for the production of Christian books, but rather Christians adopted it uniformly and consistently as a format for copies of texts for public, liturgical use. That is to say, with few exceptions, the codex was used for "professional" copies of the Bible, while the format for other works was flexible.[45] So, the fact that a third-century fragment of the Gospel of Thomas is found in codex format may point to fluctuations in its presumed normative character.[46] Even so, the dearth of comparative material discourages definitive statements on the matter.

2.2. Why the Codex?

The clear preference of the codex for biblical texts has motivated the search for the reason(s) for it. Numerous attempts have been made to explain it. One proposal, for example, is that Mark "published" his gospel in this format, and, as he was the first to compose it, his model was extended to

---

43. Nongbri, *God's Library*, 279.

44. Bagnall, *Early Christian Books*, 79, 88–89. See also Martin Wallraff, *Kodex und Kanon: Das Buch im frühen Christentum* (De Gruyter, 2013), 18–19. This is also the picture offered by the texts found in Oxyrhynchus (see Nongbri, *God's Library*, 273–80).

45. Papyrus and parchment, on the other hand, are used independently of their religious usage, although perhaps the latter is associated with the codex format. The difference between a papyrus and a parchment codex is the difference between an ordinary and a deluxe codex (see Bagnall, *Early Christian Books*, 79).

46. The writings that belong to the group of the so-called apocrypha found in Nag Hammadi are not considered, since they are later (second half of the fourth century).

the other apostolic books.[47] Others maintain that it was not Mark's Gospel but Paul's letters that, once gathered in a codex, led other works to be copied using this model.[48]

Economic reasons have also been advanced for the codex's adoption. Since the roll was written only on the inner side of the papyrus, the verso was left unused, making it less economical than the codex, which had the text copied on both sides.[49] There may also have been practical reasons for its adoption, such as the convenience of using the codex as opposed to the roll, especially if one wished to take a book on a journey or needed to locate a passage within the book more easily. According to this view, Christian itinerant missionaries would have contributed to spreading the preference for the codex insofar as they could easily carry it and quote the memoirs of the apostles, or testimonies of the Scriptures that had their fulfillment in Christ, or other texts that were to be read in liturgical gatherings or used for catechesis.[50]

Scholars have also observed that this format did not conflict with the type of book used by the Jews, for whom the scroll of the law gradually took on the character of a sacred text and received greater veneration in its materiality and its wording, something that does not seem to have occurred

---

47. Colin H. Roberts, "The Codex," *Proceedings of the British Academy* 40 (1954): 169–204. Roberts later modified this position. For a summary of the main hypotheses proposed on the Christian preference for the codex, see Hurtado, *Earliest Christian Artifacts*, 61–83.

48. See Gamble, *Books and Readers*, 58–65. It is worth mentioning the more recent proposal of Matthew D. C. Larsen and Mark Letteney, "Christians and the Codex: Generic Materiality and Early Gospel Traditions," *JECS* 27 (2019): 383–415. The authors introduce the concept of "generic materiality," which connects the literary genre with the material format in which it is presented. This approach suggests that early readers of the gospels, particularly Mark's, did not consider them books in the traditional sense, with clearly identified authors, but rather as ὑπομνήματα or *commentarii*, i.e., notes or memoranda. These types of texts, the ὑπομνήματα, tended to circulate in practical formats such as *tabulae* or codices, which would point to a close relationship between the content and its material presentation. Thus, in the view of these authors, the remarkable prevalence of the codex among biblical manuscripts between the second and fifth centuries could be understood, at least in part, as the result of deeply rooted generic expectations that linked certain textual genres with specific formats.

49. See Gregory H. R. Horsley, "Classical Manuscripts in Australia and New Zealand and the Early History of the Codex," *Antichthon* 27 (November 1993): 60–85.

50. Michael McCormick, "The Birth of the Codex and the Apostolic Life-Style," *Scriptorium* (1985): 150–58.

with the first Christian books.[51] Moreover, the codex's adoption may have had a cultural significance and may not have been simply a matter of convenience. The codex could have served Christians as a mark of identity.[52] Yet as Bagnall argues, the codex's implementation may not have emerged from an evolving and diffuse set of contemporary practices and trends. External factors may have played a role. In particular, he suggests—bearing in mind the Roman origin of the codex—that the codex's widespread use would have been favored by the unifying influence of Romanization, perhaps in the mid-second century, when the spread of Roman habits and technologies throughout the empire was exercising a determinative role also in Egypt.[53]

In light of the various explanations, it is possible to maintain a more nuanced position—that is, the preference for the codex could respond to a set of practical factors and to the use that was made of it in some influential sectors, perhaps reinforced by an explicit or implicit attempt by early Christians to distinguish themselves from Judaism. What does seem cer-

---

51. It is possible the Christians wished to distinguish themselves from the Jewish religion by adopting this format. This is the opinion of Parsons, *City of the Sharp-Nosed Fish*, 200. Skeat had also mentioned it, pointing out that by using the codex Christians distinguished themselves from both the parchment roll of the Jewish world and the papyrus roll of the pagan world. See Theodore C. Skeat, "Early Christian Book-Production: Papyri and Manuscripts," in *The Collected Biblical Writings of T. C. Skeat*, ed. J. Keith Elliott, NovTSup (Brill, 2004), 51.

52. Hurtado refers to this adoption as a Christian mark, as a convention that could have had semiotic significance (*Earliest Christian Artifacts*, 79).

53. The influence exerted by Rome because of the role it played in the Mediterranean proposed by Bagnall resembles in part the hypothesis offered by Skeat, who, first in a joint paper with Roberts, had suggested Jerusalem and Antioch as possible foci of authority and influence leading to the use of the codex, something that for the first and early second centuries might prove anachronistic. Later, Skeat proposed Rome instead of Jerusalem and Antioch. See Roberts and Skeat, *Birth of the Codex*, 53–58; Theodore C. Skeat, "The Origin of the Christian Codex," *ZPE* 102 (1994): 267–68. Unlike them, Bagnall thinks that the unifying influence was not necessarily early. It could have occurred in the middle of the second century rather than at the beginning. He argues that the combination of the use of the Greek language for the Scriptures, the location of almost the entire narrative of early church life in the Greek East, and the fact that it was the Roman authorities who had crucified Jesus have led scholars of early Christianity to focus much on the Greek world and little on the Roman. However, Bagnall states, "The codex may be one of the signs of just how Roman the world of early Christianity was" (*Early Christian Books*, 88).

tain is that Christians used the codex for books of probable liturgical use and for other writings that were sometimes considered to have the same status as these. However, for the latter (Gospel of Thomas, Gospel of Peter, etc.) the codex format is not as uniform as in the case of books that would eventually be included in the canon, perhaps because their public use was not as widespread as that of those that would later enter the canon.

3. *Nomina Sacra*

The use of *nomina sacra* constitutes another distinctive element of the Christian papyri. The practice, already attested in the earliest Christian manuscripts, consists of copying words of apparent theological significance in abbreviated form. These are easily recognizable by the horizontal line drawn over the abbreviation.[54] The first words to receive this treatment (or at least those written with much greater regularity) were *God* (ΘEOC), *Lord* (KYPIOC), *Christ* (XPICTOC), and *Jesus* (IHCOYC). The practice was a remarkable novelty in the literary production of the time due to the concrete way of executing the abbreviation. Unlike the abbreviations of the time, by suspension, that is, without writing the entire word, the abbreviation of the *nomina sacra* is mostly by contraction, that is, keeping the letters at the beginning and end of the word (e.g., $\overline{KC}$ for KYPIOC).[55] It is possible that this novel way of abbreviating would have favored drawing a horizontal line above the abbreviation, as was done with numerals, alerting the reader that what was below that line was a word and not a number.

That ΘEOC is abbreviated and that the other three *nomina* refer to Jesus is a graphic way of expressing that Jesus, as Lord and Christ, receives the same treatment as God and is on the same level as him. In other words, the four *nomina sacra* constitute the basic doctrinal framework for under-

---

54. The literature on the *nomina sacra* is very extensive. Classic works include Ludwig Traube, *Nomina Sacra: Versuch einer Geschichte der christlichen Kürzung* (Beck, 1907); Anton H. R. E. Paap, *Nomina Sacra in the Greek Papyri of the First Five Centuries* (Brill, 1959). See also José O'Callaghan, *Nomina sacra in papyris Graecis saeculi III neotestamentariis* (Biblical Institute Press, 1970). For an assessment, see Roberts, *Manuscript, Society and Belief*, 26–48. For a more recent overview, see Hurtado, *Earliest Christian Artifacts*, 95–134 (for a brief description, 106–8). See also Scott D. Charlesworth, *Early Christian Gospels*, PF 47 (Edizioni Gonnelli, 2016), 97–119.

55. In any case, some manuscripts attest abbreviated forms by suspension, leaving only the beginning of the word (e.g., $\overline{ιη}$ for Ἰησοῦς).

standing the figure of Jesus and serve to visibly encapsulate the Christian confession of faith during the first century.[56] Similarly, the later practice of also writing the words *Father, Spirit, man,* and *cross* as *nomina sacra* (and more irregularly *Son, Savior, Mother, heaven, Israel, Jerusalem,* and *David*) appears to attest to the early identification of key terms (albeit inconsistently) that resonate with the theological distinctives of the Christian tradition.[57]

The fact is that the oldest Christian manuscripts attest to the *nomina sacra*'s use. As with the preference for the codex, however, we do not know when and how this practice began to spread. Some have proposed that it began as a desire to show a reverence for God and Jesus similar to that which the Jewish scribes showed for the Tetragrammaton, the divine name in the Scriptures of Israel. This reverence led to the fact that in Greek LXX manuscripts the name of God (יהוה) was sometimes transcribed in Paleo-Hebrew characters.[58] Nevertheless, these Jewish manuscripts do not make use of the supralinear line when writing the Tetragrammaton, nor do they use the abbreviation by contraction.[59] On the other hand, it is striking how soon the use of the *nomina sacra* surfaces, how uniformly it is used, and

---

56. See, e.g., Roberts, *Manuscript, Society and Belief,* 41; Larry W. Hurtado, *Lord Jesus Christ: Devotion to Jesus in Earliest Christianity* (Eerdmans, 2003), 625–27.

57. In any case, probably because the system was not consolidated, there are records of other words abbreviated as *nomina sacra* that are not included in the fifteen indicated and that appear sporadically. This is the case, for example, in P.Egerton 2, which abbreviates *Moses, Isaiah, prophet,* and *king,* or in P.Oxy. 76.5072, which abbreviates *kingdom*. On the other hand, fluctuations in abbreviating *nomina sacra* within the same manuscript are also frequent. See, e.g., Roberts, *Manuscript, Society and Belief,* 27–28, 83–84; Christopher M. Tuckett, "'Nomina Sacra': Yes and No?," in *The Biblical Canons,* ed. Jean-Marie Auwers and Henk J. de Jonge (Peeters, 2003), 435–41 (Tuckett is criticized in some points by Hurtado, *Earliest Christian Artifacts,* 122–33); Haines-Eitzen, *Guardians of Letters,* 92–94.

58. In Greek manuscripts of Jewish provenance, the practice varies, but the common factor seems to be the concern to distinguish the Tetragrammaton from the surrounding text (see Chapa, "'Jewish' LXX Papyri from Oxyrhynchus," 213–15).

59. George Howard proposes that the origin of the *nomina sacra* lies in the fact that the Christian scribes, in copying the LXX version, abbreviated the names Κύριος ("Lord") and Θεός ("God") in a manner analogous to the Hebrew divine name, which had no vowels. See Howard, "Tetragrammaton in the New Testament," *ABD* 6:392. But, as Hurtado objects, not only did the Tetragrammaton lack vowels, but the rest of the Hebrew text did not have them either (moreover, $\overline{\text{κς}}$ for Κύριος implies the omission of vowels and a consonant; see Hurtado, *Earliest Christian Artifacts,* 111).

how it is applied not only to the name of God but also to Jesus. It therefore seems preferable to think that the practice of abbreviating specific names of special theological import was a distinctive mark created by Christian scribes.[60]

We cannot rule out, of course, that the scriptural usage of Jewish scribes was an influence, while Christian scribes may have simultaneously sought to distinguish their own practices from their Jewish counterparts.[61] In any case, it is likely that scribes and readers perceived these *nomina sacra* as referring to the name of God and of Jesus Christ and that they should accordingly be treated with reverence.[62] This is the reason some suggest that a codex, in which the *nomina sacra* are recognized at a glance, could have in itself an iconic value for Christians, even for those who could not read, and even more so if the reader and/or the people displayed their reverence to a sacred name with an external sign, such as a bow of the head.[63] Something similar occurred in the Jewish world when the celebrant pronounced the name of God during the feast of Yom Kippur and, upon hearing it, all the people prostrated themselves.[64] We know that centuries later a similar custom was fixed in liturgical usage, when the Second Council of Lyons (thirteenth century) prescribed that the celebrant should bow his head whenever the name of Jesus was pronounced during the eucharistic celebration.[65]

Hurtado further argues that Howard's proposal does not explain the motivation that led to such a consolidated use of *nomina sacra*.

60. Recently Candida Moss has called attention to the role that secretaries, especially those who were slaves or former slaves, may have had in the origin of this practice. See Moss, "The Secretary: Enslaved Workers, Stenography, and the Production of Early Christian Literature," *JTS* 74 (2023): 20–56, esp. 52–54.

61. See Parsons, "People of the Book?," 49–50.

62. "Nomen Dei non potest litteris explicari; quando purum hominem significat, per omnes litteras scribitur." Christianus Druthmarus, *Exp. Matt.* 1 (PL 106:1278D; quoted in Traube, *Nomina Sacra*, 6).

63. Larry W. Hurtado, "The Earliest Evidence of an Emerging Christian Material and Visual Culture: The Codex, the Nomina Sacra, and the Staurogram," in *Text and Artifact in the Religions of Mediterranean Antiquity: Essays in Honour of Peter Richardson*, ed. Stephen G. Wilson and Michel Desjardins, SCJ 9 (Wilfrid Laurier University Press, 2000), 271–88.

64. See David C. Parker, "Jesus in Textual Criticism," in *Jesus in History, Thought and Culture: An Encyclopedia*, ed. J. Leslie Houlden, 2 vols. (Oxford University Press, 2003), 2:837–38.

65. Council of Lyons, 1274, canon 25 (31): "When that glorious name is remem-

In any case, copyists were not always aware of the *nomina sacra*'s sacred meaning. At times they abbreviated words that were used in a non-sacral manner.[66] In most cases these are unintentional scribal errors. In others, we cannot rule out a theologically motivated abbreviation, such as in parables where *lord* (referring to the lord of the vineyard, the lord of the house, or the lord who demands to receive an account of the talents) appears abbreviated as a *nomen sacrum* because the scribe seems to identify this lord with Jesus.[67] As such, the use of these *nomina sacra* already constitutes an interpretation of the text.

In short, the *nomina sacra* exhibit insider usage intelligible to Christians and are an expression of Christian faith and devotion. They are proof of a visual and material Christian culture, manifested above all in biblical texts.[68] The staurogram pertains to the same category, a monogram (sometimes called Christogram) formed by writing the Greek letter *rho* over the *tau*, which may have been one of several ways early Christians referred to Jesus. Larry Hurtado believes the staurogram was a pictogram or numerical symbol used to refer to the crucifixion/cross of Jesus and reflects the importance given to the crucifixion of Jesus at the devotional level at least since the end of the second century.[69] In any case, the *nomina sacra* constitute clear proof of the existence of certain common criteria in the production of Christian books.

---

bered, especially during the sacred mysteries of the Maas, all should bend the knees of their hearts, which they can do by a bow of their heads."

66. They are also used in private letters (see Luijendijk, *Greetings in the Lord*, 62–67). Sometimes the *nomina sacra* are misinterpreted by the scribe when copied from the exemplar, as in P46 (see, e.g., Royse, *Scribal Habits*, 259–60, 358), or come to be used for demonic spirits. See Juan Hernández Jr., "Codex Sinaiticus: An Early Christian Commentary on the Apocalypse?," in *Codex Sinaiticus: New Perspectives on the Ancient Biblical Manuscript*, ed. Scot McKendrick et al. (British Library, 2015), 124.

67. It would be something similar to what happens in many Syriac manuscripts in which the scribes add "our Lord" when the name of Jesus appears (see Parker, "Jesus in Textual Criticism," 837).

68. Hurtado suggests, although it is difficult to prove, that these resources may have had something mysterious and reverential about them, especially for those who could not read (Hurtado, *Earliest Christian Artifacts*, 121, 132–33).

69. Hurtado, *Earliest Christian Artifacts*, 35–154; see also Hurtado, "Earliest Evidence"; Larry W. Hurtado, "The New Testament in the Second Century: Text, Collections and Canon," in *Transmission and Reception: New Testament Text-Critical and Exegetical Studies*, ed. Jeff W. Childers and David C. Parker (Gorgias, 2006), 12–13.

4. Other Formal Features

Along with the codex format and the presence of *nomina sacra*, the oldest Christian New Testament (and Old Testament) manuscripts display evidence of being copied for reading at liturgical gatherings.

As customary at the time, all these manuscripts are written in *scriptio continua*. However, they often have accompanying diacritical marks (e.g., distigmai, apostrophes, breathing marks) and paratexts (page numbering, etc.) that reflect attempts to make the task of communicating orally the contents of a manuscript easier.[70] In any case, the primary function of the so-called reading aids or reading signs is not to facilitate a performative reading, although they do serve this purpose, but rather to clarify semantic ambiguities or highlight unusual word endings, in order to aid reading without vocalization.[71] Additionally, perhaps due to Jewish influence, blank spaces and other visual aids such as the paragraph (a horizontal dash between lines), the *ekthesis* (the projection of the first letter of the first full line of a new paragraph on the left margin), a dot (high dot, middle dot, or low dot), or a colon are visible between words in many manuscripts. The origin of this practice is debated. Colin Roberts suggests that it would come from copying documents, which would have led to the introduction of various types of sense divisions and other indicators similar to those appearing in documentary manuscripts.[72] Not everyone agrees, however. For example, the larger initial letter preceded by a blank space is also found

---

70. For literary works, see Turner, *Greek Manuscripts of the Ancient World*, 8–12. For Christian works, see Dan Batovici, "Reading Aids in Early Christian Papyri," in *From Scrolls to Scrolling: Sacred Texts, Materiality and Dynamic Media Cultures*, ed. Bradford A. Anderson (De Gruyter, 2020), 35–50; Mugridge, *Copying Early Christian Texts*, 71–91. See also Roberts, *Manuscript, Society and Belief*, 21–22; Charlesworth, *Early Christian Gospels*, 32–35; Hurtado, "New Testament in the Second Century," 1–12.

71. Jan Heilmann, "Reading Early New Testament Manuscripts: *Scriptio continua*, 'Reading Aids' and Other Characteristic Features," in *Material Aspects of Reading in Ancient and Medieval Cultures: Materiality, Presence and Performance*, ed. Anna Krauß, Jonas Leipziger, and Friederike Schücking-Jungblut (De Gruyter, 2020), 183–90. Dan Nässelqvist suggests that they were rather aids to private reading. See Nässelqvist, "Reader's Aids for Whom? The Use of Lectional Signs in Early Christian Manuscripts," in *The Scriptural Universe of Late Antiquity*, ed. Emmanouela Grypeou, AAG 3 (Editorial Sindéresis, 2021), 93–104.

72. Roberts, *Manuscript, Society and Belief*, 17–18.

in the manuscript of the Minor Prophets of Nahal Hever (50 BCE–50 CE), written in Greek, in which the verses are also marked by wider spaces, most likely to facilitate liturgical reading. Emanuel Tov demonstrates that the practice of using spaces to mark units of meaning or reading (phrases, verses, or longer units) was already present in the copying of Hebrew texts (biblical and nonbiblical literary texts but not documentary ones). He argues, therefore, that Jewish scribes would have continued this practice in copying biblical texts and that Christian scribes continued to do so.[73] What is certain is that the practice of separating sentences for the reading of Scripture, which at least seems to be attested in the second century, continues to appear in later manuscripts, albeit without a uniform criterion. For example, P66 and 032 display a basic correspondence, but the punctuation marks in P66 and P75 do not always match, which might suggest the procedure was still in emergence when these codices were copied. On the other hand, P45 and P46 show that the practice was not consolidated since punctuation surfaces only occasionally in the two codices. In any case, the punctuation marks display an interest in establishing the units of meaning perceived by the copyist or the reader to facilitate the reading and understanding of the text and imply a particular way of interpreting the New Testament text.[74]

---

73. Emanuel Tov, *Scribal Practices and Approaches Reflected in the Texts Found in the Judean Desert*, STDJ 54 (Brill, 2004), 131–63. See also Tommy Wasserman, "Beyond Palaeography: Text, Paratext and Dating of Early Christian Papyri," in *The Chester Beatty Biblical Papyri at Ninety*, ed. Garrick V. Allen et al. (De Gruyter, 2023), 145–49. See also the comments of Peter Parsons in Emanuel Tov, Robert A. Kraft, and Peter J. Parsons, *The Greek Minor Prophets Scroll from Naḥal Ḥever (8ḤevXIIgr)*, DJD 8 (Clarendon, 1990), 23. For other details, see Hurtado, *Earliest Christian Artifacts*, 183–85.

74. Hurtado, *Earliest Christian Artifacts*, 181–82. Hurtado points out: "It is certainly clear, and notable, that by about 200 some Christian scribes were registering sense-unit divisions in biblical texts by various scribal devices ... [which] reflect something of how these texts were read liturgically, by about 200. Moreover, it is unlikely that our earliest evidence of these devices represents the first instances of them in Christian scribal tradition. So we have to project the use of these devices at least somewhat earlier than the extant manuscripts, which makes their import all the greater for historical purposes. Studies of the early Christian reception of these texts, the canonization process, early liturgical practices, and related matters should all take due notice of this evidence" (181). In his detailed and most useful study of the codicological conventions of the earliest papyri of the Gospels, Charlesworth also includes detailed analyses of the divisions of the text (*Early Christian Gospels*, 31–91).

Along with reading aids, the study of the materiality of manuscripts can also reveal the use for which they were designed. Scott Charlesworth has suggested that when a gospel codex has a specific size, a specific type of script (ranging from semiliterary to majuscule letters), the presence of reader aids (e.g., text divisions and punctuation), and especially when the hand of a proofreader is visible, then we are dealing with manuscripts produced for public use in Christian gatherings. Charlesworth takes these features to reveal a "catholicity," that is, they indicate the existence of guidelines agreed on by Christians of the time, which would imply a production process subject to a certain degree of control.[75] Conversely, manuscripts that are not that size, were copied with an informal or documentary hand, and do not have reading aids would have been produced for private use.[76] On the basis of these assumptions, Charlesworth calculates and proposes that, of the thirty oldest gospel manuscripts he studies, sixteen were copied for public use and fourteen for private. On the other hand, he fails to find indicators of "catholicity" in manuscripts that did not enter the canon subsequently, such as the Gospel of Thomas and the Gospel of Mary. Charlesworth believes these texts were copied for private use. He considers the fragments of the Gospel of Peter and the Egerton Gospel more difficult to evaluate.[77]

Charlesworth's analyses are useful and contain a kernel of truth. But the data he provides about the use to which the early gospel accounts

---

75. Scott D. Charlesworth, "Indicators of 'Catholicity' in Early Gospel Manuscripts," in Hill and Kruger, *Early Text of the New Testament*, 39: "The term 'catholicity,' which as used here has no reference to later periods, should be understood to connote cooperative collaboration and not hierarchical uniformity." Charlesworth has developed his thesis more fully in Charlesworth, *Early Christian Gospels* (see esp. 255–61).

76. Charlesworth, *Early Christian Gospels*, 31–91 (summary in table 2.1). See also Scott D. Charlesworth, "Public and Private: Second- and Third-Century Gospel Manuscripts," in *Jewish and Christian Scripture as Artifact and Canon*, ed. Craig A. Evans and H. Daniel Zacharias, LSTS 70 (T&T Clark, 2009), 148–75; Charlesworth, "Indicators of 'Catholicity,'" 38.

77. See Charlesworth, *Early Christian Gospels*, 121–54 (summarized in table 4.1). AnneMarie Luijendijk thinks that at least P.Oxy. 1.1 was used in the cult. See Luijendijk, "Reading the Gospel of Thomas in the Third Century: Three Oxyrhynchus Papyri and Origen's Homilies," in *Reading New Testament Papyri in Context—Lire les papyrus du Nouveau Testament dans leur contexte. Actes du colloque des 22-24 octobre 2009 à l'Université de Lausanne*, ed. Claire Clivaz and Jean Zumstein, BETL 242 (Peeters, 2011), 256.

were put should not be pushed too far.[78] A book was written primarily to be read aloud in Greco-Roman times. Although there was private or individual reading, reading was often a social activity, a source of entertainment in which a reader would read the book to a group of friends.[79] How should this reading be understood: public or private? In fact, one of the extant papyri of the Gospel of Thomas (P.Oxy. 4.654) is a roll and contains numerous reading aids. We could imagine then that it was used for a public reading like other literary works of its time but perhaps not for liturgical use. It is true that it is not a codex, but we cannot say with certainty whether "public use" in this case is to be understood as applying to a gathering of friends, to a teaching activity, or to a liturgical assembly.[80] Can we be sure that a codex of the gospels that shows traits of having been produced for private use was not also used in the liturgy?[81]

Ultimately, we lack the evidence to know whether an apparently private copy could also have been intended for or used in a public liturgical setting. The actual situation was probably complex, and we do not have sufficient data to establish a clear differentiation between public and private, nor to determine a definitive relationship between public use and authoritative character. As stated regarding the origin of these often very fragmentary texts, the data are sparse and leave many questions unanswered. The rich variety of life is more powerful than our imagination.

---

78. As Charlesworth recognizes ("Indicators of 'Catholicity,'" 42 n. 22). On the other hand, the arguments he proposes based on the indicators of catholicity of the manuscripts to criticize the lack of solidity of Bauer's thesis on the "heterodox" character of the groups that dominated primitive Christianity are more questionable (46–48). It is certainly possible that the scribal conventions that appear in the oldest papyri could have derived from a certain desire for control, but the data that have come down to us are not sufficient to prove it. Nor does this mean that there was no such control (see, e.g., Luijendijk, *Greetings in the Lord*, 62–67).

79. On this question, see William A. Johnson, *Readers and Reading Culture in the High Roman Empire: A Study of Elite Communities* (Oxford University Press, 2010) 3–31; Johnson, "Towards a Sociology of Reading in Classical Antiquity," *AJP* 121 (2000): 593–627. See Guglielmo Cavallo, "Between Volume and Codex: Reading in the Roman World," in *A History of Reading in the West*, ed. Cavallo and Roger Chartier (Polity, 1999), 71–83; also Juan Chapa, "Book Format, Patterns of Reading, and the Bible: The Impact of the Codex," *Segno & Testo* 16 (2018): 134–38.

80. See Luijendijk, "Reading the Gospel of Thomas," 264–66.

81. The conclusions reached by Dan Batovici in his study of reading aids are along the same lines as those presented here ("Reading Aids in Early Christian Papyri," 46–48).

5. Texts to Be Heard

From what we have seen so far, we can conclude that at least in the second century a set of conventions emerged among scribes who copied Christian texts that spread rapidly.[82] But, over and above convention, these common scribal practices reveal an attitude toward the content of the books. As we have seen, uniformity, especially regarding the codex format, occurs without hesitation in writings that would later acquire the status of Scripture, while it oscillates in works that were similar in genre to the future canonical writings but did not become part of the canon. The use of reading aids also suggests that the books were copied to be read in public, possibly in liturgical settings. However, contrary to what one might think, liturgical use does not appear to invest them with a special sacred character. Initially, at least, Christian manuscripts give the impression of having a practical function, especially when compared to literary works of the time. We can see this function first of all in the choice of the codex format. The first codices in the non-Christian sphere were used for practical purposes. They served mostly to record ephemera, write notes or drafts, or transmit para-literary texts. Early Christian codices are more like notebooks than literature books. We could say that they came to be objects of daily use, as if they were manuals of the first communities.[83] They were generally small in size, a fact that some consider decisive for their diffusion. The oldest ones have a similar size of 11.5–14 cm wide by a height of at least 3 cm greater than the width. There were also larger ones, however. The variety surely depended on the places and tastes of the time, and we are unable to identify a definitive difference between Christian and non-Christian codices, nor establish a clear correlation between their sizes and the question of whether they were meant for public or private use.[84] In any case, they

---

82. Skeat, "Early Christian Book-Production," 51. The rapid spread of these conventions suggests that the relations between the churches were more extensive than was believed a few years ago (see Epp, "New Testament Papyrus Manuscripts," 35–56; Stanton, *Jesus and the Gospel*, 134–35.

83. Gamble, "Literacy, Liturgy, and the Shaping," 34. As Roberts says, they were fundamentally "books for use, not, as Jewish Scrolls of the Law sometimes were, almost cult objects" (*Manuscript, Society and Belief*, 15). On the Gospels as practical texts, see also Coogan, "Gospel as Recipe Book," 50–60.

84. Hurtado, *Earliest Christian Artifacts*, 165. Many codices are elongated due to the size of the papyrus roll with which they were manufactured. The bifolia were obtained from a roll made of papyrus sheets between 19 and 33 cm in height and

differed in their external appearance from the traditional books and also from the sacred books of Israel.

The calligraphy on the pages of these codices was also not that of literary books. The writing, as noted, was somewhere between literary and documentary. Regardless of isolated cases (and bearing in mind the caution with which this data must be used), the kind of writing in Christian texts is characterized by its simplicity. It has been sometimes defined as a writing for daily use or a simple writing, as the text seems to have been copied by unskilled scribes. But it would be better to define it as a writing that is easy to read, in which legibility and intelligibility take precedence over aesthetics.[85] The page layout also suggests this. The margins are wide, and almost all of the oldest codices present the text in a single column.[86] They generally contain few lines per page and few letters per line, which could also suggest a text layout intended to facilitate public reading.[87] Moreover, the presence of corrections, sometimes by the scribe, sometimes by one or more correctors, reveals little aesthetic concern and confirms the practical character of these books.[88] The

---

20–25 cm in width. When folded, each leaf of the codex was about half of that. See William A. Johnson, *Bookrolls and Scribes in Oxyrhynchus* (University of Toronto Press, 2004) 88–91; Johnson, "Ancient Book," 257. There are miniature codices for personal reading, but they probably date from a later period, from the end of the third century onward, and occur in greater numbers from the fourth century onward.

85. In this sense, it does not seem that our extant Christian manuscripts were written with a plain type of writing because they were copies for private use. Comparison with literary works shows that the private copies were written in a quick and much more careless handwriting.

86. Among the oldest New Testament manuscripts, P4—and P64, if it belongs to the same codex (which appears unlikely; see n. 7)—is the only one written in two columns. Some speculate that P113 (a third-century fragment of Romans) may have belonged to a codex written in two columns, but the fragment is quite small. It is possible that the second-century P.Bad. 4.56, which contains some fragments of Exodus and Deuteronomy, was written in two columns, but this is also unclear. In any case, the two columns are not exclusive to biblical texts but are also used in other noncanonical writings, although evidence from the ancient codices is scarce (see Turner, *Typology of the Early Codex*, 35).

87. Turner, *Typology of the Early Codex*, 85–87. see also Michael J. Kruger, "Manuscripts, Scribes, and Book Production within Early Christianity," in Porter and Pitts, *Christian Origins and Greco-Roman Culture*, 18–31; Hurtado, *Earliest Christian Artifacts*, 172–74.

88. Particularly interesting are the corrections by the scribe himself, who goes

overall impression is that they were not copied with external elegance in mind but to enable reading.[89]

Finally, as we have also noted, the fact that Christians discarded codices worn by use—tearing their pages and throwing them in the trash—confirms the attitude of Christians toward these texts.[90] This treatment contrasts with Judaism's general attitude toward the sacred books, as their books were buried next to the rabbis or in places set aside for this purpose.[91] We get the impression that the early Christian codices may have been disposable. Those who wrote and used them did not appear to treat them as sacred objects, especially if we compare these texts with liturgical books of later times, when the canonization of the text has been extended, so to speak, to the manuscript that preserves it. Of course, a few early Christian codices are carefully copied and display a manicured external appearance, but these are exceptions. Most of them do not appear to be endowed with a special dignity in their formal appearance.

We find, therefore, that the texts that had a normative character for Christians (including Old Testament books) were not considered, at first glance, sacred. This appears to be a novelty against the backdrop of the religious and literary practices of the time. There were hardly any specific books for cultic rites in the Greco-Roman world.[92] Where they existed, they were read rather as ritual texts whose power lay in particular utterances. The texts were subordinate to the efficacy of the specific rites they

---

back and corrects his text, sometimes comparing it with another copy and detecting errors (accidental omissions, omissions, misspellings, or other mistakes). Corrections made by a hand contemporary with that of the original scribe may suggest that the copy was collated and corrected by another hand or by a corrector. In both cases, the original scribe and the contemporary corrector show that they are concerned with producing a faithful copy (Hurtado, *Earliest Christian Artifacts*, 189). Scholars debate whether one should see the existence of scriptoria behind these corrections. See, on this subject, e.g., Haines-Eitzen, *Guardians of Letters*, 83–91; Royse, *Scribal Habits*, 29–30.

89. Of this opinion is also Gamble, "Literacy, Liturgy, and the Shaping," 35.

90. It does not seem to be understood as contempt for the text or that they ended up there because of persecution against Christians (see Luijendijk, "Sacred Scriptures as Trash," 217–40).

91. See Abraham M. Habermann, "Genizah," *EncJud* 7:460; Luijendijk, "Sacred Scriptures as Trash," 236 n. 69.

92. Hurtado, "New Testament in the Second Century," 12–13. On the relationship between the concept of sacredness and the fidelity required in copying, see Royse, *Scribal Habits*, 22–31.

accompanied; that is why they could not be altered. In contrast, Christian texts, with their surplus of variants, display a different attitude. As Harry Gamble points out,

> We might expect that Christians would have taken towards their books attitudes that could be described as esoteric, or cultic, or ritualistic—attitudes that were natural in the larger religious environment of antiquity. For example, because most people were illiterate, texts were frequently viewed as mysterious objects, harbouring secrets difficult to access. Or again, texts might be thought holy, and given special handling, that showed deep reverence toward them. Thus in Judaism texts of the Torah were most carefully and exactly transcribed according to fixed conventions, and special gestures accompanied their use. Yet again, texts might be thought to have a certain potency that prompted ritualistic regard and use. But in fact we see nothing of such attitudes toward books in early Christianity.[93]

The book's efficacy does not depend on its ritualistic use.[94] The very fact that it was translated into other languages early on counters ritualistic notions. Its importance lies in its content and in the fact that, as we have seen from the formal features of the codices, they were books to be read aloud.[95] These were texts that in a certain sense had a functional role. This characteristic also explains, in part, the abundance of variants.

---

93. Gamble, "Literacy, Liturgy, and the Shaping," 33–34; see also Royse, *Scribal Habits*, 22–31. It should be noted, however, that Gamble's statement about the precise conventions in the manner of copying Torah manuscripts would apply to a later period, considering the manner of copying texts that existed in the second temple. See, e.g., Sidnie White Crawford, *Rewriting Scripture in Second Temple Times* (Eerdmans, 2008); Molly M. Zahn, *Genres of Rewriting in Second Temple Judaism: Scribal Composition and Transmission* (Cambridge University Press, 2020).

94. This does not mean, of course, that Christians did not use biblical texts for apotropaic or magical purposes. See Brice C. Jones, *New Testament Texts on Greek Amulets from Late Antiquity*, LNTS 554 (T&T Clark, 2016).

95. This does not mean that it was always so (see Johnson, "Towards a Sociology of Reading"; Keith, *Gospel as Manuscript*, 18–19). There is a greater appreciation for the practice of reading aloud in the field of textual criticism today. The liturgical use of these manuscripts would go a long way to explain textual variants that appear as small improvements designed to facilitate a better understanding of the text read. An example of these are some of the expansions in Codex Sinaiticus that appear to reflect liturgical motifs (see Hernández, "Codex Sinaiticus," 118). In addition, the fact that the four canonical gospels were read in liturgical celebrations could also explain the

Table 1.1. Oldest papyri and majuscule manuscripts of the New Testament[96]

Book	Manuscripts
Matthew	P1, P37, *P45*, *(P53)*, P64, (P62), P70, (P71), P77+P103?, (P86), P101, P102, P104, P110, (058), 0106, *0171*
Mark	*P45*, (P88), P137
Luke	P4, P7, *P45*, P69, *P75*, P111, P138, P141, *0171*
John	P5, P22, P28, P39, *P45*, P52, P66, *P75*, P90, P95, P106, P107, P108, P109, P119, (P120), P121, P134 (0162)
Acts	P8, P29, P38, *P45*, (P48), (P50), *(P53)*, P91 (0189)
Romans	P10, P27, P40, *P46*, P113, P118, P131 (0220)
1 Corinthians	P15, *P46*, P123
2 Corinthians	*P46*, (P117)
Galatians	*P46*
Ephesians	*P46*, P49, *P92*, P132
Colossians	*P46*
Philippians	P16, *P46*
1 Thessalonians	*P30*, *P46*, P65, *P92*
2 Thessalonians	*P30*
1 Timothy	P133
2 Timothy	
Titus	P32
Philemon	P87, P139
Hebrews	P12, P13, P17, *P46*, P114, P116, P126
James	P20, P23, P100
1 Peter	*P72*, (P81), (P89), (P82), P125, (0206), (0228)
2 Peter	*P72*

---

greater or lesser number of variants. A liturgical reading sets limits to the changes. It is understandable, then, that Mark, the gospel least read in liturgical celebrations, is the one with the most variants, while Matthew, the gospel most used, presents a more stable and fixed text (see Hurtado, "New Testament in the Second Century," 13, and especially Wasserman, "Liturgical Influences on the Text," 49–79, and his conclusion on 72).

96. Manuscripts with doubts about their early date are indicated in parentheses. Those attesting to more than one book are in italics.

1 John	P9
2–3 John	
Jude	P78
Revelation	P18, (P24), P47, P98, P115, (0169), 0308

Table 1.2a. Dating of oldest papyri and majuscule New Testament manuscripts[97]

Second century	P52, P90, P104
Second–third century	P4, P30, P64, P137, 0171
Third century	P1, P5, P12, P18, P20, P22, P23, P27, P29, P32, P37, P39, P40, P45, P46, P47, P69, P77+P103?, P87, P91, P95, P98, P100, P101, P103, P106, P107, P108, P109, P111, P113, P114, P118, P119, P121, P131, P138, P141, 0308
Third–fourth century	P7, P9, P13, P28, P38, P49, P65, P66, P75, P92, P115, P125
Fourth century	P8, P15+P16, P10, P17, P24, P48, P53, P50, P70, P71, P72, P62, P81, P82, P86, P88, P89, P102, P110, P116, P117, P120, P123, P126, P132, P134, P139, 058, 0160, 0162, 0169, 0189, 0206, 0220, 0228

The dating of the oldest New Testament papyri and rolls proposed by Orsini and Clarysse[98] is presented in table 1.2b. They consider some

---

97. Those mentioned in Hill and Kruger, *Early Text of the New Testament*, 86–87, 116, 139, 141, 157, 176–77, 211, 226, are included but completed by those prior to 400, according to the proposal of Orsini and Clarysse, "Early New Testament Manuscripts," 469–72. For those published later, I follow the dating of the *editio princeps* of each papyrus. Wasserman includes P35 among the early papyri (Hill and Kruger, *Early Text of the New Testament*, 86), noting, however, that its dating is disputed. Orsini and Clarysse date it to between 450 and 500, so it has not been collected. Later proposals by Orsini ("I papiri Bodmer: scritture e libri," 77) and Nongbri (*God's Library*) have been considered. For the most important, and for this reason most discussed and analyzed witnesses (P52, P45, P46, P47, P66, P75), we follow the dating that seems to have more support (other dating proposals for these papyri can be found in Nongbri, *God's Library*, 132, 170, 172). For P64, I pick up that of Gathercole, who dates these fragments to the end of the second/beginning of the third century ("Earliest Manuscript Title").

98. Orsini and Clarysse, "Early New Testament Manuscripts," 469–72. They go as far as P118 and exclude the manuscripts they consider later than 350 CE from their

earlier dating proposals, including those in the final pages of the Nestle-Aland edition. As we can see, the list attempts to offer more precise dating, suggesting for some papyri dates spanning a period of fifty years or, in some cases, twenty-five years. As noted, the proposals run the risk of being understood as definitive dating, when they are in fact tentative, especially those dating to a short period of time. They are offered here as an example of dating carried out by competent paleographers, without indicating full agreement with the dates.

Table 1.2b.	
100–200	P104
125–200	P52
150–200	P90
175–200	P4, P64
175–225	P30, P137, 0171
200–225	P46, P95
200–250	P45, P87, P98
200–300	P1, P5, P18, P20, P27, P29, P32, P40, P47, P69, P91, P100, P101, P103, P106, P107, P108, P109, P111, P113, P114, P118, P119, P121, P131, P138, P141
250–300	P12, P22, P23, P37, P77, 0308
250–350	P7, P13, P28, P38, P49, P65, P66, P92, P115, P125
275–300	P39
275–325	P9, P75
300–350	P8, P10, P70, P72, P116, 0160
325–375	(P48)

list: P6, P24, P25, P35, P48, P51, P53, P57, P71, P80, P85, P88, 0188, 0206, 0220, 0232, 0312. They include 058 and 0228 (see 460), although these are not listed in the table at the end of their article. They treat P64+P67 and P15+P16 as single witnesses but do not consider P77 and P103 as fragments of the same codex. They have modified some of their list, considering Orsini, "I papiri Bodmer: Scritture e libri," 77, and included in brackets the manuscripts whose dating is in doubt but are found in the Orsini and Clarysse list within the four hundred. Those after P118 have been added following the dating of the *editio princeps*.

300–400	P15+P16, P17, (P50), (P62), (P82), (P86), (P89), P102, P110, (P117), (P120), P123, P126, P132, P134, P139 (058), (0162), (0169), (0189), (0228)
350–400	(P24), (P53), (P81), (P88), (0206), (0220)
375–400	(P71)

Variants That Matter

The capacity to introduce errors during transcription is, of course, well known and practically unlimited. Perhaps the most glaring of all scribal blunders is found in the fourteenth-century Codex 109. This four-gospel manuscript, now in the British Library, was transcribed from a copy that must have had Luke's genealogy of Jesus (3:23–38) in two columns of twenty-eight lines each. However, instead of transcribing the text by following the columns in succession, the scribe appeared to copy the genealogy by following the lines across the two columns. As a result, not only is almost everyone made to be the son of the wrong father but, because the names apparently did not fill the last column of the exemplar, God now stands within the genealogy instead of at its close (it should end, of course, "Adam, the son of God"). So, in Codex 109, God is said to have been the son of Aram, and the source of the whole race is not God but Phares![1]

Although such cases are rare, the example draws attention to the fact that scribes were not always particularly skillful or careful when copying the New Testament books. At times, they were not entirely qualified to do so, or, even if they were, the circumstances in which they worked were difficult, and the work was exhausting.[2] Hence the frequent commission of errors.

The scribal inclination to error was already widespread in the first centuries of Christianity and did not go unnoticed by ecclesiastical

---

1. Bruce M. Metzger and Bart D. Ehrman, *The Text of the New Testament: Its Transmission, Corruption and Restoration* (Oxford University Press, 2011), 259.

2. The colophon of one manuscript reads, "Writing bows one's back, thrusts the ribs into one's stomach, and fosters a general debility of the body." In the colophon of an Armenian manuscript of the gospels, the scribe laments about the huge snowstorm raging outside, to the point that the ink froze, his hands were frozen, and his pen fell out of his fingers (see Metzger and Ehrman, *Text of the New Testament*, 29).

authors. Origen complains, "The differences between the manuscripts [of Matthew] at this point have been produced either by the negligence of copyists, or by the perverse audacity of others, or by those who do not care to check what they have transcribed, or by those who, in the process of correction, add or omit according to their opinions" (*Comm. Matt.* 15.14).[3] Jerome, for his part, laments the scribes who "do not copy what is before them but what they think it means; and while they try to rectify the errors of others, they simply manifest their own."[4] And he says something similar about Latin translations when he writes to Pope Damasus, "tot enim sunt exemplaria paene quot codices," "there are as many versions as manuscripts."[5]

Scribal errors are therefore abundant and varied. In most cases, they are involuntary (errors of sight, hearing, memory, judgment on marginal notes, skips, etc.). In others, they appear to be deliberate (spelling or grammatical changes, harmonizations, amplifications, historical or geographical clarifications, changes for doctrinal reasons, etc.). Some do not alter the text's meaning, but others may affect its interpretation. This chapter will demonstrate how the text is modified when it is copied and explore the implications of the acceptance or rejection of textual variants for the interpretation of the text and for questions about its authority. Since there are many examples of textual variation, we will limit our discussion to gospel passages with significant textual variants in the Greek papyri. We begin with the most obvious examples (passages of doubtful authenticity), proceed to less problematic variants (due to harmonization), and conclude with the most difficult and debated changes (variation that may reflect a theological motive).

---

3. GCS 10.387.28–388.7. The Alexandrian teacher, who had performed text-critical tasks with the text of the LXX, "did not dare" to do the same with the New Testament text, although he realized that this too was susceptible to criticism.

4. Jerome, *Ep. ad Lucinum* (*Ep.* 71.5; PL 22:671). See also *Praefatio in Quatuor Evangelia* (PL 29:527), where he mentions "errors which were exposed by incompetent translators, or which were erroneously revised by inexperienced, presumptuous and wicked persons, or which were added or changed by sleeping scribes."

5. Jerome, *Praefatio in Quatuor Evangelia* (PL 29:526). Augustine also complains about the audacity and, apparently, the lack of competence of the first translators of the Bible into Latin when he writes, "As soon as someone got hold of a Greek manuscript, and imagined himself to have facility in both languages, however small it might be, he set about translating it" (*Doctr. chr.* 2.11 [16]; PL 34:43).

1. Extensive Passages of Doubtful Authenticity Attested by Papyri

We know that there are some relatively extensive passages in the gospels whose inclusion or omission could affect our perception of the figure of Jesus and, by extension, aspects of the gospel message. These are passages that are usually considered to have been composed and added during the second century. Mark's long ending (Mark 16:9–20) is the most striking. However, there is no extant early papyrus of this gospel that attests to its absence. On the other hand, we have evidence of the absence of a very notable passage: the story of the adulterous woman (John 7:53–8:11). The following instances of variation, though shorter, are also important: the passage where Jesus is consoled by an angel and sweats, as it were, drops of blood during the agony in Gethsemane (Luke 22:43–44); a Jesus saying about keeping the Sabbath in Luke 6:4 (according to a variant of D); Jesus's intercession to the Father on behalf of his executioners (Luke 23:34); or the stirring of the waters of the pool of Bethesda in John 5:4. Unfortunately, no extant papyrus attests to all these variants in one way or another. We will therefore briefly examine only the omissions for which we have evidence in some papyri, namely, the absence of the *pericope adulterae* in P66 and P75 and the omission of some verses of the Lukan passage of Jesus's prayer in the garden attested by P75. The observations and implications that follow from the presence or absence of these passages in the two papyri are also applicable to other more or less extensive passages.

1.1. The Pericope of the Adulterous Woman (John 8:1–11)

P66 and P75, as is well known, lack the passage of the adulterous woman. In this they agree with important codices such as Sinaiticus (01), Vaticanus (03), Washingtonianus (032), and Athous Lavrensis (044). Some 250 majuscule codices, the Syriac tradition, most Coptic versions, and some manuscripts of the VL also omit it.[6] On the other hand, most manuscripts,

---

6. If it had been copied, the passage would have been among the missing leaves in codices A and C, but it is estimated that there is not enough space for its inclusion. The bibliography is very extensive. See, e.g., the most recent works: Chris Keith, *The Pericope Adulterae, the Gospel of John, and the Literacy of Jesus*, NTTSD 38 (Brill, 2009), 119–40; David A. Black and Jacob N. Cerone, eds., *The Pericope of the Adulteress in Contemporary Research* (Bloomsbury, 2016); and, above all, the comprehensive

Codex Bezae, some Latin manuscripts, and the Vulgate include it after 7:52. The manuscripts that attest to it note the problematic character of the pericope. This is the case with some Byzantine manuscripts that copy it accompanied by asterisks and obeli. On the other hand, the manuscripts that transcribe the passage do not always place it where we are accustomed to find it, between chapters 7 and 8 of John, but in other places. For example, family 1 of minuscule manuscripts adds it at the end of the Fourth Gospel as an appendix, and family 13 places it after Luke 21:38, where it appears to fit naturally. On the other hand, the text of the pericope has not been uniformly transmitted either. Codex Bezae, for example, offers more variants than the other manuscripts.

Here we will not analyze its stylistic features, which are not typically Johannine and present a greater resemblance to Lukan style. Instead, as far as content is concerned, the passage can be related to the story of a woman whose many sins Jesus forgives, which occurs in a version of the Gospel of the Hebrews and in the Syriac version of the Didascalia Apostolorum (fourth century) and which Papias appears to know.[7] In any case, it is likely that the tradition about Jesus forgiving a woman has its origin in a text prior to the second half of the second century, since the Protevangelium of James also seems to know it.[8] No satisfactory explanation has yet emerged, however, as to when it was added to the Fourth Gospel or as to its presence or absence in various manuscripts.

---

examination by Jennifer Knust and Tommy Wasserman, *To Cast the First Stone: The Transmission of a Gospel Story* (Princeton University Press, 2019).

7. Ehrman thinks that the pericope is the result of the fusion of two stories: the one testified by Papias about a woman accused of many sins who is brought before Jesus—also collected in the Didascalia—and another one found in the Gospel of the Hebrews and known by Didymus the Blind, in which Jesus stops an attempt of stoning. According to Ehrman, Didymus would have known the story already in some copies of the Gospel of John located in Alexandria and in the Gospel of the Hebrews. See Bart D. Ehrman, "Jesus and the Adulteress," *NTS* 34 (1988): 24–44. On this thesis and other explanations, see Knust and Wasserman, *To Cast the First Stone*, 49–65. Knust and Wassermann believe that the allusions found in authors such as Origen and Papias, as well as the reference to the Gospel of the Hebrews, suggest that the story may have circulated independently before being incorporated into some manuscripts of John.

8. William L. Petersen, "ΟΥΔΕ ΕΓΩ ΣΕ [ΚΑΤΑ]ΚΡΙΝΩ. John 8:11," in *The Protevangelium Jacobi and the History of the Pericope Adulterae, Sayings of Jesus: Canonical and Non-canonical; Essays in Honour of Tjitze Baarda*, ed. Petersen, Johan S. Vos and Henk J. de Jonge, NovTSup 89 (Brill, 1997), 191–221.

Given the manuscript tradition, the logical temptation would be to eliminate the passage or relegate it to another place in order to have a purer Johannine text for the sake of the interpretation of the gospel. Certainly, Jean Zumstein, analyzing P66's textual variants from the perspective of an exegetical analysis of the Fourth Gospel, is right when he points out that the insertion of the adulterous woman episode between 7:52 and 8:12 causes a spatial and temporal change in the development of the narrative.[9] The debate that follows in chapter 8 emerges as a new polemical episode between Jesus and his opponents, as if the controversies during the Feast of Tabernacles narrated in the preceding verses constituted a distinct group from those collected in chapter 8. On the other hand, if we eliminate the passage of the adulterous woman, there is a clear thematic and argumentative continuity between chapters 7 and 8. To Jesus's opponents, who challenge his messianic claims, Christ responds with one of the "I am" sayings (8:12). In this way, the evangelist makes a progressive shift in his teaching from Jesus's divine condition (7:37–52) to the question of monotheism (8:12–20). The shift demonstrates that "the debate on Christology is inseparable from the debate on monotheism; moreover, the question of God is the central question of Johannine Christology."[10] In this way, P66, P75, and the other manuscripts that do not preserve the passage offer a concrete contribution to this interpretation of John's Gospel worthy of note.[11] It would, therefore, seem obvious (at least from a text-critical perspective) that it would be best to eliminate this passage, as some modern editions do, and thereby preserve the original purity of John's Gospel.

This option is not without its risks, of course. What would happen if we were to dispense with chapter 21 as well?[12] Despite the fact that it is not missing in any manuscript, it is widely considered an addition.

---

9. Jean Zumstein, "Quand l'exégète rencontre le manuscrit: le P66," in *Reading New Testament Papyri in Context*, ed. Claire Clivaz and Jean Zumstein (Peeters, 2011), 230–31. See also Rudolf Schnackenburg, *The Gospel according to St John* (Crossroad, 1968), 2:168–71.

10. Zumstein, "Quand l'exégète rencontre le manuscrit," 231.

11. Zumstein also points out other exegetical consequences derived from some readings of P66 (see "Quand l'exégète rencontre le manuscrit," 231–38).

12. On the remote possibility that John's Gospel was transmitted without ch. 21, see Christian Askeland, "A Coptic Papyrus without John 21?," in *The New Testament in Antiquity and Byzantium: A Festschrift for Klaus Wachtel*, ed. Hugh A. G. Houghton, David C. Parker, and Holger Strutwolf, ANTF 52 (De Gruyter, 2020), 95–97.

Moreover, although it is believed to come from the Johannine community, it shares Lukan elements with the adulterous woman passage.[13] Moreover, the fact that chapter 21 is found at the end does not pose a serious structural problem, insofar as it is considered an appendix added subsequently to the gospel. Its elimination could be justified in the name of a more Johannine gospel. But it is evident that the gospel's interpretation would be notably compromised without the appendix. The same could be said of other Fourth Gospel passages that appear to have been added later and break the narrative sequence. For example, chapters 15–17 also imply a break in the narrative of the farewell discourse.[14] Interpreters also discuss other possible additions in successive redactions of the gospel. Certainly, the difference between these passages and the *pericope adulterae* is that no manuscript witnesses in the cited cases suggest their elimination, and the style is more Johannine. However, all of them share with the passage of the adulteress their suspected status as later additions. What criteria should we follow, then, to ascertain whether a passage should or should not be considered part of the text? Will textual criticism alone determine it? We will return to these questions below.

1.2. The Agony of Gethsemane (Luke 22:43–44)

Luke 22:43–44 is another relatively extensive passage omitted in much of the textual tradition. The gospel narrates that Jesus is consoled in the agony of Gethsemane, as bloodlike sweat drips from him: "An angel from

---

13. It is clear that the *pericope adulterae* has features closer to Luke than to John. See David C. Parker, *The Living Text of the Gospels* (Cambridge University Press, 1997), 101; Raymond E. Brown, *I–XII*, vol. 1 of *The Gospel according to John* (Yale University Press, 1995), 336. The same is true of ch. 21 of John. In fact, Boismard, who analyzed it in detail, concluded that its author was Luke. See Marie-Émile Boismard, "Le chapitre XXI de saint Jean: essai de critique littéraire," *RB* 54 (1947): 473–501. His opinion has not been followed, but it shows that the final appendix of John presents remarkable Lukan traits. See also Kyle R. Hughes, "Lukan Special Material and the Tradition History of the *Pericope Adulterae*," *NovT* 55 (2013): 232–51.

14. As is well known, the end of ch. 14, "Arise, let us depart from here," fits very well with the beginning of ch. 18: "Having said this, Jesus went out with his disciples to the other side of the brook Kidron." Chapters 15–17 seem to have been added later, perhaps as a rereading (though probably by the same evangelist). See Johannes Beutler, *A Commentary on the Gospel of John* (Eerdmans, 2017), 389.

heaven appeared to him and comforted him. And as he entered into agony he prayed more earnestly. And there came upon him a sweat as it were drops of blood falling down to the ground."[15] P69 and P75 do not preserve these verses. Here they agree[16] with the first corrector of Sinaiticus, Vaticanus, Alexandrinus, and many other important witnesses (022 029 032 579 1071* *l* 844 *pc* 10 sy^s sa bo^{pt}; Hier^{mss}). Traditionally, based on the omission by P75 and the first corrector of Codex Sinaiticus (i.e., two manuscripts historically considered to attest to a solid Alexandrian textual tradition), these verses of Luke have been understood as an antidocetic interpolation that fits the doctrinal concerns of the second century.[17] The seemingly logical consequence, as in the case of the adulterous woman passage, would be to eliminate this text as spurious.

These verses may be an interpolation. Claire Clivaz, however, has questioned this hypothesis, underscoring the importance of the testimonies of Justin, Clement of Alexandria, Origen, and Athanasius about this passage. All of them know the story of the angel who comforted Jesus in agony and about his sweating drops like blood. In her opinion, these weighty witnesses support its originality. Additionally, Clivaz points out that the Alexandrian tradition was not uniform, as evidenced by the fact that Sinaiticus's original scribe and the manuscript's second corrector include the verses by marking them with obeli.[18] For this reason, Clivaz believes not that P75's scribe eliminated Luke 22:43–44 but that this text had already been eliminated in the scribe's exemplar. The deletion would have been made in response to a possible "gnostic" reading of the passage that represented Jesus as an "agonist," a fighter, an archangel fighting

---

15. For a study of this passage's textual tradition, see Claire Clivaz, *L'ange et la sueur de sange (Lc 22, 43–44) ou comment on pourrait bien encore écrire l'histoire*, BTS 7 (Peeters, 2010).

16. P69's agreement with 01, 03, etc., is only partial, insofar as it omits more than 22:43–44.

17. Bart D. Ehrman, *The Orthodox Corruption of Scripture: The Effect of Early Christological Controversies on the Text of the New Testament* (Oxford University Press, 2011), 220–27.

18. There is also another tradition attested in P69 where not only is Luke 23:43–44 deleted but also v. 42. Thus, Claire Clivaz proposes that P69 (third century) is a Marcionite version of Luke. See Claire Clivaz, "The Angel and the Sweat Like 'Drops of Blood' (Lk 22:43–44): 𝔓^{69} and f^{13}," *HTR* 98 (2005): 419–40. See, however, Juan Hernández Jr., "The Early Text of Luke," in Hill and Kruger, *Early Text of the New Testament*, 123–24, who is skeptical about this.

against the demiurge, as, for example, appears in *Exc.* 58.1.[19] According to Clivaz, to avoid the risk of such an interpretation, some Christians would have thought to omit these verses (together with 23:34a: "And Jesus said, Father, forgive them, for they know not what they do"), as reflected in P75. We would, then, have before us a textual correction for theological reasons, albeit for reasons that differ from those proposed by Bart Ehrman. On the other hand, Clivaz adds that those same Christian scribes would have added 24:51b: "he began to rise up to heaven."[20] Thus, they wanted to avoid possible special revelations of Jesus to his disciples after the resurrection, as some circles attempted to do that also interpreted verses 43–44 in a "gnostic" way.[21]

Clearly there are speculative elements in Clivaz's proposal that are unprovable, but it does offer an alternative to the widespread assumption that Luke 22:43–44 is a later interpolation. So, if (in keeping with the aforementioned understanding of the passage of the adulterous woman) we choose to omit these verses from New Testament editions in order to preserve a more authentic interpretation of the Lukan figure of Jesus, Clivaz's observations remind us of the risks of eliminating it. On the other hand, even if these verses were not part of the original text, it is undeniable that the figure of Jesus in Luke's Gospel is enriched by the representation

---

19. "Thus, after the kingdom of death, which had made a beautiful and seductive promise, but which, in spite of everything, had been a ministry of death, when it had rejected all principalities and divinities, the great fighter, Jesus, having assumed in himself the Church in potency, … brought to salvation and on high what he had assumed." I follow the edition of Manlio Simonetti, *Testi gnostici in lingua latina e greca* (Fondazione Lorenzo Valla, 1993), 380. Simonetti points out in n. 369 that the idea of Christ ἀγωνιστής is also found in the treatise Authorized Teachings from the Nag Hammadi library (NHC VI 3 26.13).

20. The original scribe of Codex Sinaiticus omitted it. It is also missing in 05, it (3 4 5 2 8 11) sy^s (see Hernández, "Early Text of Luke," 137 n. 100). Ehrman argues that the addition is intended to emphasize the bodily ascension of Jesus and his return as judge (*Orthodox Corruption of Scripture*, 266–67). Arie W. Zwiep maintains that the omission of this part of Luke 24:51 is due to a rejection of the idea of the bodily ascension as gnostic. See Zwiep, "The Text of the Ascension Narratives (Luke 24.50–53; Acts 1.1–2, 9–11)," *NTS* 42 (1996): 219–44. See also Eldon J. Epp, "The Ascension in the Textual Tradition of Luke-Acts," in *New Testament Textual Criticism: Its Significance for Exegesis; Essays in Honour of Bruce M. Metzger*, ed. Eldon J. Epp and Gordon D. Fee (Oxford University Press, 1981), 131–45.

21. Clivaz, *L'ange et la sueur de sang*, 609–18.

of him as a man who is moved and struggles in Gethsemane, as later tradition understood him.

In short, the papyrus witnesses to the omission of more or less extensive passages can support the readings of other important manuscripts and back what we already know from later witnesses. In some cases, such as that of the *pericope adulterae*, they would underscore the advantage of eliminating those New Testament passages and relegating them to the rank of spurious and pious traditions. Undoubtedly, this is an option. But it is also worth asking whether more is lost than gained by removing passages that have formed an integral part of books that have undergone a long process of composition. The consideration is especially important when we insist on the fluidity of the text of the gospels in the second century and note that they were read from very early on in Christian communities. Our assessment on the value of these papyrus variants must therefore be more modest. What we can affirm is that the oldest manuscripts, as privileged witnesses of a community of faith's foundational text, are valuable but not necessarily definitive about what can constitute an authentic tradition about Jesus.

2. Harmonizations Attested in Papyri

P66, as noted, is a very important witness for textual criticism. The last chapters copied in this codex, however, are fragmentary. Even so, the manuscript adds a few words from Luke 5:5 to John 21:6, after the risen Lord instructs the disciples to cast their nets on the right side of the boat: "And they said, 'We have been struggling all night and have caught nothing; but in your name (?) I will let down the nets.'"[22] We are clearly dealing with a harmonization, one of the phenomena that most contributes to altering the copy of a manuscript text. This phenomenon was known in the transmission of works of classical literature and is attested in the manuscripts of all New Testament books. Predictably, it also occurs in practically all the oldest gospel papyri.[23] That it appears in these four books in abundance

---

22. The reading "in your name" is doubtful, but it seems likely that instead of ἐπὶ δὲ τῷ ῥήματί σου, as Luke's text reads, P66's scribe has harmonized with the earlier context of 20:31, where it reads ζωὴν ἔχητε ἐν τῷ ὀνόματι αὐτοῦ. Other manuscripts that also add Luke 5:5 are 01[1] 034 vg[mss] sa.

23. Logically it is detected above all in the Synoptics, but the same is true of other biblical books, not only of the New Testament but also of the Old Testament.

could be due to the flourishing of gospel harmonies from the middle of the second century that may have influenced the scribal copying process.[24]

Harmonizations are mostly simple alterations in word order that draw one text closer to another.[25] In other instances they are additions of phrases or longer texts from other gospels, as in the passage of John 21:6 in P66. In any case, many of a manuscript's singular readings are explained by some kind of harmonization, which sometimes alters a single manuscript but sometimes affects an entire textual tradition. Even so, harmonization may not produce a text identical with its parallel text. In fact, sometimes it is difficult to determine whether a variant arises from harmonization. Moreover, it does not always occur between parallel passages, as one might assume, but also between different texts. We can therefore distinguish several types of harmonization: (1) those that occur within the same context in the same gospel; (2) those that occur within the same book; (3) those produced between parallel places in different books, especially parallel gospel passages; and (4) those caused by frequently occurring expressions of general use. The most common kinds of harmonization are those that occur within the same passage or the same book. Matthew is the least harmonized of the Synoptic Gospels because it was considered the oldest and contained most of the material collected in Mark and Luke. For these reasons it was the most widely used and, with good reason, was considered the ecclesiastical gospel. In fact, Luke and Mark's texts tended to conform to it, although exceptions naturally exist.[26] Consequently, centuries of harmonization have masked some of the differences between the gospel texts. Textual criticism's task is to try to uncover these.

See Emanuel Tov, "The Nature and Background of Harmonization in Biblical Manuscripts," *JSOT* 31 (1985): 3–29; see also Cambry G. Pardee, *Scribal Harmonization in the Synoptic Gospels*, NTTSD 60 (Brill, 2019).

24. The first of the harmonies of which we have clear evidence is the *Diatessaron* of Tatian. But we cannot rule out that there were earlier ones. Petersen thinks that Justin already made use of a harmonization of gospel passages. See William L. Petersen, "From Justin to Pepys: The History of the Harmonized Gospel Tradition," StPatr 30 (1997): 93–96. See also Alvaro Pereira Delgado, "Uno de cuatro, cuatro y no uno: El Diatésaron de Taciano y el Evangelio cuadriforme," *ScrTh* 52 (2020): 285–312.

25. For this question I basically follow David C. Parker, *An Introduction to the New Testament Manuscripts and Their Texts* (Cambridge University Press, 2008), 338–41.

26. 042 is a counterexample, according to Elijah Hixson, *Scribal Habits in Greek Purple Codices*, NTTSD 61 (Brill, 2019), 206–49: "[The scribe] has a strong tendency to harmonize Matthew to Mark" (245).

The phenomenon of harmonization is well attested in the most ancient papyri, and many of their singular readings are its product. In fact, James Royse's analysis of the scribal habits of the most extensive Greek New Testament papyri, carried out precisely on the basis of singular readings, shows that there is a generalized tendency to harmonization in all of them. Specifically:

1. The scribe who copied P45 (a manuscript whose scribe does not seem very disciplined but who nonetheless attempts to transmit his text in a manner that reads well, making stylistic and grammatical improvements along the way) includes frequent instances of harmonization among his "improvements."[27] These have been produced by the general usage of the New Testament, by the context, and by parallel passages.[28] Royse notes that, of 210 significant singular readings, forty-six stem from harmonization, and of these, eight are singular readings that have their origin in parallel locations.[29]

---

27. For a detailed analysis, see Royse, *Scribal Habits*, 103–97. See also Juan Chapa, "The Early Text of John," in Hill and Kruger, *Early Text of the New Testament*, esp. 150–52.

28. In general, P45's scribe copies the text sentence by sentence or clause by clause, focusing on the content of the idea rather than on the exact word order. This does not mean that he does not want to reproduce his source or betrays it, for in fact he has hardly any meaningless singular readings (see Royse, *Scribal Habits*, 124). Barbara Aland argues that the P45 scribe's way of copying is "both intelligent and liberal: intelligent, because the sense of the exemplar is quickly grasped and in essence precisely reproduced; and liberal, because involved expressions and repetitious words are simplified or dropped." See Barbara Aland, "The Significance of the Chester Beatty Papyri in Early Church History," in *The Earliest Gospels: The Origins and Transmission of the Earliest Christian Gospels; The Contribution of the Chester Beatty Gospel Codex P45*, ed. Charles Horton, JSNTSup 258 (T&T Clark, 2004), 112.

29. Matt 20:31a: πόλ]λῳ (cf. Mark 10:48 = Luke 18:39); Mark 8:10: Μαγαδ]άν (cf. Matt 15:39); Mark 8:12a: σημεῖον αἰτεῖ (cf. Matt 12:39, 16:4, Luke 11:29, 1 Cor 1:22); Mark 9:28b: omission of εἰς οἶκον (cf. Matt 17:19); Luke 9:30: συνλαλοῦντ[ες] (cf. Matt 17:3, Mark 9:4); Luke 10:11a: omission of κολληθέντα (cf. Matt 10:14, Luke 9:5); Luke 11:12: ἄρτον (cf. Matt 7:9); Luke 12:24a: τὰ πετεινὰ τοῦ οὐρανοῦ κα[ὶ] τοὺς κόρακας (cf. Matt 6:26, Luke 12:24). See Royse, *Scribal Habits*, 186–89. The most common harmonizations are with the immediate context and less frequently with general usage, among which are some typical expressions in the gospels. Royse further indicates that harmonizations produce additions and substitutions and play almost no role in omis-

2. P66 reflects an analogous situation. This manuscript offers a faithful copy of the text it copies, despite constant corrections not only of obvious errors but also in light of another exemplar.[30] The most numerous instances of harmonizing are due to the immediate context and, less frequently, to general usage. However, there are also five unique readings that are harmonizations to parallel passages, although perhaps only two may be influenced by the Synoptic Gospels.[31]
3. P75, whose scribe intended to transcribe faithfully the exemplar before him (despite also making many spelling mistakes or creating numerous meaningless readings, mainly due to errors of one or two letters),[32] has a few singular readings created by harmonizations, the most frequent ones influenced by the immediate context (John's Gospel). It also presents other harmonizations due to general usage and five significant singular readings that were introduced by a harmonization with parallel passages.[33]
4. The rest of the papyri with gospel texts, which are extant only in fragments, also offer readings that are explicable by harmonization with the other gospels.[34]

---

sions and transpositions. He concludes that harmonization is a frequent cause of error, the most important being that of the immediate context (197). See also Juan Hernández Jr., *Scribal Habits and Theological Influences in the Apocalypse: The Singular Readings of Sinaiticus, Alexandrinus, and Ephraemi*, WUNT 2/218 (Mohr Siebeck, 2006), 76–81; and the observations of Haines-Eitzen, *Guardians of Letters*, 72.

30. Royse, *Scribal Habits*, 399–544. See a synthesis in Chapa, "Early Text of John," 143–46.

31. John 18:38c: ἐγὼ οὐδεμίαν εὑ[ρίσκω] αἰ[τία]ν ἐν αὐτῷ (cf. Luke 23:4); John 19:2: ἐξ [ἀ]κανθ[ῶ]ν [σ]τέ[φα]νον (cf. Mark 15:17). See Royse, *Scribal Habits*, 536–37.

32. For a detailed analysis, see Royse, *Scribal Habits*, 615–704; also Chapa, "Early Text of John," 147–50.

33. Luke 3:22: omission of τὸ before πνεῦμα (cf. Matt 3:16), Luke 8:21: αὐτόν (cf. Matt 12:48); Luke 12:31: omission of αὐτοῦ (cf. Matt 6:33); John 6:5a: ἑαυτοῖς (cf. Matt 14:15, Mark 6:36; but the reading is doubtful); John 6:5b: [ἀγωράσ]ωσιν (cf. Matt 14:15, Mark 6:36). See Royse, *Scribal Habits*, 690–91. Haines-Eitzen doubts that there is harmonization in Luke 3:22, 8:21, and 12:31 (*Guardians of Letters*, 71). On the other hand, with regard to the so-called non-Western noninterpolations, P75 takes the majority line and presents the long non-Western readings. Practically all of them are explained by harmonization with parallel passages to John or to other NT books (see Hernández, "Early Text of Luke," 133–38).

34. It is not clear that some of the variants in P37 may be due to harmonization

The papyri are therefore not unique, as they share the same tendency to harmonize as other manuscripts. They are witnesses to a phenomenon that occurred early in the textual tradition and is analogous to what is reflected in the harmonies of the four gospels. The harmonizing tendency reveals an interesting fact, however: it bears witness to well-consolidated gospel traditions and shows that the four gospel accounts were in fact considered a single gospel from very early on.[35] The harmonizing tendency that runs through the long ending of Mark 16:9–20 demonstrates this and suggests that Mark's Gospel was not interpreted in isolation but that its text was improved to render it more compatible with the other gospels.[36] Along with a tetramorphic understanding of the gospels, other reasons

---

with the context or with a parallel. See Tommy Wasserman, "The Early Text of Matthew," in Hill and Kruger, *Early Text of the New Testament*, 91. Wasserman also indicates the following cases of harmonization in the other fragments of Matthew: in P64, there is a possible case of harmonization of Matt 26:31 with Mark 14:27, though not clear, since it depends on a reconstruction of the text; in P70, the reading γ[ινώσκει in Matt 11:27 is probably a harmonization with the parallel of Luke 10:22. P77 seems to have omitted ἔρημος in Matt 23:38, harmonizing with Luke 13:34–35. It is possible that in P101 the reading of Matt 4:2 μ̄ (τεσσεράκοντα) ἡμέρας is a harmonization with Mark 1:13; that ὡς instead of ὡσεί in Matt 3:16 is a harmonization with Mark 1:10 and Luke 3:22; and that the omission of καί also in Matt 3:16 is a harmonization with Mark 1:10. For P103, a harmonization of a possible [ὧδε πρὸς ἡμᾶς] in Matt 13:56 with Mark 6:3 has been proposed; the original omission of εἰσῖν in the same verse could also have been caused by the parallel in Mark. In P110, the substitution of ἐφ' ὑμᾶς for πρὸς ὑμᾶς in Matt 10:13 could be a harmonization with Luke 10:6, and the omission of ἔξω in Matt 10:14 could be a harmonization with Luke 9:5. Majuscule 0171 has six variants that could be explained mainly by harmonization with parallels (Wasserman, "Early Text of Matthew," 94–103). In the Luke fragments it is possible that, of the four singulars of P4 due to harmonizations, that of ῥήγνυσι in 5:37 is due in part to the reading of ῥήγνυνται from Matt 9:17. See Hernández, "Early Text of Luke," 126; Peter M. Head, "Observations on Early Papyri of the Synoptic Gospels, Especially on the 'Scribal Habits,'" *Bib* (1990): 240–47. In the earliest papyri fragments of John, there are no traces of harmonization with parallels, perhaps because of the peculiar character of the gospel or lack of data. See Peter M. Head, "The Habits of New Testament Copyists: Singular Readings in the Early Fragmentary Papyri of John," *Bib* 85 (2004): 399–408.

35. Petersen thinks that the reasons that led Tatian to compose his work must have been very varied, probably reflecting the complexity of the harmonized tradition of the gospels. See Petersen, "From Justin to Pepys," 71–96; and Pereira Delgado, "Uno de cuatro, cuatro y no uno," 285–312.

36. Peter M. Head, "The Early Text of Mark," in Hill and Kruger, *Early Text of the New Testament*, 111.

that contributed to the scribal harmonizing of some texts with others were apologetic concerns and, surely, liturgical practices, since the use of these texts in such gatherings facilitated their memorization.[37] We ought to remember, moreover, that the gospels were the most used and most familiar texts of the early Christian movement because they were considered the most authoritative. It is likely that they were memorized in many cases and that their knowledge influenced the scribe, so that the scribe unconsciously used forms of speech taken from a gospel different from the one being copied.[38]

The phenomenon of harmonization is significant for understanding the text in its transcribed materiality. That a large part of variants stem from contextual influences—that is, by the influence, both particular and general, of the contexts of the four gospels or other New Testament books—shows the scribes' familiarity with writings whose authoritative character had the capacity to influence the copying process, whether consciously or unconsciously. This does not preclude that copyists at times may have deliberately changed the book to be copied. The motives for doing so could be many, but, without doubt, among them were those prompted by theological concerns.

---

37. Haines-Eitzen shows that it occurs mostly in P72 (*Guardians of Letters*, 72–73). In any case, this author considers that intentional harmonization in the oldest papyri is very infrequent. She admits that in a few cases they are the result of remote harmonization (68–73). On apologetic concerns, see Wayne C. Kannaday, *Apologetic Discourse and the Scribal Tradition*, TCS 5 (Society of Biblical Literature, 2004), 82–100.

38. A study of New Testament quotations in Clement of Alexandria shows that there is greater harmonization in the gospels, especially in the Synoptics, than in the Pauline letters. "The Lord's teaching was for Clement the most authoritative and important element in the whole collection of the Scriptures. It is, therefore, antecedently probable that his familiarity with the Bible will here be at its highest, and his tendency to quote memoriter consequently more pronounced than elsewhere. This is borne out by the fact that his quotations from the Gospels (and these are mainly quotations of teachings: incidents are referred to but rarely in the ipsissima verba of the text) are less closely in accordance with the MSS. than quotations from other New Testament books." Richard B. Tollinton, *Clement of Alexandria* (Williams & Norgate, 1914), 2:183–84, quoted in Carl P. Cosaert, "Clement of Alexandria's Gospel Citations," in Hill and Kruger, *Early Text of the New Testament*, 397.

3. Alterations of the Text for Theological Reasons as Attested in Papyri

In the second volume of his work *Jesus of Nazareth*, Benedict XVI comments in these terms on the figure of the humiliated and mocked Jesus presented in the passion according to John:

> Thus caricatured, Jesus is led to Pilate, and Pilate presents him to the crowd—to all mankind: "Ecce homo," "Here is the man!" (Jn 19:5). The Roman judge is no doubt distressed at the sight of the wounded and derided figure of this mysterious defendant. He is counting on the compassion of those who see him.[39]

Rudolf Bultmann, on the other hand, with whom Joseph Ratzinger dialogues several times in his book, does not see compassion in the attitude of the governor. He translates the original Greek ἰδοὺ ὁ ἄνθρωπος, the Latin *ecce homo*, of Pilate as "look at this pitiful figure." He understands that the Roman prefect, by presenting him in this way, sought to move the accusers to withdraw the request for death against Jesus. *Ecce homo* was a way of underscoring how ridiculous it was to take such a miserable figure seriously. Still, for Bultmann, Pilate's scorn is not the most important detail. What is really important is that "to the mind of the Evangelist the entire paradox of the claim of Jesus is in this way fashioned into a tremendous picture. In very truth, such a man it is who asserts that he is the king of truth! The declaration ὁ λόγος σὰρξ ἐγένετο [the word became flesh] has become visible in its extremest [*sic*] consequence."[40] The scandal of the incarnation is confirmed.[41]

Curiously, P66, which, as said, is one of the oldest witnesses to John's Gospel, omits any reference to Pilate's words in its original wording. According to this manuscript, the chief priests and officials call for

---

39. Joseph Ratzinger, *Jesus of Nazareth: From the Entrance into Jerusalem to the Resurrection* (Ignatius, 2011), 199.

40. Rudolf Bultmann, *The Gospel of John: A Commentary*, trans. George R. Beasley-Murray (Basil Blackwell, 1971), 659.

41. Rudolf Bultmann, *Theology of the New Testament*, trans. Kendrick Grobel, (SCM, 1965), 2:41: "John at the end brings this *skandalon* drastically into view when he has Pilate present the scourged and thorn-crowned Jesus to the crowd with the words, 'Behold the man!' (19:5 KJ) and, 'Behold your king' (19:14 KJ). Here and in the inscription over the cross (19:19) the paradoxical stumbling-block of Jesus' claim is presented in a symbol of tremendous irony."

Jesus's crucifixion when he is led out with the purple robe and crown of thorns, without Pilate making any presentation of the accused to the Jewish authorities. That is, the papyrus completely omits the moment Pilate presents Jesus with *Ecce homo*, which raises a handful of questions: Did the scribe who copied the manuscript or the community to which he belonged perceive the scandalous character of presenting Jesus as a poor man? Wouldn't pointing out the Son of God as a wretched man be taking things too far? Wouldn't such a humiliating reference have to be eliminated? We do not know, but if this were the reason, we would be dealing with a deliberate textual change, a change motivated by the theological concerns of those who copied the manuscripts and, therefore, with a variant that tells a story.

Ehrman thinks so. He believes that the omission of the words "and he says to them: behold the man" (καὶ λέγει αὐτοῖς—ἰδοὺ ὁ ἄνθρωπος) is an example of an "orthodox refusal" to present Jesus as "merely" human. In an alleged anti-adoptionist context in which, according to Ehrman, P66's scribe would be placed, the omission of Pilate's words was meant to prevent readers from identifying Jesus with a mere mortal.[42] His interpretation would be supported by the fact that these same words are also missing in some VL manuscripts unrelated to this codex (it [3, 2, 8, 14] ly), which would show that the omission was not accidental. Moreover, the deliberate nature of the change would appear to be confirmed by the reading of these same words in another of our oldest codices. Indeed, the article ὁ has been omitted before ἄνθρωπος in Codex Vaticanus, so that, according to Ehrman, Pilate would not be saying, "Behold the man" but "Behold a man." By omitting the article, the text would indicate that this mocked and dejected Jesus is merely "a mortal." For Ehrman, Codex Vaticanus's reading, which in his opinion was the most widespread, would have prompted P66's copyist to eliminate the entire phrase: "Scribes found its implication troubling; for them, even though Jesus had been bloodied and reviled: he was not a mere mortal. Pilate's statement to the contrary could best be dismissed by being excised."[43]

---

42. Ehrman, *Orthodox Corruption of Scripture*, 110. See Jeremiah Coogan, "Rethinking Adoptionism: An Argument for Dismantling a Dubious Category," *SJT* 76 (2023): 1–13.

43. Ehrman, *Orthodox Corruption of Scripture*, 110. So also Royse, who thinks that it does not appear that the omission is due to the scribe skipping a line in copying: "Ehrman is, as far as I can tell, correct in noting that there is no cause for accidental

It is not at all evident, however, that this omission corresponds to a theological motivation, as we will explore below. But what is of interest now, apart from this specific case, is to demonstrate that changes for theological reasons are not improbable.[44] Undoubtedly, the most striking example of this kind of change was Marcion's edition of the gospel and Pauline Letters.[45] Unfortunately, we hardly know how these texts read after his revision. Nor do we have any data about the changes made by Artemon's followers, who apparently used pagan criteria of literary criticism to "correct the Scriptures," according to Eusebius (*Hist. eccl.* 5.28.15–17).

However, there are other changes that, while less noticeable, may reflect a scribal interest in presenting a text more in line with a scribe's theological ideas. We know for example, of Mark 1:41, where Codex Bezae and the versions (3, 5, 8², 14*, Diatess^Ephrem)" show Jesus "angry" (ὀργισθείς) with the leper, while most of the textual tradition says that he "was moved to compassion" (σπλαγχνισθείς), perhaps to avoid an image of a Christ subject to less noble passions.[46] Another case is that of Mark 1:1, where some manuscripts add the title "Son of God" to Jesus Christ to avoid possible associations with adoptionism that could be read into Mark 1:11,

---

omission in Greek, Latin, or Coptic, and we can hardly suppose that precisely these words were written as one line in exemplars in all three languages" (*Scribal Habits*, 460). See below for a contrary opinion.

44. This type of alteration falls within what are sometimes called "deliberate" or "intentional" variants, as opposed to those called "accidental" or "errors." From a philosophical point of view, it is very complicated to determine what is meant by intentional, what is accidental, and what is an error. If we include the sometimes adduced "failed act" or Freudian slip, by which something different or contrary to the intention of the subject is expressed, the question becomes more complicated (see Parker, *Living Text*, 37; Parker, *Introduction to the New Testament Manuscripts*, 152). See also Royse, *Scribal Habits*, 97 n. 108; on the differences between intentional and accidental changes, see 96 n. 105, with quotations from fathers and ecclesiastical authors in this regard, and other bibliographical references. See also Haines-Eitzen, *Guardians of Letters*, 177 n. 10, with other references.

45. See Ulrich Schmid, *Marcion und sein Apostolos: Rekonstruktion und historische Einordnung der marcionitischen Paulusbriefausgabe*, ANTF 25 (De Gruyter, 1995); Dieter T. Roth, *The Text of Marcion's Gospel*, NTTSD 49 (Brill, 2015).

46. See Peter J. Williams, "An Examination of Ehrman's Case for ὀργισθείς in Mark 1:41," *NovT* 54 (2012): 1–12; Tjitze Baarda, "Mk 1:41: ὀργισθείς: A Reading Attested for Mar Ephraem, the Diatessaron, or Tatian," *ZNW* 103 (2012): 291–95. See also Peter Lorenz, "Counting Witnesses for the Angry Jesus in Mark 1:41: Interdependence and Insularity in the Latin Tradition," *TynBul* 67 (2016): 183–216.

"You are my Son the beloved, in you I am well pleased." With the addition in verse 1 it is clear from the beginning of the gospel that Jesus was God's Son and not simply the beloved son.[47] Another example is in Mark 15:34, where the word *despised* (ὠνείδισας), which appears in Codex Bezae, has probably been replaced by *forsaken* (ἐγκατέλιπες), to avoid a separationist reading of the text that would show a distance between the Father and the Son. Yet another case is Luke 2:43, where numerous manuscripts replace the reference to Jesus's "parents," who were unaware that the child had remained in Jerusalem, with "Joseph and his mother," thus showing that Jesus did not have a human father.[48]

It is possible that some of the unique readings in the oldest surviving papyri are theologically motivated. Even so, it is always necessary to weigh each case carefully to determine whether a reading was in fact deliberate and, if so, whether it was created for theological reasons or otherwise. It is true that some of the variants the papyri share with other manuscripts appear to reflect a deliberate change. For example, P75 reads "the only God" (μονογενὴς θεός) in John 1:18 instead of "the only son" (μονογενὴς υἱός), which some textual critics prefer on the basis of the internal evidence (and even then, it is disputed).[49] However, it is not clear that the variant of P75 and other supporting manuscripts emerged in an anti-adoptionist polemical context to show that Jesus is not a "mere man" rather than for other kinds of reasons. There may, of course, have been theological motives in the variant's origin, but they did not necessarily have to be polemical. Moreover, we could easily imagine that the change was initially produced for more prosaic reasons, such as a scribal error in copying the *nomen sacrum* "son" (ΥΣ) instead of "God" (ΘΣ), or by the influence of the ὁ ὤν that follows (see Rev 1:8: κύριος ὁ θεὸς ὁ ὤν, which has a strong liturgical character). In any case, it is not a singular reading, nor do we know when it originated.[50]

---

47. For a defense of the originality of the longer reading, see Tommy Wasserman, "The 'Son of God' Was in the Beginning (Mark 1:1)," *JTS* 62 (2011): 20–50.

48. Examples taken from Parker, "Jesus in Textual Criticism," 839–40.

49. They share reading with P75 01ᶜ 33 850 Syᵖ Syʰᵐᵍ copᵇᵒ Irᴸᵃᵗ Or. They have the same reading but without the article of P66 01* 03 04* 019 and several fathers, including most Alexandrians. The reading υἱός of the Byzantine text is attested by 02 04³ 032ˢ 033 037 038 044 045 063 0141 f¹ f¹³ 157 397 579 700 1071 1424 Maj Lat Syᶜ Syʰ Syᵖ arm geo Tert Hipp Clᴾᵗ Chrys. See Ehrman, *Orthodox Corruption of Scripture*, 92–96; Alexander Smarius, "Another God in the Gospel of John? A Linguistic Analysis of John 1:1 and 1:18," *HBT* 44 (2022): 158–59.

50. P66 shares with P75 the reading of μονογενὴς θεός instead of μονογενὴς υἱός,

On the other hand, P75's reading "not even a single thing" (οὐδὲ ἕν), instead of P66's "nothing" (οὐδέν), in John 1:3 (i.e., "without him nothing was done"), which could be a stylistic variant (οὐδὲ ἕν and οὐδέν are sometimes interchangeable in Greek) or simply an *epsilon* dropping out οὐδε[ε]ν), may have arisen in response to gnostics. In fact, Origen and Heracleon respectively discern different theological significances in this variant. For Heracleon, the Logos's creative activity did not extend to the divine pleroma (which is at the margin of creation), so he understood 1:3 to say "nothing [οὐδέν] comes into existence outside of it," that is, nothing except the pleroma. For Origen, however, there is nothing, "not even a single thing [οὐδὲ ἕν]," that exists in which Christ has not intervened.[51]

Also, P75 agrees with most manuscripts when it attests to the reading τοῦ κυρίου Ἰησοῦ in Luke 24:3 ("[the women who went to the tomb] on entering did not find the body of the Lord Jesus"), which was perhaps added for pious or theological reasons.[52] On the other hand, other P75 variants in Luke, which have been suspected of theological motives, are best explained as a product of scribal harmonization (with the context or with various parallels), an oversight, stylistic improvements, or simply the reading of the *Vorlage*.[53]

Several readings have been identified as the product of theological motives in P66. We have already alluded to the omission of Pilate's words

---

but omitting the article before μονογενής. For Ehrman, the variant arises in a typically Alexandrian anti-adoptionist context, so that Christ is not simply described as the "only Son" but is God, the "only God," distinct from the Father but his coequal (*Orthodox Corruption of Scripture*, 92).

51. Bart D. Ehrman, "The Use and Significance of Patristic Evidence for NT Textual Criticism," in *New Testament Textual Criticism, Exegesis and Church History: A Discussion of Methods*, ed. Barbara Aland and Joel Delobel (Pharos, 1994), 128–29. See also Schnackenburg, *Gospel according to St John*, 1:239–40.

52. This is one of the "Western noninterpolations," the omission of which is maintained by 05 and VL (see Hernández, "Early Text of Luke," 134; Ehrman, *Orthodox Corruption of Scripture*, 256). The same can be said of the addition of 24:51b, already noted above.

53. Mikeal C. Parsons, "A Christological Tendency in P75," *JBL* 105 (1986): 474–75; Parsons, *The Departure of Jesus in Luke-Acts* (Sheffield Academic, 1987). Parsons investigates the theological tendency in the case of Western noninterpolations (passages that appear in almost all manuscripts but are omitted in Codex Bezae [05] and related witnesses to it) and complements his analysis of P75 with 05. See Royse's detailed critique of Parsons in *Scribal Habits*, 698–703; Hernández, "Early Text of Luke," 132 n. 66.

in John 19:5, which Ehrman considers an attempt to avoid presenting Jesus as a mere man. Ehrman proposes other variants: (1) the inclusion of "truly" (ἀληθῶς) in Nathanael's confession in John 1:49: "You are truly the son of God" (σὺ εἶ ἀληθῶς ὁ υἱὸς τοῦ θεοῦ), to emphasize that Jesus was truly the Christ; according to Royse, however, this variant is the product of a harmonization with the context or a parallel passage (e.g., in the confession of the disciples after Jesus calms the storm in Matt 14:33, and also in Matt 27:54, Mark 15:39; in all these cases the confession is accompanied by ἀληθῶς, "truly."[54] (2) The accentuation of irony through indirect style by substituting ὅτι for οὐχ in 6:42, altering, "And they said, 'Is not this Jesus, the son of Joseph?'" to "And they said that this is Jesus, the son of Joseph," in order to avoid an adoptionist interpretation (which for Ehrman would be confirmed by the addition of μου after ὁ πατήρ in 6:44, thereby highlighting that Jesus comes from heaven); Royse, however, demonstrates that they are neither related nor intentional: the scribe corrected his error in 6:42, and the addition in 6:44 is likely a harmonization to the immediate context, since ὁ πατήρ μου surfaces frequently in John (it appears in 5:17, 43; 6:32).[55] (3) The inclusion of the article τόν before "God" (θεόν) in 10:33, so that, by saying, "Being a man you become God" (σὺ ἄνθρωπος ὢν ποιεῖς σευτὸν τὸν θεόν), Jesus does not appear as equal "to a god" but as really God, something that, according to Ehrman, was noted by the correcting hand of the same P66 who then deleted the article, because he understood that the text ran the risk of being interpreted incorrectly (as the patripassians later did).[56] In any case, Royse believes the addition is best explained as a dittography (σεαυτὸν τὸν θεόν), which the scribe corrects.[57]

Ehrman also sees in other readings of this codex an attempt to stress the orthodox understanding of Jesus's human and divine natures. He argues, for example, that P66's scribe modified the text of John 9:33,

---

54. Ehrman, *Orthodox Corruption of Scripture*, 188; Royse, *Scribal Habits*, 457.

55. Ehrman, *Orthodox Corruption of Scripture*, 67; Royse, *Scribal Habits*, 509–10 n. 578.

56. Ehrman, *Orthodox Corruption of Scripture*, 99.

57. Royse, *Scribal Habits*, 459. Peter M. Head considers Ehrman's emphasis on the absence of the article to be exaggerated and subscribes to Royse's explanation. See Head, "Scribal Behaviour and Theological Tendencies in Singular Readings in P. Bodmer II (P66)," in *Textual Variation: Theological and Social Tendencies?*, ed. Hugh A. G. Houghton and David C. Parker (Gorgias, 2008), 66–67.

which reads "if this [οὗτος] were not from God, he could do nothing," by adding "man" (ὁ ἄνθρωπος) in order to emphasize Jesus's human nature. Most manuscripts lack this word.⁵⁸ The same tendency would be observed in 7:46. The words uttered by the high priests' envoys according to most manuscripts, "Never did a man speak thus" (οὐδέποτε ἐλάλησεν οὕτως ἄνθρωπος), are ambiguous. Is Jesus the best teacher among all men, or, rather, are the teachings of Jesus not those of a mortal? P66's scribe would have resolved the ambiguity by writing, "Never did a man speak thus as this man speaks" (οὐδέποτε οὕτως ἄνθρωπος ἐλάλησεν ὡς οὗτος λαλεῖ ὁ ἄνθρωπος ὁ ἄνθρωπος), as other manuscripts do. Thus, servants of the Jewish authorities would be claiming that no person in Israel ever spoke like Jesus, that is, they would be emphasizing his humanity, so as to avoid a docetic interpretation.⁵⁹

Finally, this antidocetic tendency would be confirmed by the omission of "that the scripture might be fulfilled" (ἵνα τελειωθῇ ἡ γραφή) in 19:28, when the evangelist notes that Jesus said, "I thirst." The reference to the fulfillment of Scripture is the reading of the other manuscripts. In Ehrman's judgment, however, its omission in P66 is not accidental. The scribe omitted those words to avoid the impression that Jesus was only thirsting for the fulfillment of the Scriptures rather than really thirsting like a suffering man: "Now Jesus really *is* thirsty in the throes of death. This is a real, human, suffering Jesus, the Jesus that proto-orthodox Christians set forth in opposition to various docetic heresies."⁶⁰ Kurt Aland, however, believes that the omission is not a variant "but only a negligence of the scribe."⁶¹ Peter Head, for his part, considers Ehrman's comments speculative and points out that his proposed theological tendency in the omission

---

58. Ehrman, *Orthodox Corruption of Scripture*, 134 n. 185. But Royse suggests that it is a desire to avoid a possible pejorative sense (*Scribal Habits*, 509–10).

59. Ehrman, *Orthodox Corruption of Scripture*, 278. The reading is from the original scribe and was later corrected, probably by the same scribe, which makes Ehrman's interpretation difficult. Readings in other manuscripts vary in word order and in the addition or omission of ὡς οὗτος λαλεῖ ὁ ἄνθρωπος. The reading of P66* is shared by ℵ* and D. However, Royse thinks that it may be the result of a correction of a previous reading he passed on to what the scribe of P66 found in his *Vorlage* and which the latter understood as an addition rather than a substitution (*Scribal Habits*, 455–56).

60. Ehrman, *Orthodox Corruption of Scripture*, 228, emphasis original. Royse accepts this interpretation (*Scribal Habits*, 460).

61. Kurt Aland, "Über die Möglichkeit der Identifikation kleiner Fragmente neutestamentlicher Handschriften mit Hilfe des Computers," in *Studies in New Testament*

of 19:28 runs in the opposite direction of the one proposed for the omission of 19:5. If, in 19:5, the scribe wanted to avoid exposing the humanity of Jesus (according to Ehrman), the omission in 19:28 would underscore precisely that humanity. For this reason, like Aland, Head believes that it is simply an error, due to the fact that toward the end of the book the scribe is less careful.[62]

All of these variants do not merit detailed discussion. Most have already been explained on more probable grounds. On other occasions, as in the omission of Pilate's words in 19:5 ("and he saith unto them, behold the man"), Ehrman's reasons are unconvincing.[63] In fact, an observation that weakens his hypothesis (that P66's scribe wanted to avoid presenting Jesus as a mere man) is that other references to Jesus as a man (using the term ἄνθρωπος) are kept in P66, without similar changes.[64] Moreover, the alleged antidocetic[65] interest present in the aforementioned readings (in 7:46, 19:28), as Head points out, does not fit well with a deliberate omission of 19:5, when Pilate's very words serve to show that Jesus was truly a man. In other words, does the scribe avoid presenting Jesus as a man so that his readers do not fall into adoptionism, or does he emphasize that he is a man so that they do not fall into docetism? The inconsistency indicates that P66's omission was probably due to a simple scribal oversight rather than the scribe's desire to ensure the copied text's orthodoxy.[66]

Language and Text: Essays in Honour of George D. Kilpatrick on the Occasion of His Sixty-Fifth Birthday, ed. J. Keith Elliott, NovTSup 44 (Brill, 1976), 34.

62. Head, "Scribal Behaviour," 70–71.

63. As Head points out, "it is more difficult to attribute motives to omissions than to other types of disturbances" ("Scribal Behaviour," 70).

64. E.g., John 4:29; 11:47, 50; 18:14 [vid], 29 [vid]) (see Head, "Scribal Behaviour," 70).

65. There is, of course, a growing consensus today that terms designating "heterodox" groups and their teachings in the early centuries are to be used advisedly insofar as they often emerge in polemical contexts prone to distortion. See Michael A. Williams, *Rethinking "Gnosticism": An Argument for Dismantling a Dubious Category* (Princeton University Press, 1996); Coogan, "Rethinking Adoptionism," 1–13.

66. Royse wonders whether in this variant of 19:5 the twenty-three omitted letters would correspond to a line of the copy that the scribe copied, and therefore the omission could have been accidental (*Scribal Habits*, 459–60). However, he thinks that, given their absence also in Latin and Coptic witnesses (it ly), the omission could have been intentional.

We note that the variant in 19:5 and other P66 variants cited by Ehrman to support the idea of orthodox corruption are found in the codex's original version and were later corrected in the same manuscript. Therefore, following Ehrman's logic, we would have to understand that a correcting hand contemporary to the original scribe, perhaps using another copy of the text, disagreed with the "orthodox corruption" and corrected it in favor of the "heterodox" reading. This does not fit well with Ehrman's basic thesis. Moreover, it is quite likely that the vast majority of P66's corrections, among which could be the insertion of the omitted words in the margins in 19:5, were made not by another hand but by the same scribe who initially copied the text.[67] Unfortunately, the papyrus is damaged, and we do not know what the corrector added. But if the corrector was the same individual who copied the rest of the book and had indicated the omitted words ("and he says to them: behold the man") in the margin, we would have to assume that, if he had omitted them for theological reasons, his "orthodoxy" was short-lived, since he appeared to resume his "heterodoxy" by correcting the very text he had changed.

These examples show that the theological motivations Ehrman identifies in P66 are suggestive but questionable. This is confirmed by Head's study of unique readings related to christological variants and attitudes toward Judaism attested in John 7:52; 8:42; 10:33; 11:4, 34, 39; 19:5, 28; 12:11; 15:25. His conclusion is clear: "Attempts to discern a theological agenda in the work of our scribe generally involve over-interpreting the variations and, in any case, result in contradictory tendencies. I think it is preferable to see these as more or less directionless variations on the part of our careless, but committed scribe."[68]

P66, of course, is not the only papyrus with variants suspected of having originated for theological reasons. Some of P45's readings also fall into this category. As with P66, however, such readings can be explained on other grounds. For example, Ehrman argues that, similar to the addition

---

67. Royse, *Scribal Habits*, 413–21.

68. Head, "Scribal Behaviour," 73. This does not mean, of course, that variants could not have been introduced for various reasons, ecclesiastical, theological, or otherwise. For example, according to Elizabeth Schrader, P66 would reflect that Martha's name was added secondarily in the episode of Lazarus's resurrection, intended to subtly avoid identifying Mary of Bethany with Mary Magdalene. See Schrader, "Was Martha of Bethany Added to the Fourth Gospel in the Second Century?," *HTR* 110 (2017): 360–92, 473–74.

of "truly" (ἀληθῶς) in John 1:49 in P66, the addition in P45 of the article ὁ before "son of God" (υἱὸς τοῦ θεοῦ) in John 10:36, where Jesus defends himself from his accusers, who brand him a blasphemer for saying, "I am the son of God" (υἱὸς τοῦ θεοῦ εἰμι), serves to emphasize that "Jesus is (truly) the Christ, the Son of God."[69] This variant does not need to be an intentional theological change, however. Regardless of whether that was the text before the scribe, the general context accounts for the addition; indeed, the article precedes the expression "son of God" (υἱὸς τοῦ θεοῦ) elsewhere in John.[70]

Theological reasons have also been suggested for variants in other, more fragmentary papyri. In particular, Juan Hernández argues for them in two cases of P4: the addition of the article τοῦ before "Lord" (κυρίου) in Luke 1:76 ("[you will] go before the Lord," ἐνώπιον κυρίου) as a way of stressing the divinity of Jesus; and the change of the adjective "bodily" (σωματικῷ) to "spiritual" (πνεύματι) in Luke 3:22 ("and the Holy Spirit came down upon him in bodily form," καὶ καταβῆναι τὸ πνεῦμα τὸ ἅγιον σωματικῷ εἴδει), to imply that the Holy Spirit descended spiritually or as a spirit, thereby avoiding any identification with a corporeal form.[71] Also, in Jesus's invocation to the Father in his prayer in the garden in Matt 26:39, "My Father," Ehrman understands that, if the original reading were just "Father," as it appears in P53, the addition of the pronoun μου, which according to the *editio princeps* was made by a hand contemporary with the first copyist, is an antipatripassian corruption to show that Jesus was truly the Son of God.[72] Finally, for P101 Tommy Wasserman has suggested that the omission of "after me" (ὀπίσω μου) in Matt 3:11 ("he who comes after me is mightier than I") might have been intended to prevent Jesus from being considered a disciple of John.[73]

It is quite possible that some of the readings examined by Ehrman in *The Orthodox Corruption of Scripture* were introduced for theological

---

69. Ehrman, *Orthodox Corruption of Scripture*, 188.

70. Royse, *Scribal Habits*, 194.

71. See Hernández, "Early Text of Luke," 126. However, it has also been understood as a scribal error (see Head, "Observations on Early Papyri," 243).

72. Ehrman, *Orthodox Corruption of Scripture*, 319 n. 42. As Wasserman points out, the reading without the pronoun is poorly attested, and so the addition of μου would be more than an "orthodox corruption," a harmonization with the context (see Matt 26:42: "My Father"; Wasserman, "Early Text of Matthew," 94).

73. Wasserman, "Early Text of Matthew," 99.

reasons.[74] His work is extensive, and his arguments are not so easily dismissed. Here we have examined only a handful of his proposals related to specific papyri. Undoubtedly, there will be other cases in which Ehrman's interpretation is compelling. However, his explanations for some of the variants in the oldest papyri are by no means self-evident, nor free of a good deal of speculation. This does not preclude that some variants may reflect the sociocultural environment in which these texts were copied. The circumstances under which manuscripts were copied are of great significance and merit study. We will turn to this below, after addressing questions related to how we attempt to establish the New Testament texts closest to the originals.

---

74. See also ch. 4 of this book.

Critical Concern to Establish the Text

Of the approximately 5,700 cataloged New Testament manuscripts, about 360 are dated prior to 800 CE. Of these, about 190 are prior to the fifth century, and of these, only four are extant that contain the entire New Testament.[1] Moreover, as already indicated, the oldest copies that have come down to us, the papyrus witnesses, are overwhelmingly very fragmentary, and none of these papyri contains a single complete or almost complete New Testament book. Neither are any of these manuscripts identical to any other. They have all undergone changes, voluntarily or accidentally, in the copying process.

1. The Textual Criticism of the New Testament

Faced with such diverse material, New Testament textual criticism is the discipline that aims to recover the text closest to the originals. This is an arduous and complex task. It requires the examination of each manuscript—both as an artifact and for its transmitted text—in an attempt to discover what the preceding manuscripts (exemplars) were like from which that particular copy is derived.

Specifically, as David Parker states, variants must be analyzed in order to determine the order of their emergence. After evaluating all that material, one should then try to establish a better text.[2]

---

1. On updated global numbers, see Leggett and Paulson, "How Many Greek New Testament Manuscripts." See also Eldon J. Epp, "Textual Criticism in the Exegesis of the New Testament with an Excursus on Canon," in *Handbook to Exegesis of the New Testament*, ed. Stanley E. Porter, NTTS 25 (Brill, 1999), 56; and table 6.10 in Epp, "Are Early New Testament Manuscripts," 94–102.

2. Parker, *Introduction to the New Testament Manuscripts*, 159; Parker, "Scripture Is Tradition," *Theology* 94 (1991): 12.

The concern to determine the best possible text of a literary work is not new. It dates back to the world of Alexandrian Hellenism, which, in the last two centuries before our era, attempted to recover the original texts of many works of classical antiquity.[3] This task was soon extended to the biblical text, especially by Origen, who, as in so many other exegetical and theological questions, was a pioneer in this.[4] Alexandria's academic tradition, which had shaped the Hexapla's author, probably contributed to this interest in establishing the best text, an interest that must not have been exclusive to him but shared by scholars of the region. This is one of the reasons manuscripts linked to Egypt's ancient capital are thought to reflect the objective of Christian scribes to preserve the best possible text of the books that would form the New Testament and why the Alexandrian manuscripts are also usually considered to be of higher quality.[5]

With the emergence of the scriptoria, probably from the fourth century onward, the production of Bible copies became more and more professional, thereby reducing the number of errors compared to previous times.[6] Later, it was the monks in particular who were responsible for copying and transmitting the Greek text throughout the Middle Ages and up to the invention of the printing press. It is in this area, from the seventh century onward, that many manuscripts were produced in the eastern part of the Byzantine Empire whose copies displayed fewer differences among themselves (without necessarily offering a better witness to the New Testament text). Meanwhile, in the West, in the face of the multiplicity of

---

3. See Rudolf Pfeiffer, *History of Classical Scholarship: From the Beginnings to the End of the Hellenistic Age* (Clarendon, 1968), 87–279.

4. See Bart D. Ehrman, "Origen and the Text of the New Testament," in *The Text of the Fourth Gospel in the Writings of Origen*, by Bart D. Erhman, Gordon D. Fee, and Michael W. Holmes, NTGF 3 (Scholars Press, 1992), 1–20.

5. Günther Zuntz, *The Text of the Epistles; A Disquisition upon the Corpus Paulinum* (British Academy, 1953), 271–76; Geoffrey W. H. Lampe, ed., *The West, from the Fathers to the Reformation*, CHB 2 (Cambridge University Press, 1969).

6. The origin of the scriptoria is not clear due to the absence of data and the lack of agreement on what they consisted of. For their possible existence in Oxyrhynchus in the third century (with further bibliography), see Alan Mugridge, "What Is a Scriptorium?," in *Proceedings of the Twenty-Fourth Congress of Papyrology, Helsinki, 1–7 August, 2004*, ed. Jaakko Frösén, Tiina Purola, and Erja Salmenkivi (Societas Scientiarum Fennica, 2007), 781–92; Lincoln H. Blumell, *Lettered Christians: Christians, Letters, and Late Antique Oxyrhynchus*, NTTSD 39 (Brill, 2012), 180.

translations of the biblical text, the Vulgate (the Latin version that Pope Damasus had entrusted to Jerome as the official Latin translation from the ancient Latin versions that had begun to appear since the second century) began to prevail. The use and diffusion of this version was such that the number of extant Vulgate manuscripts almost doubles that of New Testament Greek manuscripts.[7]

The invention of the printing press, together with the love of literature and the passion for classical antiquity that characterized the Renaissance, made possible the recovery and printing of the New Testament Greek text, especially in the West, where it had been practically relegated to oblivion by the almost exclusive use of the official Latin version.[8] After Desiderius Erasmus's *editio princeps*, published in 1516, the work of Robert Estienne (known as Stephanus) marks a milestone in the history of critical editions of the Greek New Testament. In 1550, Estienne published the third edition of the New Testament text established by Erasmus, enriching it with annotations that highlighted the differences between the fifteen manuscripts he himself had handled. Since then, critical editions have multiplied. The first edition with an extensive critical apparatus was John Mill's (1645–1707); Mill, after thirty years of work, published in 1707 an edition of the New Testament, printing the textus receptus published by Estienne in 1550 and a critical apparatus featuring about a hundred Greek manuscripts, quotations from the fathers of the church, and Latin, Syriac, and Coptic versions. The edition he produced presented a text with more than thirty thousand variants, which he introduced with a prolegomena that discussed the New Testament canon and the text's transmission, described thirty-two printed New Testament editions, and discussed 3,041 of the almost eight thousand verses it contains.[9] Subsequently, the seventeenth- and eighteenth-century contributions of Richard Simon, Richard Bentley, and Johann Salomo Semler led to refinements in text-critical method, and the editions of Johann Albrecht Bengel (1734), Johann Jakob Wettstein (1751–1752), Johann Jakob Griesbach (2nd ed., 1796–1806) and Karl Lachmann (1831 and 1842–1850) paved the way for those of Constantin von Tischendorf

---

7. Bruce M. Metzger, *The Early Versions of the New Testament: Their Origin, Transmission and Limitations* (Clarendon, 1977), 293.

8. For a detailed history, see Metzger and Ehrman, *Text of the New Testament*, 137–204.

9. Metzger and Ehrman, *Text of the New Testament*, 154.

(8th ed., 1869–1872), Brooke Foss Westcott and Fenton John Anthony Hort (1881), and Hermann von Soden (1902–1910/1913), true masterpieces of scholarship and science.[10]

In any case, it was in the twentieth century when access to an increasing number of manuscripts opened new channels for New Testament textual criticism and led to the publication of more accessible critical editions. After those by Bernhard Weiss (1894–1900) and Alexander Souter (2nd ed., 1947)—and here we include those published by Catholic scholars such as Heinrich Joseph Vogels (4th ed., 1955), Augustinus Merk (1933), José Maria Bover (1943), and Bover and José O'Callaghan (1977)—some critical editions were published that enjoyed great popularity. These editions not only contributed to the stabilization and diffusion of a text that would be widely considered the standard New Testament text but also posed new challenges and shed light on a more fundamental problem: to what extent it is possible to speak of the original text, how to arrive at it, and, if feasible, how to recover it.

1.1. Modern Critical Editions: NA and UBS/GNT

Among the various critical editions of more recent times, the one prepared by Eberhard Nestle (1851–1913), who in 1898 published a manual edition of the Greek New Testament that reflected the text critical consensus of his time, stands out.[11] Numerous reprints were published. In 1950, Kurt Aland (1915–1994) began working on the Nestle edition, which was already a very popular hand edition. Starting with the twenty-fifth edition, it took the name Nestle-Aland.[12] Almost simultaneously, the United

---

10. For the history of this and the following period, see Metzger and Ehrman, *Text of the New Testament*, 156–94.

11. This consensus was represented by Constantin von Tischendorf, Westcott-Hort (Brooke F. Westcott and Fenton J. A. Hort; and Richard F. Weymouth, at first), and Bernhard Weiss. Nestle's son, Erwin Nestle (1883–1972), published in 1927 the thirteenth edition, with a critical apparatus made from Hermann von Soden's edition, in which there were references to manuscripts, versions, and fathers. See Moisés Silva, "Modern Critical Editions and Apparatuses," in *The Text of the New Testament in Contemporary Research: Essays on the Status Quaestionis*, ed. Bart D. Ehrman and Michael W. Holmes (Eerdmans, 1995), 285. In this work's second edition (2013), the author of the chapter with the same title is Juan Hernández Jr.

12. See Gregory S. Paulson, "Die Geschichte des Novum Testamentum Graece/Nestle-Aland," in *Biblica Monasteriensia*, ed. Holger Strutwolf and Jan Graefe (LIT,

Bible Societies set out to produce a critical edition designed especially for Bible translators in 1955. The result was the *Greek New Testament*, which was first published in 1966, accompanied by a textual commentary prepared by Bruce Metzger.[13] But Aland's presence in both the Bible Societies' and the Nestle-Aland project helped to join forces in the production and dissemination of a new Greek text, the twenty-sixth edition of the Nestle-Aland (NA[26]), which appeared in 1979 and adopted the same text as the 1975 third edition of the Bible Societies. In 1993, using the text of UBS/GNT[4] and NA[26], NA[27] was published with a modest but significant number of improvements.[14]

A new development came with the 2012 publication of the twenty-eighth edition of Nestle-Aland (NA[28]). For the first time in the history of Nestle-Aland editions, there are two methodologies operative in the reconstruction of the Greek New Testament. The Catholic Letters present a new text—the result of a revision of the previous text published in the second edition of the *Editio Critica Maior*—as opposed to the remaining New Testament books, whose text continues to be that of the previous editions, albeit all collated *ex novo*.[15] The new method of revision used for

---

2024), 5:85–99; Simon Crisp, "Eugene Nida and the UBS Greek New Testament," in Βιβλικές μεταφράσεις – Ιστορία και πράξη: Επετειακός επιστημονικός τόμος για τα διακόσια χρόνια της Ελληνικής Βιβλικής Εταιρίας, ed. Maria Schick and Kostas Tsiknakis (Athens, 2021), 89–105.

13. The World Association of Bible Societies was founded in 1946. The committee was originally composed of Kurt Aland, Matthew Black, Allen Wikgren, and Bruce Metzger. The second edition—with Carlo M. Martini joining the committee to replace Arthur Vööbus—was published in 1968. In 1982, Barbara Aland and Johannes Karavidopoulos joined the committee. Commentary: Bruce M. Metzger, *A Textual Commentary*, first published in 1971 and of which a second edition was published in 1994.

14. Although the text remains unchanged, the main contribution was a revision of the critical apparatus with regard to the manuscripts cited and the inclusion of Variae Lectiones Minores (an appendix that breaks down the contents of the manuscripts that appear in parentheses in the critical apparatus). The edition also included new papyri (which for the eighth reprint of 2001 counts the 116 papyri published to date) and employs 239 majuscules, 219 minuscules, and nine lectionaries (as opposed to the 69 lectionaries of the UBS[4]). In addition, some of the variant entries were rewritten, giving greater prominence to the minuscule manuscripts, some of which are included for the first time among the "consistently cited witnesses," replacing some of the majuscules cited in the previous edition.

15. The result is thirty-three different passages with respect to the Nestle-Aland edition, in addition to 125 cases whose original reading is unknown and which in *ECM*

the Catholic Letters will be adopted in the future for the New Testament edition as a whole.[16] In the meantime, an editorial committee appointed by the United Bible Societies is preparing NA[29].[17]

1.2. Modern Critical Editions: International Greek New Testament Project

Alongside the publication of subsequent critical editions for manual use, in recent years various projects have been developed aimed at obtaining a greater clarification of the Greek text of the New Testament. In chronolog-

---

second edition are presented in an open manner, dividing the text into two parallel lines. In these cases, NA[28]'s text maintains a single line but preceding the reading with a diamond-shaped sign. The critical apparatus has also been completely revised to make it clearer and more user-friendly but retains the same basic structure as the twenty-seventh edition. The general revision and correction work includes an update of the list of newly discovered papyri to date, abandons the distinction between first and second order of consistently cited witnesses, excludes conjecture, stops adding *pauci* and *alii*, eliminates inaccuracies, reduces and translates Latin texts, etc. Consistently cited witnesses have also been defined, following the method by which the *ECM* text was produced (see below), and the Gothic letter 𝔐, which indicated the reading of the majority text, has been replaced by "Byz." Likewise, marginal references have been revised, and a standard method has been adopted in spelling, affecting a total of over two hundred readings.

16. Since it first appeared in 2012, several reprints of NA[28] have been published, correcting some errata; the latest is the fifth reprint of 2016. It is also available in digital format. In 2014 the fifth edition of the UBS/GNT was published, with the same text of NA[28].

17. It will consider the considerable progress that the *ECM* has made since the publication of NA[28]. The main stages of the revision are the incorporation of all textual changes of the *ECM* in the Gospel of Mark (*ECM* 1.2), Acts (*ECM* 3) and Revelation (*ECM* 4), published between 2017 and 2024; the revision of the text-critical apparatus (witnesses and selection of variants) in Mark, Acts, and Revelation; and the adaptation of the permanent witnesses in the Pauline Letters in accordance with the preliminary work on the Pauline corpus within the framework of the *ECM*. In addition, manuscripts (papyri) discovered or accessible in the meantime have been incorporated into the apparatus, as well as numerous selected adjustments. The most notable change, however, will probably be that the order of the twenty-seven NT writings will be adapted to the order found in the vast majority of ancient manuscripts. In these, the Acts of the Apostles is usually transmitted together with the so-called Catholic Letters. Thus, in NA[29], the Acts of the Apostles will be followed by the Catholic Letters. These will be followed, in turn, by the letters of St. Paul, within which there will also be small changes corresponding to the manuscripts. See "Ausblick: Nestle-Aland 29," Deutsche Bibel Gesellschaft.

ical order, the International Greek New Testament Project, which began in 1949 within the American Society of Biblical Literature, follows the Critical Greek Testament project initiated in 1926.[18] The International Greek New Testament Project was directed by an international committee of experts in textual criticism from Europe and America. The first volume, Luke, was published in the 1980s.[19] In 2005 the International Greek New Testament Project committee merged with the Institute for New Testament Textual Research—Institut für Neutestamentliche Textforschung—in Münster and assumed responsibility for the *Editio Critica Maior* of John.[20] Once completed, it will undertake the edition of the Pauline Letters, which is expected to be completed in 2031.

A second important project is the Gospel according to John in the Byzantine Tradition, which is part of a more ambitious project on the Byzantine or Majority Text.[21] Its origin dates back to 1999, when the Bible

---

18. See the International Greek New Testament Project, http://www.igntp.org/.

19. The American and British Committees of the International Greek New Testament Project, eds., *The New Testament in Greek: The Gospel according to St. Luke*, 2 vols. (Oxford University Press, 1984, 1987).

20. Transcriptions of the New Testament manuscripts made so far, electronic editions, and other resources, together with an abundant bibliography, can be found on the project's website. The IGNTP editions in John can be found online at www.iohannes.com. See Klaus Wachtel and David C. Parker, "The Joint IGNTP/INTF Editio Critica Maior of the Gospel of John" (paper presented at the Meeting of the Society for New Testament Studies, Halle, 15 August 2005), https://tinyurl.com/SBL7016e. The members of the editorial team for the Gospel of John are Wachtel, Parker, Holger Strutwolf, Ulrich Schmid, Gerd Mink, and Bruce Morrill. The following have been published: William J. Elliott and David C. Parker, eds., *The Papyri*, vol. 1 of *The New Testament in Greek IV: The Gospel according to St John*, NTTS 20 (Brill, 1995); Ulrich B. Schmid, William J. Elliott, and David C. Parker, eds., *The Majuscules*, vol. 2 of *The New Testament in Greek IV: The Gospel according to St. John*, NTTSD 37 (Brill, 2006). These aim to present a critical apparatus that is as broad as possible. The sociohistorical dimensions of early Christianity latent in the diversity of variants are also considered. The restoration of the text is deferred by more immediate codicological concerns. See Silva, "Modern Critical Editions and Apparatuses," 293–94; Juan Hernández Jr., "Modern Critical Editions," in Ehrman and Holmes, *Text of the New Testament in Contemporary Research* (2nd ed.), 700.

21. As is known, the Byzantine text is a text type represented by many manuscripts. For some scholars, it is the closest text to the canonical autographs, being the archetype from which other text types are derived. Hernández points out, however, that the lack of evidence for an early and dominant Byzantine text undermines this thesis ("Modern Critical Editions," 694–95). The oldest manuscript is from the fifth

78   The Textual Transmission of the New Testament

Societies held a meeting at El Escorial (Madrid). Delegates from the Orthodox churches came to that meeting requesting the preparation of a critical text of the Byzantine text that could be used for translations into vernacular languages. The project, which began with the Gospel of John, is an example of a text reconstructed to meet the needs of the Eastern Orthodox churches.[22]

1.3. Modern Critical Editions: *Editio Critica Maior*

Of particular relevance is the aforementioned *Novum Testamentum Graecum: Editio Critica Maior*. It is a work designed by the Institut für Neutestamentliche Textforschung in Münster, which is a milestone in the history of critical editions. For the first time in decades (NA[26] in 1979), a section of the New Testament text has been reconstructed afresh from previously unused manuscript data. The new advances in theory and method of textual criticism have also been considered. In 1997, the fascicle for the Letter of James appeared. Later 1–2 Peter (2000), 1 John (2003), and 2 John–Jude (2005) were published. The second edition was published in 2013. Each fascicle has two parts: the text with an apparatus and a volume with supplementary material.[23] The aim is to establish the text and trace

---

century, and patristic testimonies prior to the fourth century do not seem to know this text type. The few early papyri that have Byzantine readings are not sufficient to speak of a priority. For this reason, the editions made by Arthur L. Farstad and Zane C. Hodges or Maurice A. Robinson and William G. Pierpont, are at most useful reproductions of one of the texts that had the widest diffusion in the history of Christianity. See Arthur L. Farstad and Zane C. Hodges, *The Greek New Testament according to the Majority Text: English and Greek Edition*, 2nd ed. (Nelson Reference and Electronic, 1985); Maurice A. Robinson and William G. Pierpont, *The New Testament in the Original Greek: Byzantine Textform* (Chilton, 2005). This does not prevent a particular ecclesiastical tradition from choosing this type of text as normative.

22. Roderic L. Mullen with Simon Crisp and David C. Parker for the United Bible Societies, eds., *The Gospel according to John in the Byzantine Tradition* (Deutsche Bibelgesellschaft, 2007). The edition presents as its base text MS 35, an eleventh-century Byzantine manuscript. See "An Electronic Edition of the Gospel According to John in the Byzantine Tradition," Electronic Editions of the Gospel According to John in Greek, Latin, Syriac and Coptic, last revised July 2014, http://www.iohannes.com/byzantine/index.html.

23. Hernández notes that the design of the ECM encourages an interaction between text and apparatus ("Modern Critical Editions," 704). To avoid repeating the citation of the full lemma in the apparatus, each word in the established text carries an

its transmission during the first millennium, from the earliest forms to the Byzantine text. Subsequently, Acts of the Apostles (2017), the Gospel of Mark (2021), and Revelation (2024) were published. Each of these adds new features to the editions, particularly Revelation. The electronic edition is also announced.

Although the first fascicle does not specify the method used to reconstruct the text, the critical method that emerges in the following volumes is the coherence-based genealogical method (CBGM).[24] It is a method designed to examine the relationships between manuscripts in order to establish the text. This method does not replace the internal and external criteria but is an additional tool along with other external criteria. It seeks to determine the plausible textual flow by examining the genealogical coherence between witnesses. An essential concept is that of the potential ancestor. One of two textual witnesses can be classified as a potential ancestor of the other if it more frequently supports a variant from which the variant of the other witness can be derived. Some witnesses have many potential ancestors; others have few or only one. The percentages of agreement between witnesses are used to rank each witness' potential ancestor(s).[25]

---

even number, while spaces carry odd numbers. Valid alternative readings are indicated by a bold dot in the first line of the text. Readers must therefore judge whether the dot signals an alternative reading of "equal value" to that of the established text or one that simply cannot be excluded.

24. See Gerd Mink, "The Coherence Based Genealogical Method. What Is It About?," Institut für Neutestamentliche Textforschung, https://tinyurl.com/SBL7016f. On this method, see Tommy Wasserman and Peter J. Gurry, *A New Approach to Textual Criticism: An Introduction to the Coherence-Based Genealogical Method*, ed. Michael W. Holmes, RBS 80 (SBL Press, 2017).

25. According to Hernández, of the thirty-three new readings in the ECM of the Catholic Letters, seven involve a return to Westcott and Hort's text, and two others had been considered by Westcott and Hort as readings that had a reasonable probability of authenticity ("Modern Critical Editions," 705). Of the seventy-six that present an alternative reading, nineteen involve a return to Westcott and Hort, and six were considered by the English scholars to be serious candidates for the text. Most of the changes concern word order or the omission of a word or part of a word. Only a few carries with them a semantic difference. Of these, for example, the selection of οὐχ εὑρθήσεται over εὑρθήσεται in 2 Pet 3:10, an unsupported conjecture from Greek manuscripts read in the Sahidic text and in some witnesses of the Philoxenian Syriac, is interesting. Other readings with semantic differences are the substitution of μέρει for ὀνόματι in 1 Pet 4:16 (a pure Byzantine reading) and of παρὰ κυρίῳ for παρὰ κυρίου in 2 Pet 2:11. For the first

Editors reconstruct the *Ausgangstext*, the "initial text," which is not the text of the author, nor that of the archetype of the manuscript tradition (nor is it identical to the eclectic text of UBS⁴/NA²⁷), but the text form that is at the beginning of a textual tradition. Put more precisely, the *Ausgangstext* is "the reconstructed hypothetical form of text from which all surviving witnesses descend, a stage of a text's history that stands between its literary formation, on the one hand, and the archetype of the extant manuscripts, on the other."[26] Theoretically, the "initial text" may correspond to the *Editio Critica Maior*'s guiding line, although we should note that a complete correspondence is not possible, since this initial text cannot be established with certainty at all points of variation. For textual reconstruction, manuscripts that have the initial text in each book are identified and ranked (from the first to the fifth level) by examining their genealogical coherence. The *Editio Critica Maior* also enters into dialogue with the Byzantine tradition (which Westcott and Hort had devalued), as seen by the importance afforded the Byzantine witnesses in reconstructing the text.[27]

The coherence-based genealogical method, of course, has its limitations, like any other method. The editors, for example, do not include versional evidence insofar as these readings cannot always be unequivocally assigned to a Greek variant. Additionally, the genealogical coherence of heavily fragmented witnesses, such as many papyri, is not as reliable as fully extant witnesses because there is much less evidence available for comparison.[28] The complexity of lectionaries' reading schedules also

---

time in a century, the eclectic text of the Catholic Letters departs from Westcott and Hort and, by extension, from Codex Vaticanus. The distance from these is even greater if one adopts some of the alternative readings. See "Textual Changes in NA28," Institut für Neutestamentliche Textforschung, https://tinyurl.com/SBL7016g.

26. Michael W. Holmes, "From 'Original Text' to 'Initial Text,'" in Ehrman and Holmes, *Text of the New Testament in Contemporary Research* (2nd ed.), 653. See also Klaus Wachtel and Michael W. Holmes, eds., *The Textual History of the Greek New Testament: Changing Views in Contemporary Research* (Society of Biblical Literature, 2011), 2–8.

27. Hernández, "Modern Critical Editions," 706. The Byzantine witnesses that have over 70 percent support agree with the established text of the Catholic Letters in most cases where there is textual variation. With this attention to the Byzantine tradition, readings that had not previously appeared in a critical apparatus are collected. At the same time, the differences between the Byzantine text and the majority text are highlighted.

28. Gregory S. Paulson, "Improving the CBGM: Recent Interactions," in *The*

poses problems for comparisons with continuous text witnesses. Work is nonetheless underway to address these limitations.[29] In spite of these, the coherence-based genealogical method represents a notable advance in New Testament textual criticism, offering a rigorous and systematic method for analyzing textual variants and reconstructing the history of their transmission. To date the method has proven to be eminently useful for large-scale projects such as the *Editio Critica Maior* that utilize massive amounts of textual data.

To lay the groundwork for the production of the *Editio Critica Maior*, the Institut für Neutestamentliche Textforschung published a number of initial projects. The first is the series Text und Textwert der griechischen Handschriften des Neuen Testaments, which was launched in order to lay the groundwork for the critical apparatus of the *Editio Critica Maior*.[30] The second is titled Das Neue Testament auf Papyrus, which presents the text of each New Testament book as attested by our extant papyri.[31] Most fundamental, however, is the Kurzgefaßte Liste der griechischen Handschriften des neuen Testaments, a catalog of all known Greek New Testament manuscripts and the basis for the aforementioned projects.

A fundamental tool for the execution of this work is the New Testament Virtual Manuscript Room, an online platform developed by the Institut für Neutestamentliche Textforschung whose main purpose is to provide a digital workspace for text-critical research. Here researchers, students, and scholars can consult high-quality images, transcriptions, the digital editions of the *Editio Critica Maior*, and data related to New Tes-

---

New Testament in Antiquity and Byzantium: Traditional and Digital Approaches to Its Texts and Editing; A Festschrift for Klaus Wachtel, ed. Hugh A. G. Houghton, David C. Parker, and Holger Strutwolf, ANTF 52 (De Gruyter, 2019), 295–307.

29. Gregory S. Paulson, "To All Things an Appointed Time: Editing a Critical Edition of the Greek New Testament Lectionary with the Aid of Digital Tools," in *Reading the Gospel in Liturgy: Rites and Rituals, Sources and Systems*, ed. Marie-Ève Geiger, Elena Velkovska, and Harald Buchinger, MB (De Gruyter, forthcoming).

30. The series is intended to show the results of a series of manuscript collations carried out by the institute. These collations have been carried out in order to differentiate Greek manuscripts containing mainly the Byzantine form of the text from those preserving other more primitive forms. The first volume, dedicated to the Catholic Letters, was published in 1987.

31. The volumes corresponding to the Catholic Letters (1986) and to the Pauline Letters, Romans through 1–2 Corinthians (1989) and Galatians–Hebrews (1994), have been published.

tament textual criticism. The New Testament Virtual Manuscript Room features hundreds of thousands of images of New Testament manuscripts, including papyri, majuscules, minuscules, and lectionary manuscripts, as well as amulets and ostraca. Users can index, transcribe, compare texts, and analyze textual variants. Moreover, the New Testament Virtual Manuscript Room provides information on the characteristics, content, dating, location, and so on of each manuscript. The site also has the advantage that researchers from all over the world can contribute to the project by uploading transcriptions, making annotations, and discussing textual variants.

2. Textual Criticism and the Problem of the Original

From the brief survey of critical editions, we observe that enormous progress has been made in the knowledge of the Greek text of the New Testament and that this knowledge carries with it an awareness that the text eludes any attempt at a definitive and fixed form. Certainly, there have been considerable advances that are the result of remarkable scholarship and the ability to access an ever-increasing number of manuscripts; moreover, there are extraordinary new possibilities offered by digital resources. But perhaps what stands out most in the recent history of the editing of New Testament Greek text is how the text is understood and the posture of textual critics toward it.

The text-critical practices that flourished following the Renaissance and reached into the last decades of the twentieth century were characterized by the pursuit of a complete and stable text. Although the objective was generally understood to be beyond reach, in actual practice, the reconstructed text was assumed to be essentially that of the original documents. Claims that our reconstructed text was nearly identical to the one to come from the hand of the authors were not uncommon. Not only was textual criticism understood as the search for the original text, but the objective was unquestioned. The original text was, of course, elusive, but its reconstruction from extant manuscripts was considered achievable. Gradually, however, textual critics came to realize that the object of the discipline resembled that of an asymptotic curve, insofar as textual criticism continually approaches the author's text but never manages to find it.[32] There

---

32. See the analysis of Holmes, "From 'Original Text,'" 637–88; also Juan Chapa, "Texto autoritativo y crítica textual: Implicaciones teológicas del concepto 'texto origi-

was nonetheless a consensus about how the discipline was defined. Textual criticism was understood as "the science and art of reconstructing the original text of a document," and it had three main aims: "gathering and organizing the evidence"; "evaluating and assessing the significance and implications of the evidence"; and "reconstructing the history of the transmission of the text to the extent allowed by the evidence." The ultimate goal was to determine "which of the variant readings *most likely* represents the original text."[33]

Defining the object of textual criticism, however, was not the only challenge the discipline would face. In the 1960s and 1970s, other complexities that made it difficult to define the nature and purpose of textual criticism became more apparent. On the one hand, it became clear that the very concept of an original text was not unequivocal. Textual critics understood it variously as the "text intended" by the author, the "autograph," the "primitive text," the "initial form of text," or as the "published text."[34] Scholars further recognized that textual criticism is not a neutral discipline but, like any historical discipline, is conditioned by the intellectual and ideological presuppositions of its practitioners. Therefore, it was natural that the variety of approaches to the text would also produce a variety of ideas about its nature and the degree of our accessibility to it. Another aspect that became evident is the lack of agreement on the antiquity of the text that can be accessed through the study and analysis of the various manuscripts. On the one hand, many authors maintain that it is possible to obtain a text reasonably close to the original. They understand that scribes intended to make a copy of a text and were not carried away by personal whims or a desire to change it. The relatively careful transcription of the oldest extant papyri demonstrates that there was at least an attempt to transmit the text faithfully.[35] On the other hand, authors such as

---

nal' del Nuevo Testamento," in *Revelación, Escritura, Interpretación: Estudios en honor del Prof. D. Gonzalo Aranda Pérez*, ed. Fernando Milán (Eunsa, 2014), 155–61.

33. Holmes, "From 'Original Text,'" 637, emphasis added.

34. Holmes, "From 'Original Text,'" 646. Holmes's excellent analysis is followed in this section.

35. Obviously, the concept of fidelity is ambiguous and admits degrees, so it is not easy to agree on how these ancient papyri were copied. In any case, these authors consider that there are certain indications that they were copied with care. For example, Barbara Aland writes regarding the "initial text": "If we do not see that later radical changes have occurred in the transmission of a text, it follows that we should not see them before the initial text. We should therefore be able to rely on the initial text

Helmut Koester, William Petersen, or David Parker are skeptical about the claim and maintain that the oldest text that can be established is, at most, the one that circulated in Christianity at the end of the second century. Prior to that period, they claim, we have only a chaotic situation of texts, as reflected in the New Testament citations of the authors of that century.[36] The disparity between the two positions derives from the analysis of different factors but above all from four main ones: the interpretation of the data provided by the oldest New Testament papyri, the value of New Testament quotations in the writings of the fathers, the presumed influence of contemporary oral culture (when the various traditions on the life of Jesus were written), and the weight of literary arguments on the composition of the texts.[37]

Another challenge textual criticism faced regarding the original text during these decades relates to the difficulty of determining what is understood by the author's text or by the autograph (which are at times understood in different ways). Without knowing an author's intentions, we are unable to determine whether an autograph is what the author of a book meant to write on papyrus or parchment, or what an amanuensis wrote. It is also obvious that we will never be able to determine the material form of the writing as it was written by its author (the concrete form of the text, its exact spelling, the physical details, etc.). Consequently, and despite the fact that we already know we cannot reconstruct the author's

---

as being fairly close to the original text" ("New Testament Textual Research," 20). See Holmes, who takes this line and in n. 117 cites other authors who follow it (e.g., Kyoung Shik Min, Tommy Wasserman, Holger Strutwolf, K. Martin Heide; Holmes, "From 'Original Text,'" 667). A similar position from another point of view is found in Parsons, "People of the Book?," 53.

36. Helmut Koester, "The Text of the Synoptic Gospels in the Second Century," in *The Gospel Traditions in the Second Century*, ed. William L. Petersen (University of Notre Dame Press, 1989), 19–37; Koester, *Ancient Christian Gospels: Their History and Development* (SCM, 1990); William L. Petersen, "The Genesis of the Gospels," in *New Testament Textual Criticism and Exegesis: Festschrift J. Delobel*, ed. Adelbert Denaux (Leuven University Press and Peeters, 2002), 33–65; Petersen, "What Text Can New Testament Textual Criticism Ultimately Reach?," in Aland and Delobel, *New Testament Textual Criticism*, 136–52; Parker, *Introduction to the New Testament Text*, 117–18, 338. See Holmes, "From 'Original Text,'" 664–66; Charles E. Hill and Michael J. Kruger, "Introduction: In Search of the Earliest Text of the New Testament," in Hill and Kruger, *Early Text of the New Testament*, 12.

37. Holmes, "From 'Original Text,'" 667–68.

text in its entirety, discussions now revolve around whether it is even feasible to establish the substance of what was written, that is, the particular sequence of words as conceived by an author from the existing witnesses. For some, this possibility is unquestionable; for others, it is not.[38]

Related to the concept of the autographic text, the concept and definition of a literary work also comes into play. Is a literary work the one written by the author or the one appropriated by other writers who use the work as their own source? Traditionally, the authorship of a book has been understood as that which is the result of the work of an author who produces a readable, closed, and complete work. But today some argue that authorship can also refer to the action of a "writer" who produces a text, whose sources are collected in a composition or network susceptible of being recomposed or rewritten by other "writers" who use the work as their own source.[39] The problem is not minor, since it affects works such as the gospels and our ability to distinguish between texts written by an author and those copied by a scribe.

In light of these developments, new attempts to define the object of textual criticism appeared in the 1990s, albeit with disparate results. Sometimes the discipline is conceived of as an attempt to establish the initial text (*Ausgangstext*); sometimes as an effort to seek an approximation of the archetypal text, that is, the oldest textual state that can be reached;[40] and sometimes as the endeavor to "identify the earliest recoverable stages of textual transmission," that is, the textual forms in which an ancient Christian writing began to circulate and be copied. This is followed by the "evaluation of the variants representing the earliest stages of the text that can be recovered, in order to assess to what extent, they are original" and reconstruct some of the characteristics of the original text.[41] All these

---

38. Holmes, "From 'Original Text,'" 668–670.

39. Holmes, "From 'Original Text,'" 678. Holmes refers primarily to the theses set forth by Parker in *Living Text of the Gospels* and Petersen in "Genesis of the Gospels," 57–62.

40. For example, the *Editio Critica Maior* of the INTF. See Holmes, "From 'Original Text,'" 651–53, who also refers on 663 to what the Oxford edition attempts to do with the OT. See Ronald Hendel, "The Oxford Hebrew Bible: Prologue to a New Critical Edition," *VT* 58 (2008): 324–51. See also Santiago Guijarro and Jorge Blunda, "Desafíos de la crítica textual a la exégesis, la teología y la pastoral," *ScrTh* 54 (2022): 127–32.

41. It is the one proposed by Michael W. Holmes himself in "The Case for Rea-

approaches leave open the possibility of investigating an initial stage in the history of the text's transmission.

Other approaches, however, deny this possibility and argue that textual criticism should not only abandon the attempt to establish an original text but should also limit itself to trying to establish "the earliest attainable text" or an edition of the Greek text that represents the *editio princeps* of the canonical edition and not earlier stages that are beyond reach.[42] This is because we only have fragments of that text prior to 350 CE, and none of them transmits the pure original text.[43]

The result of all these factors is that today, not only is it assumed that obtaining the original text is impossible, but even the very expression "original text" has fallen into disuse.[44] This is evident in the different objectives that have been set by the most commonly used critical editions. As we have noted, the third edition (1975) of the Bible Societies and the twenty-sixth edition (1979) of Nestle-Aland (UBS³/NA²⁶) printed the same text. It was an eclectic text reconstructed mainly following manuscripts traditionally thought to represent the Alexandrian text type, from the oldest and "best" manuscripts, particularly Codex Vaticanus. As such, the edition was not very different from that of most of which appear here in English for the first time and Hort. The editors of the two editions, UBS³/NA²⁶, or at least some of them, saw the work done as a recovery of the wording of the original text, or at least as a close approximation of that wording. They did not claim to be infallible but presumed NA²⁶'s text to be, for all intents and purposes, the same as the original text. In contrast, the twenty-seventh Nestle-Aland edition of 1993 exhibits a change. It expressly states that its text is provisional and encourages the edition's users to deploy the critical

---

soned Eclecticism," in *Rethinking New Testament Textual Criticism*, ed. David A. Black (Baker, 2002), 77–100. See also Holmes, "From 'Original Text,'" 656–62.

42. The former would be the case of Eldon J. Epp, "It's All about Variants: A Variant-Conscious Approach to New Testament Textual Criticism," HTR 100 (2007): 282–86, 308. See Holmes, "From 'Original Text,'" 648–51. The latter position is observed in the thesis of David Trobisch, *The First Edition of the New Testament* (Oxford University Press, 2000). See Holmes, "From 'Original Text,'" 654–55.

43. In a similar vein Holmes points to Reuben J. Swanson, ed., *New Testament Greek Manuscripts: Variant Readings Arranged in Horizontal Lines against Codex Vaticanus: Romans*, 9 vols. (Tyndale House and William Carey International University Press, 1995–2005). See Holmes, "From 'Original Text,'" 655–56.

44. See Holmes, "From 'Original Text,'" 645–46; Hernández, "Modern Critical Editions," 703. See also Guijarro and Blunda, "Desafíos de la crítica textual," 122–26.

apparatus to verify or correct that text. It no longer claims that the text of the edition is a standard text but that it has three characteristics: it is a critically reconstructed text, it is a well-founded text, and it is practical to work with.[45] The change in posture is also evident in the aforementioned joint project of the International Greek New Testament Project and the Institut für Neutestamentliche Textforschung Münster for the *Editi Critica Maior*, the aim of which is to establish the "initial text." We therefore encounter a situation in which text and critical apparatus are in a symbiotic relationship, each taking its place in the reconstruction and history of the text.[46]

3. Where to Place the Initial Text vis-à-vis the Original

Abandoning the pursuit of the original text and espousing the goal of establishing the initial text does not solve all our text-critical problems. The question of where/when to situate the initial text is complex, and no consensus exists about how to answer it. As already noted, there is a temporal and conceptual space between the original and the initial text that is difficult to map. This is because data come into play about which there is little agreement. The information that can be extracted from the fragments of the oldest New Testament papyri is debatable; the way the church fathers quote the New Testament is understood in different ways; the role of orality in the composition of the gospels is a matter of debate; and the literary arguments in the formation of the autographic texts are susceptible to different interpretations. On the other hand, as already noted, textual criticism is not an exact or objective science and is therefore subject to epistemological limitations like any other discipline, and many text-critical results depend on the hermeneutical presuppositions of its practitioners.[47]

These and other questions account for why different views prevail about the relationship between the original and the initial text. However, they can be grouped into two camps: the view that defends the existence of a (varying) distance between these two texts and the view that advocates a proximity between them.

---

45. NA[27] (3rd ed.), "Introduction," 2*: "This text is a working text.... It is not to be considered as definitive, but a stimulus to further efforts toward defining and verifying the text of the New Testament." See also Holmes, "From 'Original Text,'" 653.
46. Hernández, "Modern Critical Editions," 703.
47. Holmes, "From 'Original Text,'" 648, 679–80.

3.1. Textual Fluctuation and Initial Distancing

We know that the New Testament text is the best attested text of the ancient world. We also know, however, that 85 percent of the manuscripts were copied in the eleventh century or later and that very little evidence survives from the end of the second century. Although there are witnesses of the gospels perhaps from the second century and witnesses of the gospels, Paul, and Revelation from the third century, no texts of the Catholic Letters are preserved until the third–fourth century. To this we add the difficulty of determining whether some New Testament books were edited more than once by their authors, whether in some cases there were truly originals as we understand them today, or whether the first copyists of these works simultaneously functioned as scribes and authors (changing words, altering the text, and making new compositions, etc.). For Parker (as well as for Epp and Petersen), the way in which the gospels were composed is analogous to what occurred, for example, in the *Odyssey*, for which ascertaining whether it had an autograph proves elusive. That is to say, the gospels would not have been formed from a single text but from the successive rewriting of original material. Michael Holmes notes that, according to this perspective, the composition process of the gospels would have been similar to that of some of the works that make up the Scriptures of Israel (e.g., Jeremiah, which is very different in Hebrew and Greek), some Jewish pseudepigraphic works (e.g., the Life of Adam and Eve), some of the early Christian writings (such as the Shepherd of Hermas, of which there were perhaps two versions at the beginning, to which other passages were added later), some Jewish works of late antiquity (Sefer Yesira, with several different recensions), or some works of medieval literature (e.g., Piers Plowman). The copyists of these works would have acted as scribes and authors at the same time, that is, they would have changed words, altered the text, and made new compositions. The integrity of the autograph would have been diluted in the many manuscripts that multiplied the text. The gospels, therefore, would be works similar to each other, in that they all belong to a tradition that can be identified vis-à-vis other traditions, but with such material and structural differences that it would not be possible to distinguish between forms of texts that were written by the authors and conceived as such by them, and texts that were copied and altered by the scribes.[48] Along these lines is Matthew Larsen's

---

48. Holmes, "From 'Original Text,'" 671–72.

much-debated work *Gospels before the Book*, which addresses issues such as unfinished texts, accidental publications, and later revisions, as well as multiple authorized versions of the same work, to argue that concepts such as "book, author and publication" are alien to the first centuries of our era.[49] He proposes to develop new theories that take textual fluency seriously rather than relying on traditional notions.[50]

Given the available data, it is therefore understandable that no agreement exists about the time period in which the hypothetical initial text should be placed. The most skeptical positions deny that there is a temporal proximity between the original and the initial text. Assuming a great fluidity of texts, not only during the first decades of their composition but also throughout the following century, those who hold this view argue that

---

49. Matthew D. C. Larsen, *Gospels before the Book* (Oxford University Press, 2018), 149.

50. Specifically, according to Larsen, the "initial text" of Mark's Gospel was a growing collection of textual traditions, seen by early readers as notes or drafts, rather than a complete book with a definite author. For a critique of his work see, e.g., Timothy N. Mitchell's review in *JETS* 62 (2019): 641–45, and the discussion of his positions in Keith, *Gospel as Manuscript*, 49–64. In addition to Larsen, other authors such as Jan Assmann, David Brakke, John Kloppenborg, Judith Lieu, Guy Stroumsa, and Tom Thatcher have developed the role of the authoritative text in giving life, thought, sense of identity, and relationships with outsiders, drawing heavily on the concept of textual community created by Brian Stock, *The Implications of Literacy: Written Language and Models of Interpretation in the Eleventh and Twelfth Centuries* (Princeton University Press, 1983). See also Jane Heath, "'Textual Communities': Brian Stock's Concept and Recent Scholarship on Antiquity," in *Scriptural Interpretation at the Interface between Education and Religion: In Memory of Hanz Conzelmann*, TBN 22 (Brill, 2018), 5–35. Equally influential has been the work of Donald McKenzie, who stresses the importance of considering material and social processes in the formation of a text, suggesting that communities not only interpret but also actively participate in the construction of textual meaning. See especially McKenzie, *Bibliography and the Sociology of Texts* (Cambridge University Press, 1999). Considering many of these aspects and in dialogue with them, Keith's *Gospel as Manuscript* studies the dynamics of the written tradition, in contrast to those who advocate the primacy of orality in the origins of the Christian tradition. The reference to the materiality of the written text serves Keith to defend the role played in that tradition by textuality, that is, the text embodied in a manuscript. Relying on the studies of Jan Assmann and William Johnson, he argues that the material manuscript allows us to see the text as process. As such a process, he considers that the text can play an important role in the construction and preservation of group identity and stresses how each gospel invoked the written medium to claim its authority within the Jesus tradition.

it is possible only to arrive at a text from the end of the second century. Some, such as Petersen, and to some extent Koester or Parker, argue that the text available to us today does not reflect the autographs at all, given the chaotic textual situation of the decades immediately following the New Testament books' composition and throughout the second century.[51] They claim we know almost nothing of the original texts and that the Greek text of modern critical editions dates back at most to the end of that century. For Petersen, proof of this resides in the fact that most of the New Testament passages apparently quoted by the apostolic fathers, and which find recognizable parallels in the present text, present different textual forms. He therefore considers that the text we know now is, at the earliest, later than 180 CE.[52] Others make this approach a little more concrete. David Trobisch, for example, argues that the archetype of practically all extant New Testament manuscripts is an edition of the New Testament made in the middle of the second century that also included the LXX.[53] That is to say, for Trobisch, the text that has come down to us reflects only the text of that canonical edition. From here derive the variants we know, without access to earlier textual forms. Textual criticism would then aim to reproduce a Greek text as close as possible to that *editio princeps* of the second century.

Although Trobisch's arguments have some appeal, they are also beset by clear weaknesses.[54] Trobisch's thesis does not sufficiently explain why so much variation exists in the order and content of our extant manuscripts, if in fact everything stems from a putative canonical edition; nor how canonical discussions continued in subsequent centuries if that canon had already existed in the second century.[55] On the other hand, many of

---

51. See above, 84 n. 36.

52. See Michael W. Holmes, "Text and Transmission," in *The Reliability of the New Testament*, ed. Robert B. Stewart (Fortress, 2011), 68–75; cf. Chapa, "Texto autoritativo y crítica textual," 160–61.

53. Trobisch, *First Edition of the New Testament*. See also his more recent work, David Trobisch, *On the Origin of Christian Scripture: The Evolution of the New Testament Canon in the Second Century* (Fortress, 2023). There he adds some analyses that, in his view, show specific editorial decisions in the books selected to form the New Testament. He argues that the New Testament is a second-century fabrication to address second-century concerns and that it was formed as an interpolated and expanded revision of the Marcionite edition.

54. See, e.g., the extensive review by David C. Parker in *JTS* 53 (2002): 299–305.

55. Holmes, "Text and Transmission," 62–65.

Petersen's assertions require substantiation.[56] Moreover, it is well known that the way the apostolic fathers quoted Scripture presents enormous difficulties.[57] It is true that, along with written traditions, there were other oral traditions that were used by the Christian authors and that some of these were different from those found in the texts of the gospels as they appear around 180 CE. This does not demonstrate, however, that the text of the gospels at the end of the first century was different from the text of those gospels around or after 180 CE.[58]

On the other hand, it is surprising that, in the case of the gospels, within the fluctuations observed in the oldest fragments that have come down to us, there is so much uniformity. If the gospels do not go back to well-defined originals and were also altered as time went by, we would expect greater diversity in the texts that were preserved. Certainly, none of the ancient New Testament fragments presents a text equal to another, but the differences do not prevent us from deducing the same original that has been transmitted with certain fidelity. Generally speaking, the variations are not substantial and do not hamper recognition of the text.

3.2. Proximity between the Original Text and Initial Text

Along with the more skeptical positions, there are those who adopt a more positive attitude about the possibility of arriving at an initial text close or very close to that of the autographs. Perhaps the best-known exponents of this position, which otherwise appears to be assumed by most practitioners of New Testament textual criticism, even if left unexpressed, are Kurt Aland and Barbara Aland. They argue in their handbook that the transmission of the New Testament's textual tradition exhibits an impressive "tenacity."[59] Once a reading appears, it stubbornly persists. They therefore believe that the original reading must sit somewhere in the textual

---

56. Holmes, "Text and Transmission," 72.
57. See Gordon D. Fee, "The Use of the Greek Fathers," in Epp and Fee, *New Testament Textual Criticism*, 191–207; Bart D. Ehrman, "The Use of the Church Fathers in New Testament Textual Criticism," in *The Bible as Book: The Transmission of the Greek Text*, ed. Scot McKendrick and Orlaith A. O'Sullivan (Oak Knoll and British Library, 2003), 155–65; Charles E. Hill, "'In These Very Words': Methods and Standards of Literary Borrowing in the Second Century," in Hill and Kruger, *Early Text of the New Testament*, 261–81.
58. Holmes, "Text and Transmission," 73.
59. Kurt Aland and Barbara Aland, *The Text of the New Testament: An Introduc-*

tradition. What we have to do is to try to identify it. They further affirm that where there is no great profusion of variants, the text has not been altered. For this reason, they consider that once the oldest text that can be recovered is determined, this text should be identified, at least practically speaking, with the "original text."

In short, for the Alands, the text of the third-century manuscripts is essentially the same as the one published by the author. The proposition has much to commend it. That is, until the appearance of evidence to the contrary, the vast majority of the original text appears to be present somewhere in the textual tradition. There are exceptions, of course, so the proposition cannot be pushed too far. There are cases where there is no certainty that a group of witnesses has preserved the original text, and at times the absence of a viable solution can create room for a conjecture in the process of textual reconstruction. In other cases, it is possible that the text of all the surviving manuscripts derives from a homoeoteleuton or another kind of error, as when the Greek text appears to make no sense, or that an original reading will be unknown until a manuscript serendipitously surfaces that transmits it. These considerations make it impossible to affirm with certainty that the original reading of every text has been preserved in parts of the extant manuscript tradition.[60] This does not preclude, of course, the general viability of the Alands' position, which, barring exceptions, admits the possibility of establishing an initial text (*Ausgangstext*) close to the original.

4. Toward an Interactive Textual Criticism

A brief survey of New Testament critical editions demonstrates that every edition is a product of its time. To this we add the fact that the increasingly comprehensive study of manuscripts and scribal copying habits has disclosed the impossibility of recovering the original text and has centered the purpose of textual criticism on the initial text, insofar as it is a text suitable for work. A penultimate goal has replaced the ultimate one, and although the textual changes are minimal, the conceptual shift is remarkable.[61] Users of the new critical editions do not have before them an edition

---

tion to the Critical Editions and to the Theory and Practice of Modern Textual Criticism, 2nd ed., trans. Erroll F. Rhodes (Eerdmans, 1989), 56.

60. Holmes, "Text and Transmission," 65–68.
61. Hernández, "Modern Critical Editions," 707.

regarded as the definitive or quasi-definitive text, but they are now invited to use the critical apparatus to revise the text themselves.

In addition, the possibilities offered by electronic editions signal a text-critical revolution.[62] The critical apparatus will be interactive. It will be possible to create editions of the Greek New Testament that offer a variety of manuscript transcriptions. Of these, any manuscript can serve as a base text, and the apparatus can appear in various formats, while transcriptions and images of selected witnesses will be made available.[63] Users will be able to check and evaluate editorial decisions for themselves. What was once reserved for a select few will now be available to all. The main variants will be linked to a discussion forum with digital images of the main manuscripts, as can be seen in the prototype of what will be the NA[28] website or on the International Greek New Testament Project website, and will serve to make available an apparatus that enables users to make their own textual decisions.[64] In Parker's words, the critically reconstructed text will function "as a peg on which to hang other kinds of information."[65] Attention has now shifted from the text to the apparatus and transcriptions. We are all invited to reconstruct our own text.[66]

The invitation is suggestive, but we should also recognize that before reconstructing our own text, we must weigh what others have done and why. As such, textual criticism will continue to rely largely on experts. There is no question, however, that we now have more means by which to judge the work of the experts.

---

62. Clivaz, "New Testament in the Time," 18–38. See also David C. Parker, *Textual Scholarship and the Making of the New Testament* (Oxford University Press, 2012), 10–14, 125–42.

63. David C. Parker, "Through a Screen Darkly: Digital Texts and the New Testament," *JSNT* 25 (2003): 395–411.

64. See "Matthew Inscriptio," New Testament Transcripts Prototype; and International Greek New Testament Project (http://www.igntp.org/).

65. Parker, "Through a Screen Darkly," 404.

66. Hernández, "Modern Critical Editions," 707.

Variants, the Living Text, and Textual Fluidity

In 1990, the journal *Speculum*, published by the Medieval Academy of America, devoted an issue to the so-called new philology.[1] This movement in Romance philology (elsewhere labeled "material philology" or "social textuality") proposes a new vision of the medieval text that follows in the footsteps of Bernard Cerquiglini's work *Éloge de la variante*.[2] Influenced by Michel Foucault and Jacques Derrida, Cerquiglini's fundamental thesis is that critics should not reduce the medieval tradition to a single text but allow textual variations to coexist. This is because, as he rather provocatively points out, "medieval writing does not produce variants; it is itself variation."[3] That is, instead of looking at variants as deviations from the norm, Cerquiglini suggests seeing them as natural products of scribal culture, a culture in which diverse readings should not be considered exceptions to the norm or textual corruptions but the norm itself.

1. The Freeing of Variants and Textual Fluidity

When the label was coined in 1990, the new philology was not entirely new. There were precedents, particularly in the work of Paul Zumthor,

---

1. The editor of that issue was Stephen G. Nichols, who in explains that the New Philology is based on "insistence that the language of texts be studied not simply as discursive phenomena but in the interaction of text language with the manuscript matrix and of both language and manuscript with the social context and networks they inscribe." See Nichols, "Introduction: Philology in a Manuscript Culture," *Speculum* 65 (1990): 9. See also Susan Yager, "New Philology," *Handbook of Medieval Studies: Terms—Methods—Trends*, ed. Albrecht Classen (De Gruyter, 2010), 1:999–1006.
2. Bernard Cerquiglini, *Éloge de la variante: Histoire critique de la philologie* (Seuil, 1989). One should note, however, that it has not been without its critics. For some criticisms, see, e.g., Alberto Varvaro, "The 'New Philology' from an Italian Perspective," *Text* 12 (1999): 49–58.
3. Cerquiglini, *Éloge de la variante*, 111.

Swiss literary critic, philologist, and medievalist, who in the 1970s stressed the importance of the fluidity of texts. Zumthor called this fluidity *mouvance*, which has become a technical term in French to describe the levels of textual variation and mobility between manuscripts.[4] Zumthor defines *mouvance* as a product of continuous change and an interference between various traditions, both oral and written. Consequently, he rejects the preference for the best manuscript, that is, the one that faithfully reflects a decisive moment in the earliest textual tradition and asserts that what is of interest is the sum total of all versions—a total that includes not only those surviving from medieval times but also more modern editions. The first version no longer has priority; all later versions are potentially comparable to it insofar as they have documentary value in the continuous development of the text in the act of making itself.[5] This development takes place through the process of reading-listening-copying that occurs over the centuries.[6]

Apart from a number of debatable aspects, the new philology has served to broaden the scope of traditional textual criticism that sought to recover the authentic form of a text from the available manuscripts, in accordance with both Karl Lachmann's Stemmatic method and Joseph Bédier's option of the best manuscript. The new philology asserts that the concerns to recover an original text and to present it as "the text" are at odds with the variety of manuscripts and copies we preserve. Each of these manuscripts is unique, and therefore neither the variation nor the nonconformity or unruliness of the texts can be dissociated from these manuscripts. Hence, textual variants should be afforded greater prominence, rather than "hidden" or "imprisoned" in a critical apparatus.[7] This represents a shift from a search for the original text to a new way of editing and studying unstable textual traditions.

This approach to variants also explains the new philology's interest in textual fluidity. Texts obviously change, accidentally or intentionally, when they are copied. A process occurs in which the text develops as it is transmitted. The consequence is what John Bryant calls *fluid text*, referring also to any literary work that exists in a variety of versions (from author's drafts

---

4. Paul Zumthor, *Essai de poétique médiévale* (Seuil, 2000). See Roy Rosenstein, "Mouvance," in Classen, *Handbook of Medieval Studies*, 1:1538.

5. Zumthor, *Essai de poétique médiévale*, 73.

6. Rosenstein, "Mouvance," 1540.

7. Cerquiglini, *Éloge de la variante*, 106.

to printer's proofs, revised editions, film adaptations, etc.). According to Bryant, all these versions must be considered in their cultural contexts because they provide a valuable record of the interaction between artist and society. The reason, Bryant believes, is that literary works are not immovable products but works in progress, which flow, move, and change according to their cultural situation.[8]

As we can see, these developments dispense with the concern for a stable text and reject the understanding of variants as a form of textual corruption. Changes introduced during transmission are considered important aspects of the text's life, as witnessed in individual manuscripts, as *snapshots* of that text. Studying texts in their fluidity shows that textual traditions are never continuously linear but that they are sometimes broken, interrupted, or profoundly transformed during the copying process. This recognition leads us to no longer consider textual criticism as simply the study of witnesses to an earlier text but as the science that asks to what extent those texts with their variants reflect the interests and concerns of their producers and owners, to what extent the "original" text can be recovered, and what degree of fluidity we can expect from the text(s) under examination.[9]

At the same time, the appreciation of variants has inspired an interpretation of texts centered on *manuscript culture*,[10] according to which the manuscript is analyzed as an artifact. The study of the text in the abstract,

---

8. John Bryant, *The Fluid Text: A Theory of Revision and Editing for Book and Screen* (University of Michigan Press, 2002). Earlier, McGann had also questioned the idea of a fixed and final text, proposing instead that texts are dynamic and constantly evolving. He introduced the concept of the textual condition, which examines how texts are products of historical and social processes. In this regard he argues, "A critical edition is a kind of text which does not seek to reproduce a particular past text, but rather to reconstitute for the reader, in a single text, the entire history of the work as it has emerged into the present." Jerome J. McGann, *A Critique of Modern Textual Criticism* (University of Virginia Press, 1992), 93. In addition, McGann has explored the impact of digital technology on the editing and interpretation of texts, arguing for a textual criticism that incorporates digital and collaborative methods.

9. Liv I. Lied and Hugo Lundhaug, "Studying Snapshots: On Manuscript Culture, Textual Fluidity, and New Philology," in *Snapshots of Evolving Traditions: Jewish and Christian Manuscript Culture, Textual Fluidity, and New Philology*, ed. Lied and Lundhaug, TUGAL 175 (De Gruyter, 2019), 9.

10. The ideas in the following two paragraphs are based on Lied and Lundhaug, "Studying Snapshots."

separated from its physical appearance and presentation, is abandoned, as the literary work does not exist outside its material embodiment. In other words, the material artifact is part of the text's meaning, since the artifact's production is determined by social, economic, and intellectual factors in both its origin and its use. Moreover, these conditioning factors provide access points to those who produced, owned, and read the manuscripts and facilitate the discovery of their sociohistorical, cultural, and religious contexts. This kind of analysis signals a distancing from questions about authorship and authorial intent and focuses more on the actual reception, reading, and use of the manuscripts. It also privileges the reader rather than the author and/or their text and thus focuses primarily on the history of transmission, in which the study of texts in their manuscript contexts can reveal "an evolving, frequently contested, multi-layered process of meaning making."[11]

This approach has generated a proliferation of studies in recent years on scribal practices, manuscript production, copying, circulation and transmission of texts, literacy, reading and memorization, orality and aurality, and other contexts related to the use of ancient texts. Through these studies, not only has the historical-critical paradigm been revised, but the way in which texts interact with their readers or with the general public has also been examined in depth.[12]

2. Narrative Textual Criticism

Devoting attention to the text-critical developments in the field of medieval philology is helpful insofar as it illustrates parallel developments in the field of New Testament textual criticism. We have already noted in the previous chapter that in the 1960s and 1970s the traditional way of practicing this discipline seemed to have reached a dead end or was at least experiencing stagnation. As we have seen, the possibility that there were two editions of Mark and Acts, or that several copies of the Letter to the Ephesians were made, or that there were versions of the gospels that were very soon altered problematized the concept of an autograph and upended the traditional notion of an author.

---

11. Michael Penn, "Monks, Manuscripts, and Muslims: Syriac Textual Changes in Reaction to the Rise of Islam," *Hugoye* 12 (2009): 251, cited in Lied and Lundhaug, "Studying Snapshots," 8.

12. Lied and Lundhaug, "Studying Snapshots," 2.

Faced with this situation, some New Testament textual critics began to take an interest in aspects that were previously seen as secondary developments within a purer textual tradition. Until then, the traditional way of doing textual criticism was based on the belief in the existence of an original text that was corrupted during transcription and whose variants were textual corruptions to be eliminated. Now, however, textual variants are worthy of study in their own right. The study of the various readings as such is of interest insofar as they are considered legitimate sources for exploring the social and religious world behind them.[13]

This perspective change is reflected in the way New Testament textual criticism has been redefined. If we compare Paul Maas's classic definition with Eldon Epp's comparatively recent one, we find significant changes. Maas's definition reads as follows: "The business of textual criticism is to produce a text as close as possible to the original."[14] Epp's 2011 definition is much more nuanced:

> New Testament textual criticism, employing aspects of both science and art, studies the transmission of the New Testament text and the manuscripts that facilitate its transmission, with the unitary goal of establishing the earliest attainable text (which serves as a baseline), and at the same time of assessing the textual variants that emerge from the baseline text so as to hear the narratives of early Christian thought and life that inhere in the array of meaningful variants.[15]

As we can see, the definition is not only more extensive and quite nuanced but also broadens its field of study and refers to the criteria used to prioritize certain readings, thereby alluding to the importance of textual variants. In fact, the textual criticism of the last decades shows an interest in vari-

---

13. For a complex view of the problems raised and a proposal in this regard, see Holmes, "From 'Original Text,'" 637–88.

14. Paul Maas, *Textual Criticism* (Clarendon, 1958), 1.

15. Eldon J. Epp, "Traditional 'Canons' of New Testament Textual Criticism: Their Value, Validity, and Viability—or Lack Thereof," in Wachtel and Holmes, *Textual History*, 127. This approach is also evident in what Epp wrote in 2007 about the goals of textual criticism: "(1) searching for the earliest attainable text and, (2) disclosing, through narrative textual criticism, the theological, liturgical, and ethical contexts of textual variants in the life of the church" (Epp, "It's All about Variants," 294). See also Epp, "Critical Editions and the Development of Text-Critical Methods: Part 2: From Lachmann (1831) to the Present," in *From 1750 to the Present*, vol. 4 of *The New Cambridge History of the Bible*, ed. John Riches (Cambridge University Press, 2015), 47–48.

ants not only as a means to recover the initial text but also as transmitters of information that provide a fuller picture of the life of early Christian communities. If previously almost all textual variants were discarded, now many of them, especially those that appear significant, merit study. They are presumed to have something to tell us. Consequently, a manuscript should not be seen simply as an object of the past that testifies to a certain evolution of an older text but as a living witness of the community from which it emerged. Applied, for example, to the gospels, textual criticism should favor an analysis that strives to discover, behind the diversity of textual variants, the variety of interpretations of the gospels and of the different figures of Jesus reflected in various manuscripts. In other words, the practice of textual criticism today understands that each copy mirrors a particular community, with its own social history, its own theology, and its particular understanding of Jesus.[16] We do not have a single image of Jesus (or even four portraits) but as many images as there are manuscripts.

This relatively recent approach has been called narrative textual criticism because it argues that textual variants have a story to tell, as they bear witness to the personal habits and understandings of scribes.[17] Ehrman's article "The Text as Window: New Testament Manuscripts and the Social History of Early Christianity" offers a good synthesis of this approach to manuscripts.[18] He reviews a variety of studies on the transmission history of New Testament texts that were undertaken as a way of entering the social world of the first centuries of Christianity. He argues that the

---

16. For more details on how the focus of New Testament textual criticism has been shifting, see Holmes, "From 'Original Text,'" 648–64, and ch. 3 of the present book.

17. Eldon J. Epp, *Perspectives on New Testament Textual Criticism: Collected Essays, 1962–2004* (Brill, 2005), 1:xxxix. See Clivaz, "New Testament in the Time," 17. The author refers to those who have used this term: David C. Parker, review of *The Orthodox Corruption of Scripture: The Effect of Early Christological Controversies on the Text of the New Testament*, by Bart D. Ehrman, *JTS* 45 (1994): 704; Eldon J. Epp, "Anti-Judaic Tendencies in the D-Text of Acts: Forty Years of Conversation," in *The Book of Acts as Church History: Apostelgeschichte als Kirchengeschichte*, ed. Tobias Nicklas and Michael Tilly, BZNW 120 (De Gruyter, 2003), 144–46; Thomas R. Shepherd, "Narrative Analysis as a Text Critical Tool: Mark 16 in Codex W as a Test Case," *JSNT* 32 (2009): 77.

18. Bart D. Ehrman, "The Text as Window: New Testament Manuscripts and the Social History of Early Christianity," in Ehrman and Holmes, *Text of the New Testament* (2nd ed.), 803–30.

analysis of scribal changes introduced during transcription allows us to reconstruct the sociohistorical context of those copyists in such a way that "variant readings are not merely chaff to be discarded en route to the original text ... but valuable evidence for the history of the early Christian movement."[19]

The works of Epp, Ehrman, and Parker illustrate this new text-critical approach. Each has, from his own perspective, contributed to a renewed interest in the study of New Testament manuscripts as witnesses to a way of reading and interpreting the text.[20] On the other hand, research that focuses on *manuscript culture* complements the aforementioned approach. The studies of Gamble, Kim Haines-Eitzen, or Hurtado, and publications on the scribal tendencies that introduce various types of changes in the manuscripts they copy, exemplify this research on manuscript culture.[21]

---

19. Ehrman, "Text as Window," 804. This approach is inseparable from the reception history of manuscript texts in the context of their *Wirkungsgeschichte*, that is, the "history of effects" or how biblical texts have been interpreted, received, and used over time. As such, the production, transmission, and interpretation of a text are seen as elements that weave together the history of its reception, analyzing ultimately what that text looks like and what it can do. See Brennan W. Breed, *Nomadic Text: A Theory of Biblical Reception History* (Indiana University Press, 2014); Breed, "What Can a Text Do? Reception History as an Ethology of the Biblical Text," in *Reception History and Biblical Studies: Theory and Practice*, ed. Emma England and William J. Lyons (Bloomsbury, 2015), 95–109.

20. See also Juan Chapa, "The Contribution of Papyrology in the Interpretation of the Gospels," in *The Gospels: History and Christology. The Search of Joseph Ratzinger—Benedict XVI*, ed. Bernardo Estrada, Ermenegildo Manicardi, and Armand Puig i Tàrrech (Libreri a Edítrice Vaticana, 2013), 128–40; Chapa, "Texto autoritativo y crítica textual," 161–63.

21. In this sense, the work of Royse, *Scribal Habits*, which analyzes in detail these habits in the six oldest and most extensive extant Greek NT papyri, is encyclopedic. Along the same lines is the study by Juan Hernández Jr., *Scribal Habits*, on the scribal practices and theological influences revealed by the unique readings of the fourth- and fifth-century codices. Almost simultaneously with this, Dirk Jongkind published *Scribal Habits of Codex Sinaiticus* (Gorgias, 2007) on those same habits present in Codex Sinaiticus. In the same field, more recently has appeared the work of Peter Malik, *P.Beatty III (P47): The Codex, Its Scribe, and Its Text*, NTTSD 52 (Brill, 2017), on P47, the oldest surviving extensive copy of the Apocalypse, as well as Hixson, *Scribal Habits*. See also the collected essays in Gregory R. Lanier and J. Nicholas Reid, eds., *Studies on the Intersection of Text, Paratext, and Reception: A Festschrift in Honor of Charles E. Hill* (Brill, 2021); Stanley E. Porter, David I. Yoon, and Chris Stevens, eds., *Studies on the Paratextual Features of Early New Testament Manuscripts* (Brill, 2023).

2.1. Eldon Epp and Bart Ehrman

Chronologically, Epp's work, published in 1966, can be considered the first in recent times to highlight the peculiar bias that a scribe can imprint on a manuscript copy. His meticulous study of the theological tendencies of Codex Bezae (05) in Acts revealed that changes in beliefs and customs affect manuscript copies.[22] In particular, he looked at the anti-Jewish tendencies of the manuscript, demonstrating that almost 40 percent of the variants in Luke's second volume may have their origin in anti-Jewish prejudice. Epp uncovers this attitude by focusing on three points in particular: how the manuscript stresses Jewish hostility to Jesus and responsibility for his death, the increased interest in the role of the Holy Spirit in distinguishing Christianity from Judaism, and the way it emphasizes texts referring to the persecution suffered by the apostles at the hands of the Jews. Although Epp's contributions were not an absolute novelty, as we find precedents in the work of Kirsopp Lake and Rendel Harris in the early twentieth century, his contribution was positively received as an innovative way of understanding the possibilities of textual criticism.[23] Subsequently, Epp

---

The work of Gamble, *Books and Readers*, deals with the production, circulation, and use of books and their readers in the early church. Haines-Eitzen, *Guardians of Letters*, studies who the scribes were who copied Christian literature in the second and third centuries, and what role they played in the copying, transmission, and interpretation of these texts. Hurtado, *Earliest Christian Artifacts*, deals with the early Christian codices as material objects that reveal a specifically Christian culture through their format, the *nomina sacra*, or the staurogram. On what has been described as the "material turn," that is, what Kim Haines-Eitzen describes as "a renewed interest in the physical features of our earliest Christian literary papyri for what they might tell us about early Christian scribes and readers" see also Keith, *Gospel as Manuscript*, 36–39. See Haines-Eitzen, "The Social History of Early Christian Scribes," in Ehrman and Holmes, *Text of the New Testament* (2nd ed.), 486.

22. Eldon J. Epp, *The Theological Tendency of Codex Bezae Cantabrigiensis in Acts* (Cambridge University Press, 1966).

23. See Kirsopp Lake, *The Influence of Textual Criticism on the Exegesis of the New Testament* (Parker & Son, 1904); J. Rendel Harris, "New Points of View in Textual Criticism," *Expositor* 7 (1914): 316–34, mentioned in Hill and Kruger, "Introduction," 5. For an overview of earlier studies that pay attention to scribal tendencies, see also Kannaday, *Apologetic Discourse and the Scribal Tradition*, 5–18. For a challenge to Epp's position, see Josep Rius-Camps and Jenny Read-Heimerdinger, *The Message of Acts in Codex Bezae: A Comparison with the Alexandrian Tradition*, 4 vols. (T&T Clark, 2004–2009). There was no lack, however, of less enthusiastic responses. For

has continued in this line and has analyzed the multivalence of the term "original text," pointing out the importance for textual criticism of giving the same recognition to significant variants, often rejected, as to the readings of the text. For Epp, these variants can reveal aspects of the life and thought of Christian communities in various periods of church history.[24]

Almost three decades later, Ehrman published *The Orthodox Corruption of Scripture*, a work that in some ways became paradigmatic of the new way in which some authors understand New Testament textual criticism.[25] His basic thesis is that the scribes of the Christian communities of the second and third centuries made changes in the New Testament texts for theological reasons, making the texts say what they thought they should say. Driven by a desire to defend the orthodoxy of the faith they confessed—that is, to avoid interpretations that they attributed to contemporary heretical understandings (especially of the adoptionist, separationist, docetic, or patripassian types), and to defend "orthodox" Christianity—they modified the words of the manuscripts and corrupted the Scriptures.[26] Scribes made these changes, Ehrman argues, to oppose

---

example, the review article by Richard P. C. Hanson, "The Ideology of Codex Bezae in Acts," *NTS* 14 (1968): 282–86; Charles K. Barrett, "Is There a Theological Tendency in Codex Bezae?," in *Text and Interpretation: Studies in the New Testament Presented to Matthew Black*, ed. Ernest Best and Robert McL. Wilson (Cambridge University Press, 1979), 15–27. Barrett thinks that the theological tendencies Epp proposes are already present in Luke's text. See also the criticism of David C. Parker, *Codex Bezae: An Early Christian Manuscript and Its Text* (Cambridge University Press, 1992), 90.

24. Eldon J. Epp, "The Multivalence of the Term 'Original Text' in New Testament Textual Criticism," *HTR* 92 (1999): 245–81.

25. Ehrman, *Orthodox Corruption of Scripture*; see also Bart D. Ehrman, "Text and Interpretation: The Exegetical Significance of the 'Original' Text," in *Studies in the Textual Criticism of the New Testament*, NTTSD 33 (Brill, 2006), 307–24; Ehrman, "Text and Transmission: The Historical Significance of the 'Altered' Text," in *Studies in the Textual Criticism*, 325–42. For various criticisms of Ehrman's method, see Ulrich Schmid, "Scribes and Variants: Sociology and Typology," in Houghton and Parker, *Textual Variation*, 1–23; Tommy Wasserman, "Misquoting Manuscripts? The Orthodox Corruption of the Scripture Revisited," in *The Making of Christian Conflicts, Contacts, and Constructions: Essays in Honor of Bengt Holmberg*, ed. Magnus Zetterholm and Samuel Byrskog (Eisenbrauns, 2012), 325–50.

26. As Ehrman literally puts it, "In the technical parlance of textual criticism—which I retain for its significant ironies—these scribes 'corrupted' their texts for theological reasons" (*Orthodox Corruption of Scripture*, xii). Epp comments, "I call this [Ehrman's thesis] a startling thesis, not because textual critics were unaware that

Jews, pagans, and heretics more forcefully and to emphasize the subordinate role of women in the church. An example of Ehrman's approach is the way he treats a well-known variant: the addition of the word *Christ* after *Jesus* in Rom 10:9, attested by P46. For Ehrman's *Doktorvater*, Bruce Metzger, the inclusion "reflects scribal piety."[27] For Ehrman, it is an "orthodox corruption" of the New Testament text introduced to combat Christologies of a separatist type.[28]

Ehrman's approach has had a great impact, and his work is often extolled as one of the first text-critical works to combine textual analysis with social history. It has also paved the way for similar work, such as that of Wayne Kannaday, who has attempted to show that scribes who transcribed the gospels modified their copies because they were motivated or influenced by apologetic interests in controversies with pagans.[29] But Ehrman's work, while undeniably addressing specific points with incisiveness and rigor and presenting issues that merit consideration, has often been overrated. Once the initial novelty wore off, many of his proposed results began to be questioned from different angles. This is not to deny that some scribes made the text say what they thought it should say. This is well known. What is criticized is the methodology employed. Epp's work on Codex Bezae demonstrates the anti-Jewish tendency in that manuscript is demonstrable. Epp makes a careful assessment, confined to a single codex, and is thereby able to detect a pattern of deliberate effort in the manuscript's scribal habits. In contrast, as Ulrich Schmid rightly points out, Ehrman's consistent references to intentional scribal modifications are, to say the least, misleading, since he does not contrast his proposals with each manuscript's possible peculiarities. That is, he does not explain his findings by contrasting them with the idiosyncrasies of particular manuscripts, nor does he carefully

---

scribes made such alterations in their manuscripts, but because of the *direction* in which Ehrman shows these changes to have moved—toward supporting and emphasizing the emerging main-stream theology, or orthodoxy, of the time—rather than following the previously common theme in textual criticism that heretics twisted the text to accredit their views" ("Multivalence of the Term," 259, italics original).

27. Bruce M. Metzger, *A Textual Commentary of the Greek New Testament* (United Bible Societies, 1971), 525 (this variant is not discussed in the 2nd ed. of 1994); cf. Royse, *Scribal Habits*, 353.

28. Ehrman, *Orthodox Corruption of Scripture*, 191.

29. Kannaday, *Apologetic Discourse*. See the critique in Schmid, "Scribes and Variants," 16.

analyze these individual witnesses to see whether their scribes reveal any discernible tendency, such as omitting short words. Such an analysis would have enabled Ehrman to effectively substantiate his proposed interpretations.[30] And on the other hand, Schmid criticizes the certainty with which Ehrman continually asserts that the scribes consciously modified the texts, for

> after being stated and read many, many times, it captures our imagination to the effect that we are inclined to envisage every single scribe who penned such a potentially orthodox corruption as effectively executing that job (or "corruption") right on the spot. We do not see just one scribe, who once created the variant that has subsequently been copied. We see "some scribes," as many as there are witnesses to that reading, who willingly authored the corruption several times.[31]

Further, after stating that scribes appear as authors or editors rather than copyists in Ehrman's work, Schmid argues that Ehrman and Kannaday

> do not try to back up this new and rather eccentric perception of scribes by seeking for supporting evidence either from New Testament manuscripts themselves (scribal hands, layout, corrections, marginalia etc.) or from other ancient sources. In other words, the concept of scribes as authors is entirely built on the interpretation of variants in almost complete isolation from their physical containers (the manuscripts) and their sociological environment (the professional setting of those who produced them).[32]

---

30. Schmid, "Scribes and Variants," 5. He also points out that Ehrman's analysis has significant methodological limitations because of the difficulty in quantifying the data he provides.

31. Schmid, "Scribes and Variants," 6. He applies the same criticism to Kannaday's work *Apologetic Discourse* (Schmid, "Scribes and Variants," 6–8).

32. Schmid, "Scribes and Variants," 8–9. Schmid suggests that the harmonizations, corrections, stylistic improvements, etc., reflect more the work of readers/users than of scribes or copyists. In this vein, Michael W. Holmes notes, "Well-intentioned but unsupervised and largely undisciplined amateurs, not professionals, will have been the most frequent transmitters of the text of the New Testament; amateurs, at least some of whom 'felt themselves free to make corrections in the text, improving it by their own standards of correctness, whether grammatically, stylistically, or more substantively' (K. Aland and B. Aland, *The Text of the New Testament: An Introduction to the Critical Editions and to the Theory and Practice of Modern Textual Criticism*, 2nd ed., trans. E. F. Rhodes [Eerdmans, 1989], 69)." See Holmes, "Codex Bezae as a

For Schmid it is clear that, when evaluating a given manuscript's variants, one must begin by considering the physical characteristics of the manuscript that preserves those variants and, from there, see what can be known about the sociocultural context its literary production/reproduction.[33]

These observations are useful for weighing and qualifying Ehrman's proposals, which, as has been said, are suggestive and in many cases compelling but which must be analyzed individually.

2.2. David Parker: The "Living Text"

Epp and Ehrman's studies were pioneers in this new way of doing textual criticism. Alongside them, however, the one who is perhaps most closely aligned with the proposals of the new philology and reaches analogous conclusions by independent paths is David Parker, emeritus professor at the University of Birmingham (UK). Parker's positions are arguably in line with the new philology's distinctive emphases, especially regarding the value of variants and textual fluidity. For Parker, New Testament textual criticism should not only renounce the recovery of the original text, as we neither have it nor will we ever be able to obtain it, but should focus on the study of specific texts, with their variants, as they are preserved in various manuscripts and examine what these texts might convey.[34]

While Parker aligns himself with Epp and Ehrman's narrative criticism, his position is far more complex. For Parker, the multiple textual variants offer alternative meanings that were latent in the texts. They reveal contemporary ethical and theological concerns and provide a glimpse into the life of the early church, when Christian scribes and readers used and interpreted scriptural texts. But he prefers to delve into the story told by each variant, especially those that have been rejected.[35]

Parker's understanding begins with an analysis of Codex Bezae (05), the same codex Epp had studied years earlier, a bilingual manuscript, in Greek and Latin, probably copied around 400 CE.[36] The codex preserves

---

Recension of the Gospels," in *Codex Bezae: Studies from the Lunel Colloquum, June 1994*, ed. David C. Parker and Christian-Bernard Amphoux (Brill, 1996), 150.

33. Schmid, "Scribes and Variants," 23.
34. Parker, *Textual Scholarship and the Making*.
35. See Epp, "Critical Editions and the Development," 47.
36. Parker, *Codex Bezae*. In his view, this codex was copied in Berytus (modern Beirut) in the fifth century, but its text dates back to the second century. Here I sum-

the text of the four gospels and the Acts of the Apostles in two parallel columns, each occupying one page: the even pages, the column of the Greek text; and the odd pages, the Latin text. Parker pays attention above all to the free character of this codex's text, in which there is a marked tendency to harmonization, to the inclusion of material about Jesus that is not in the canonical gospels, and to rewrite or alter the text, often in a more colloquial style. A well-known example of the inclusion of material absent in the other gospels is the episode in Luke 6:4, where the Pharisees reproach Jesus's disciples for plucking ears of corn on the Sabbath. After Jesus's words about how David entered the house of God, took the shewbread, and ate it, the codex adds: "On the same day, when he saw one working on a Sabbath, he said to him, Man, if you know what you are doing, you are blessed; if you do not know, then you are cursed and a transgressor of the law." The addition clearly is not small. In the case of Acts, D's text is considerably longer than usual (by almost 8 percent), to the extent that it could be described as a different version of the same work or, at least, as a second edition. An example of such a discrepancy surfaces in the Jerusalem Council letter of Acts 15:23–29. In verses 20 and 29, where it says, "abstain from things sacrificed to idols, from blood, from strangled animals and from fornication," Codex Bezae omits the reference to "strangled animals" and adds, "and whatever you do not want to happen to you, do not do to another [or to 'others']" at the end of the verse.

From a detailed manuscript analysis, Parker concludes that the codex's text can be traced back to the second century, that is, to a period that in the opinion of some textual critics is fundamental for understanding the New Testament's transmission.[37] These authors think that almost all the significant Greek New Testament textual variants were introduced for the first time before the year 200, and they advance several hypotheses for this:

1. the change of attitude about the oral tradition, as Eusebius testifies when speaking of Papias's preference for oral traditions, which would have led to the introduction of textual variants from oral sources;
2. the discussion of the number of gospels, with the choice of only one by Marcion (Luke), and the harmonization of the four into a

---

marize and gloss what Parker comments in "Scripture Is Tradition," 12–14. See also Parker and Amphoux, *Codex Bezae*.

37. Here I recap what is summarized by Parker in "Scripture Is Tradition," 13–14.

single account by Tatian, which probably had an important impact on harmonizations in Mark's Gospel;
3. the text's possible alteration or enlargement in the process by which the gospels achieved literary status (it is possible that Mark's nonliterary status may have extended to the other gospels until the physical form of the codex was adopted from a simpler format, such as the roll or the notebook);
4. the possible existence of material about Jesus that would have been preserved and transmitted orally with certain freedom and that ended up being written down in the form we know of the Gospel of Thomas, similar to how it was transmitted in the hypothesized Q source, regardless of whether this gospel is authentic or not.

Parker considers these possibilities and believes that Codex Bezae's textual variations reveal that at the beginning the New Testament text, including Jesus's sayings, could be treated quite freely. If in the earliest stages, he argues, the exact tenor of Jesus's words did not matter, there must have been a free textual form in the second century that bore a resemblance to how Jesus's teachings were transmitted before the gospels were written.

On the basis of these observations and hypotheses, Parker subsequently wrote another influential work, *The Living Text of the Gospels*.[38] In it he looks at the multiplicity of existing texts of some specific gospel passages (e.g., the Lord's Prayer, Jesus's sayings on marriage and divorce, Mark's various endings, the peculiar textual history of the story of the adulterous woman, the variants of the three final chapters of Luke) or of broader texts (e.g., the Fourth Gospel's development and transmission) to show the existence of a collection of reinterpretations of these texts throughout history. Parker stresses that the Lord's Prayer, for example, which might be thought to have been fixed very soon in a single textual form due to its popular character, displays such a number of variants that it is impossible to know which is the original text. In any case, establishing the original text is not what really matters, according to Parker, but the fact that the different forms of this prayer contribute to understanding the tradition of

---

38. His positions are also found in other important contributions: Parker, *Introduction to the New Testament Manuscripts*; David C. Parker, *Manuscripts, Texts, Theology: Collected Papers 1977–2007* (De Gruyter, 2009). See also the implications of his thesis in relation to the "original text" noted by Epp, "Multivalence of the Term," 264–66.

Jesus. So, although a reader might consider the variants of little theological importance, what Parker emphasizes is that "the significance rests not in the character of the variants, but simply in the fact that the variants exist."[39]

The same is true of Jesus's sayings on marriage and divorce, in which the many variants reveal a collection of interpretive rewritings of a tradition, which, in Parker's view, prevent establishing a moral law on marriage and divorce based on a literal reading of Jesus's words. Hence, he provocatively asserts, "Given the number of textual forms in which these sayings exist, the question of their value in establishing authoritative moral teaching is posed incisively. We conclude that the early church rewrote the sayings in its attempt to make sense of them, and it is not possible to recover a single authoritative statement. It follows that there is no precept of the Lord which the discipline of the Church can invoke as authoritative."[40] We note, however, that Parker is not questioning the biblical text's authority. He warns only against the temptation to rest the foundation of a specific teaching of Jesus on a particular text. As he underscores, "The words of Jesus can be found only in the tradition and not behind or beyond it. They are available to us only in the manuscript continuum in which they were written down."[41]

For his part, Mark's various endings show that there are different ways of reading the Second Gospel, since "to provide a new ending is to rewrite a story."[42] The same is true of the textual tradition that tends to expand the text in Luke's final three chapters to underscore its orthodoxy. In the case of both Mark and Luke, what is observed—and this is what matters to Parker—is a continued textual growth, which entails a reinterpretation:

---

39. Parker, *Living Text of the Gospels*, 74.

40. Parker, *Living Text of the Gospels*, 183. He also says, "The recovery of a single original saying of Jesus is impossible" (92).

41. Parker, *Living Text of the Gospels*, 93. See also Parker, *Textual Scholarship and the Making*, 124.

42. Parker, *Living Text of the Gospels*, 183. Earlier he had stated: "Even if one insists on a single original text of Mark, one cannot escape the need to be aware of the fact that all the text forms affect our interpretation of it. This fact is true whichever ending one believes to be original. So, while readers of the Bible are in disagreement with regard to the text of Mark which they read, they have this in common—the different forms in which the text exists" (147). On the use of prior material in Mark's long ending, see James A. Kelhoffer, *Miracle and Mission: The Authentication of Missionaries and Their Message in the Longer Ending of Mark*, WUNT 2/112 (Mohr Siebeck, 2000), 123–56.

"The Gospel story continues to grow within as well as beyond the canonical pages. We might say that Luke is not, in these early centuries, a closed book. It is open, and successive generations write on its pages."[43] Parker believes that something analogous happens with other gospel passages, as with the peculiar textual history of the story of the adulterous woman or with the Fourth Gospel's development and transmission. These are examples of how a collection of reinterpretations is created throughout history that not only prevents us from having to choose a specific original text but also allows us to discover that this text exists in different variations that surfaced over time.[44]

In other words, Parker understands that the existence of textual variety precludes the choice of a single text, because the gospels exist only within a manuscript tradition that grew freely from the very beginning. That is why, at the end of his text-critical manual, he states that one of the key issues in gospel research is the possibility that, whatever the textual forms were in the year 100, these forms were very different from those of the late second century that remain available to us.[45] For him, any interpretation

---

43. See Parker, *Living Text of the Gospels*, 174. In *Textual Scholarship and the Making*, the concept is summarized as follows: "Every written work is a process and not an object" (21). See also the aforementioned work by Larsen, *Gospels before the Book*.

44. Regarding the *pericope adulerae*, the work of Knust and Wasserman, *To Cast the First Stone*, shows that, beyond questions of its authenticity or inauthenticity as an original text of John, the pericope has a significant value in Christian history and tradition, revealing the complex interaction between texts, liturgical practices, and reception and interpretation over time. The pericope is more than a story, it is a witness to the very process of gospel transmission (see passim and "Concluding Reflections," 343–44).

45. Parker, *Introduction to the New Testament*, 346. Petersen expresses himself in the same vein but more forcefully, emphasizing the text's chaotic character: "It is of the utmost importance to remember that whatever sort of text (or oral tradition) early (pre-180) Christian writers were accessing, it was very different from the text we now find in our critical editions" ("Genesis of the Gospels," 62, italics original). Epp, on the other hand, is less radical and argues that the existence of numerous manuscripts is best viewed positively, since they "represent a rich accumulation of texts, preserving diverse interpretations that have emerged from life experiences in the churches" ("Papyrus Manuscripts of the New Testament," 26). That a text's character is less controlled and more likely to change until the early fourth century is a fairly common opinion. See the quotations from Colwell, Hort, Birdsall, Alands, etc., in Royse, *Scribal Habits*, 20–22. In any case, there is no clear agreement on what is meant by accuracy in copying.

and theological formulation must begin with this reality. The text, Parker states, is sometimes very free, but more than anything else it is a living text and must remain so.[46] In his opinion, this way of understanding the text changed during the Renaissance with the invention of the printing press. With the publication of the New Testament in print, the text was reduced to a single text. The text was mummified, losing the character of vitality it had until then, and the printed text became identified with an authoritative text.[47] In this way the very concept of Scripture is betrayed because the plurality of readings reflects precisely the attitude adopted by Christians of the first generations in transmitting Jesus's words.[48] It was a free transmission, which highlighted the relationship between the written text and the oral tradition.[49] For Parker, texts reflect tradition and are also tradition. In this sense it is worth quoting his own words:

> Written tradition is only a part of the tradition. The oral tradition is often seen as ending at some point in the early church, so that we today are wholly dependent on the written text. But it is not so. One should think instead of an oral tradition extending unbroken from the lips and actions of Jesus, since people have never stopped talking about the things he said and did. Sometimes the oral tradition has been influenced by the written tradition, and sometimes the influence has been in the opposite direction. The written and oral tradition have accompanied, affected and followed one another. It is as the written tradition which has survived and as the oral tradition which we have received that the tradition lives. The surviving manuscripts and the spoken word are not simply bearers of some prior living tradition. They are the living tradition.[50]

---

46. As such, the expression "living text" as such is not new. Aland and Aland spoke of "living text" in the sense of the fluidity of the New Testament text (*Text of the New Testament*, 69). See also Epp, *Perspectives on New Testament Textual Criticism*, 1:xxxvi, xl; Epp, "Textual Criticism in the Exegesis," 48: "Exegetes … should never consider the New Testament text to be static or inert, for it was and remains a living text that, in turn, reveals the living church that transmitted it" (italics original).

47. Parker, *Living Text of the Gospels*, 189.

48. Parker wonders whether the fact that in the early days the text was remarkably free does not preserve "the spirit of the primitive use of Jesus' words, precisely because the letter has been altered" (*Living Text of the Gospels*, 189).

49. Parker, *Living Text of the Gospels*, 209.

50. Parker, *Living Text of the Gospels*, 210. See also Parker, "Scripture Is Tradition," 11–16, esp. 15: "This [free] text indicates that to at least some early Christians, it was more important to hand on the spirit of Jesus' teaching than to remember the

Thus, he argues, the search for a single authoritative text is a distortion of the tradition because the concept of an authoritative text widely used today is foreign to that tradition. Parker thus argues that the object of text-critical study should be the manuscripts in their variety as they have come down to us and insists that the textual fluidity embodied in the plurality of our extant texts shows that the notion of a single authoritative text is alien to the tradition of origins.[51] Consequently, since the printed text runs the risk of being interpreted as the authoritative text, which never existed in that form, the interpretation of texts must be about what the manuscripts, as material artifacts, attempt to convey and not about the hypothetical original (and therefore authoritative) text.

3. The Danger of the Textualization of the Scriptures

Parker's insights are the product of enormous erudition and merit serious attention. Some of his proposals, however, are highly debatable and have in fact received forceful criticism.[52] The main objection concerns his understanding of the early period of New Testament formation, when in his view there was a *remarkably free text*.[53] This is a much-debated question. It is quite likely that those who transmitted Jesus's words orally did so with a certain flexibility, but we lack sufficient evidence to affirm that there were no specific gospel texts or to sustain the notion that copyists altered these texts at their convenience. That is to say, until proven otherwise, the data indicate that there must have been some relatively fixed originals of the gospels and that the scribes who copied them sought to reproduce a text, even if they sometimes took liberties and altered it, more often accidentally and less often consciously. If the text had been free at the beginning, we should have more witness to that freedom rather than

---

letter… The material about Jesus was preserved in an interpretative rather than an exact fashion."

51. See also the implications of his thesis regarding the "original text" noted by Epp, "Multivalence of the Term," 264–66.

52. See, e.g., the long review of Moisés Silva of David C. Parker, *The Living Text*, *WTJ* 62 (2000): 295–302; or John C. Poirier, "Living Text or Exquisite Corpse?," *ExpTim* 119 (2008): 437–39; and that of Peter J. Williams of Parker, *Manuscripts, Texts, Theology*, *TC* (2013), https://tinyurl.com/SBL7016h. Nevertheless, those who have made such criticisms admit the honesty and rigor of the analysis of Parker's work.

53. Parker, *Living Text of the Gospels*, 202.

the uniformity (in spite of the variants) we see in the extant manuscript tradition.[54]

Moreover, to affirm that the putative free text of the earliest stages of Christianity is "very different" from the one we have can be understood in a number of ways. What do we mean by "very different"? Do we mean different word sequences that do not alter the message conveyed within the context in which they are inserted or sequences that convey a completely different meaning? Are not the translations of the New Testament in the same language also "very different" from each other, even though they have been made from practically the same Greek text? And yet, any reader can recognize one and the same book in each of these translations. On the other hand, supposing some manuscripts change the meaning of a passage, can we give equal value to all witnesses, no matter how old they are? Logically, the problem lies in defining how we understand freedom or fluidity and what we understand by the authoritative text.

It is perhaps understandable that Parker might find it difficult to reconcile the extant manuscript tradition with the idea of an untouchable original text that has, for all intents and purposes, been converted into the ultimate referent of faith and has been largely severed from the tradition.[55] His thesis, however, has implications for questions about the authority of Scripture. The variety of manuscript texts adduced by Parker, which in his opinion demonstrates that there was a remarkably free text in the beginning, does not mean that there was no belief in an authoritative text. Certainly, there was no single normative text in the beginning, as there is none today, but there was and is, as the Catholic tradition would put it, an authoritative Word that is partially attested in a text that takes on various

---

54. See the discussion above.

55. Parker's defense of tradition is noteworthy and even appears to echo Catholic distinctives with its emphasis on the role of the Spirit: "The crux of the matter is that the definitive text is not essential to Christianity, because the presence of the Spirit is not limited to the inspiration of the written word…. Belief in single authoritative texts gives the Spirit an important role in the formation of Scripture and almost none in the growth of tradition. Once the distinction has been abolished in the way we have attempted above, it is possible to recognize fully that the very life itself and the whole life of the Church is in the Spirit" (Parker, *Living Text of the Gospels*, 211). The Catholic tradition, of course, differs critically insofar as it holds that the action of the Spirit in the formation of the gospels through the apostolic community is unrepeatable and to be distinguished from the Spirit's action in guiding the church in the postapostolic period.

forms.[56] In this sense, it is true that the variety of texts containing Jesus's sayings on marriage and divorce does not allow us to establish a literal teaching of the Lord in this regard. Texts and traditions alone and in isolation cannot constitute the last word on what Christians should believe, unless we admit the impossibility of finding in the Christian faith any other foundation than what is contained in the Bible: the multiplicity of texts testifies to an authoritative Word that is not circumscribed by these texts.

That said, it is worth noting that, from the point of view of the Catholic tradition, Parker's insistence that Scripture is tradition is interesting. It is an assertion that has led him to draw criticism from certain quarters. In this, we seem to be reliving the past insofar as the criticisms are analogous to those levied against Richard Simon for claiming in the seventeenth century that manuscripts had suffered unintentional alterations and that, if they were rejected for this reason, "there would not be any version of the New Testament, Greek, Latin, Syriac or Arabic, that could be truly called authentic because not one of them in whatever language is completely free from interpolations." He added, "I can even say that … Greek copyists took great liberties when making their manuscripts."[57]

Simon, by stressing that we cannot know the exact words of Scripture due to the variations between manuscripts, defended the necessity of tradition and showed that the principle of *sola Scriptura* did not hold. These affirmations drew criticism from the Protestant world, mainly in England and Germany. This reaction, on the other hand, had a fruitful side. The challenge posed by the existence of a multiplicity of variants prompted in those countries, and where the Reformation had triumphed, the development of textual criticism and the search for the original words of the New Testament, which would counter attacks on the principle of the priority of Scripture.[58]

---

56. On this, see, e.g., Vicente Balaguer, "La economía de la Palabra de Dios: A los 40 años de la Constitución dogmática Dei Verbum," ScrTh 37 (2005): 424–39.

57. Richard Simon, *Histoire critique du Texte du Nouveau Testament* (Leers, 1689), 79. For the English quotation, see Simon, *Critical History of the Text of the New Testament, Wherein Is Established the Truth of the Acts on Which the Christian Religion Is Based*, trans. Andrew Hunwick, NTTSD 43 (Brill, 2013), 69.

58. See Bart D. Ehrman, *Misquoting Jesus: The Story behind Who Changed the Bible and Why* (HarperCollins, 2005), 102–5.

It seems that, with the passing centuries, Simon appears to have been right, at least in a certain sense. The emphasis on the biblical text by the Reformation's biblical heirs has dominated exegetical practices, leading in some cases to a reading that is very dependent on a quasi-sacred reconstructed text. This does not mean that the same has not occurred within the Catholic tradition. On a popular level, one could say that there is a widespread tendency to identify the Bible's text in critical editions with the original (or near-original) text and therefore with a text written by God. Perhaps recent advances in textual criticism can serve to balance the scales and avoid the dangers of biblicism. Thus, the efforts to show that we cannot arrive at the autographic text from the available manuscripts, and that a Christian religion based on the identification of God's Word with the exact wording of a supposed printed text has no foundation, weigh in Parker's favor.

At the same time, the multiplicity of texts on which Parker looks bears witness to an authoritative Word, oral and written, that is not confined to those texts, for texts and traditions alone and in isolation cannot constitute the final normative word on what Christians should believe. These texts are in direct relationship with other unwritten traditions. If the text's authority depends on its status as an original autographical text, then it is reasonable to question that authority, since we do not know which text the author wrote. If, on the other hand, these books are understood to have been composed in a community of faith (Israel and the church) that existed before the books, their authoritative status is guaranteed by the faith of that community of believers. Christians who were baptized at the dawn of the early Christian movement were not given a Bible, but with baptism they made a profession of faith, in which they grew and were strengthened by the nourishment of the Word and the Eucharist (see Did. 9–10; Justin, *1 Apol.* 66–67). It is significant that the church does not canonize texts but books, something that is even more evident in the case of the Old Testament. The church fathers were aware of the multiplicity of texts but did not opt for a particular form of them.[59] What mattered

---

59. See J. Keith Elliott, "Manuscripts, the Codex and the Canon," *JSNT* 63 (1997): 112: "The *text* of the New Testament that was found in the manuscripts was not of importance to those who pronounced on the canon. Jerome, Origen and others recognized certain books as approved, canonical scripture, but they did not try to specify a particular or precise form of the text to be found in the manuscripts even though these Fathers were alert to textual variation in manuscripts" (emphasis original).

was that these books were interpreted in accordance with the faith of the community that transmitted them. The faith of the church keeps us from diminishing Scripture (by circumscribing it to a hypothetical text) and lets Scripture be what it is and have the authority it has.[60]

---

60. For more details, see Chapa, "Texto autoritativo y crítica textual," 172–75, and ch. 7 of the present book.

Translations as a Living Text

One of the risks of theological work is the desire to domesticate the biblical text, presuming we have the original autographs. As we have seen, the practice of textual criticism serves as a permanent reminder to avoid falling into this trap. Manuscript culture and new approaches to New Testament textual criticism show that, despite our inability to recover the original text, we can use manuscripts as witnesses to an ever living text. The text is attested by a diversity of manuscripts that are part of the tradition insofar as they are in conformity with the faith of the communities that read the same texts as authoritative. But this vitality is not limited to the Greek text. It is ratified by the ancient translations as well, which not only make it possible to demonstrate the impossibility of establishing a presumed original text as authoritative but also show the inseparable relationship between the text and the community of faith in which it was born and in which it is read.

For the same reason, the diversity of ancient versions is valuable because it testifies to the text from which each one derives and, as witnesses of a living tradition, allows us to study aspects of the social world in which these versions arose. That is to say, just as the New Testament versions are valuable for recovering part of the Greek text translators used and for disclosing geographical information about the circulation of the text (Syria, Egypt, etc.), these same translations also offer clues about how a given passage was understood in a particular time and place, evident in the language, exegesis, and interpretation of those texts.[1]

The analysis below will serve to illustrate these points by focusing specifically on the Latin translations, as they occupy a prominent position among the New Testament versions. Certainly, like other versions, the Latin translations present methodological problems for establishing

---

1. Parker, *Introduction to the New Testament Manuscripts*, 118–19; Parker, *Living Text of the Gospels*, 14.

the underlying Greek text, since the various VL texts and the Vulgate display mixed readings and need to be disentangled.[2] In addition, the VL's language presents the additional challenge of being unpolished. There is no single form of the VL text, as Jerome himself acknowledged when Pope Damasus asked him to prepare the revision of the Latin translation that ended up as the Vulgate of 383 CE. Moreover, we do not yet know whether the VL emerged in North Africa at the end of the second century or elsewhere.[3]

1. Unexplained Intentionality or Orthodox Corruptions?

In any case, as the Greek text was translated and copied, various changes were introduced. Some were due to the history of the version itself and the requirements of the target language. Others show the text's living character, since at times these changes implied an interpretation or gave the text a new meaning. Particularly illuminating are those variants that appear to have been made deliberately, as they potentially showcase the reasons for those changes. We note, however, that it is very difficult definitively to determine intentionality, and given the variety of possible causes, each case should be analyzed individually.

For example, the versions attest a handful of variants that seem to have arisen in a clearly deliberate manner but reflect only local preferences. The value of such cases is merely anecdotal, and the information they transmit is dubious. This is the case, for example, with texts that preserve the names of the thieves crucified with Jesus. In Matt 27:38, Mark 15:27, and Luke 23:32, some VL codices (6, 11, 14) add the names of the two thieves.

Most curious, however, is the fact that they do not use the names we know from the apocryphal literature, Demas and Gestas, but add more obscure ones: in Codex Colbertinus (6), the thief on the right is called Zoatham and the one on the left Camma in Matt 27:38 (but Zoathan and Cammatha in Mark 15:27); in Codex Rehdigeranus (11), they were Joathas and Maggatras (Luke 23:32), and in Codex Usserianus (14), at least one of

---

2. The vast number of manuscripts of these versions that have been preserved—specifically more than ten thousand, of which fifty (dated between the fourth and thirteenth centuries) are representatives of the VL—makes this necessary (see Parker, *Living Text of the Gospels*, 14).

3. See Jacobus Petzer, "The Latin Version of the New Testament," in Ehrman and Holmes, *Text of the New Testament* (1st ed.), 113–30.

them was called Capnatas (Luke 23:32; the name of the other thief is missing). Such examples are rare. In any case, they are of interest because they illustrate community preferences in fixing local traditions.[4]

Another, more interesting example pertains to variants that appear to reflect some kind of doctrinal question. This seems to be the case with the variant attested in Luke 1:3: ἔδοξεν κἀμοὶ παρηκολουθηκότι ἄνωθεν ἀκριβῶς ("it seemed also to me, after I had been accurately informed of everything from the beginning"), where several VL manuscripts (and the Gothic version), instead of reading *visum est et mihi* ("it seemed also to me"), read *visum Spiritu Sancto et me* ("it seemed to the Holy Spirit and to me"). In this case, whoever introduced this reading perhaps thought that the Third Evangelist required divine assistance to write his work and remedied it by adopting the expression of Acts 15:28: "visum est enim Spiritui Sancto et nobis" ("it seemed to the Holy Spirit and to us").[5]

Another example of a variant that could be related to contemporary doctrinal disputes is the rendering of some Latin manuscripts for the Greek text of Luke 2:33, 48. When the evangelist refers to Joseph as Jesus's father in 2:33, the preferred text, according to some Greek manuscripts (01 03 05 019 032 1 700 1241 *l* 2211), the Vulgate, and other versions, reads καὶ ἦν ὁ πατὴρ αὐτοῦ καὶ ἡ μήτηρ θαυμάζοντες ἐπὶ τοῖς λαλουμένοις περὶ αὐτοῦ ("His father and mother were amazed at the things that were said about him"). On the other hand, the Greek majority text, with the VL and some Vulgate manuscripts, as well as the Syriac and Coptic versions, reads, "Joseph and his mother" (Ἰωσὴφ καὶ ἡ μήτηρ; Lat. *Ioseph et mater eius*). The change of πατὴρ αὐτοῦ ("his father") to Ἰωσήφ ("Joseph") is usually explained as having been motivated by apologetic reasons. Scribes introduced the changes because of the apparent difficulty of understanding the Greek text correctly in the context of disputes with some Judeo-Christians and other adoptionist Christians, who held that Jesus was fully human, the

---

4. Metzger and Ehrman, *Text of the New Testament* (2nd ed.), 270, with references to Rendel Harris's articles on the subject. See also Gerard Mussies, "Reflections on the Apocryphal Gospels as Supplements," in *Reflections in Empssychoi Logoi—Religious Innovations in Antiquity: Studies in Honour of Pieter Willem van der Horst* (Brill, 2008), 597–611. The most important in attesting these names is the twelfth-century Codex Colbertinus (6), which presents a text of the VL considered European but contaminated with the Vulgate (see Metzger and Ehrman, *Text of the New Testament* [2nd ed.], 103; Metzger, *Early Versions of the New Testament*, 341).

5. Metzger and Ehrman, *Text of the New Testament* (2nd ed.), 266–67.

son of Joseph and Mary.⁶ This avoided referring to Joseph as the father of Jesus. However, this concern does not appear in the Greek manuscript tradition of Luke 2:48: ἰδοὺ ὁ πατήρ σου κἀγὼ ὀδυνώμενοι ἐζητοῦμέν σε ("See that your father and I, being distressed, were looking for you"), where the words ὁ πατήρ σου ("your father") are solidly attested. Only a fifth-century Greek manuscript appears to read οἱ συγγενεῖς σου κἀγώ ("your relatives and I"). The Greek text of Luke 2:27, 41 is also consistent when it refers to Joseph and Mary as "parents" (γονεῖς) of Jesus (though not in 2:43, where the Byzantine text changes γονεῖς to Ἰωσὴφ καὶ ἡ μήτηρ, "Joseph and his mother"). These readings could suggest that the variant of Luke 2:33 is due to stylistic issues rather than theological problems. Even so, two VL manuscripts (2, 26) read "kinsmen" (*propinqui*) in Luke 2:48, while most manuscripts of this version (3, 4, 8, 7) omit "your father and I," leaving simply *ecce dolentes quarebamus te* ("See how anxious we were looking for you"). All this shows that some Latin versions of Luke 2:33, 48 appear to support the more "orthodox" readings and point to a doctrinal concern along the lines indicated above.

2. Original Readings?

Also, in the context of possibly deliberate changes, the Latin versions offer an important type of witness to the original Greek text. It is quite possible that there are passages in which the Latin translation preserves a reading closer to the original Greek text that has since then disappeared (perhaps for doctrinal reasons) or, conversely, in which the Latin translation reflects doctrinal concerns that existed at the time the manuscript was copied. We can illustrate the problem with two examples from the Fourth Gospel.⁷

The first is that of John 13:10: ὁ λελουμένος οὐκ ἔχει χρείαν εἰ μὴ τοὺς πόδας νίψασθαι ("He who has bathed has no need to wash more than his feet"). Here, three VL manuscripts (Colbertinus [6], Würzburg Univ. 67, and the Fragmentum Milanense [ρ (24)]) translate the Greek text with "qui lotus est semel non indiget (nisi ut pedes lavet)" ("he who has been bathed

---

6. Ehrman, *Orthodox Corruption of Scripture*, 65–66; Metzger and Ehrman, *Text of the New Testament* (2nd ed.), 285.

7. For an overview of the VL manuscripts of the Fourth Gospel, see Hugh A. G. Houghton, *The Latin New Testament: A Guide to Its Early History, Texts, and Manuscripts* (Oxford University Press, 2008), 165–67. A complete transcription of the manuscripts of John's VL can be found at http://www.iohannes.com/vetuslatina.

once needs only to wash his feet").⁸ That is, these versions add the adverb *semel* ("once"), which has no equivalent in Greek manuscripts. This raises the question as to whether the Latin text reflects a lost Greek variant, or whether the presence of *semel* is a way of indicating the character of the Greek perfect tense (a definitive action presented in stative aspect), or whether the adverb was introduced in the context of a theological controversy about the repetition of baptism.⁹ Several of Augustine and Ambrose's works support the latter possibility, which present *semel* together with the words *qui lotus est* ("he who has bathed") to translate the Greek participle λελουμένος, as in the aforementioned manuscripts.¹⁰

Determining which of the three options is preferable is not simple. That it is a way of translating the Greek perfect, highlighting the state of affairs resulting from the action, does not seem probable, although it is difficult to demonstrate that it is not. That it is due to controversies about the repetition of baptism is also difficult to determine and in any case not very plausible. At the very least, it does not seem that the occasions on which it appears in Augustine's works are due to the fact that the bishop of Hippo deliberately introduced this adverb because it was favorable to him for the polemic against the Donatists. It is more likely that he had already found it in the tradition.¹¹ In fact, Tertullian (*Bapt.* 12.3) and Optatus (*Parm. Donat.* 4.4, 5.3) also read *semel* in this verse (even Jerome reads in *Jov.* 2.3 something similar: "qui lotus est non necesse habet uti iterum lauet" ["he who has bathed has no need to wash again"]).¹² Perhaps we must consider that the VL manuscripts that read *semel* are transmitting an original text that has left no trace in the Greek manuscript tradition. The question, however, remains open.¹³ In any

---

8. Sangermanensis primus (g¹ [7]) and some Vulgate manuscripts change the word order and read *qui semel lotus est*.

9. See Philip Burton, "The Latin Version of the New Testament," in *Text of the New Testament* (2nd ed.), 195; Houghton, *Latin New Testament*, 166.

10. Hugh A. G. Houghton, *Augustine's Text of John: Patristic Citations and Latin Gospel Manuscripts* (Oxford University Press, 2008), 304–5; Petersen, *Tatian's Diatessaron*, 380–84.

11. Houghton, *Augustine's Text of John*, 75, 305.

12. For the testimonies of the fathers on this subject, see Marie-François Berrouard, *Oeuvres de saint Augustin. Homélies sur l'Evangile de saint Jean LV–LXXIX: Traduction, introduction et notes*, BA 74a (Institut des Études Augustiniennes, 1993), 404.

13. In any case, we should add that the Codex Colbertinus, though important, is the last of the witnesses to John's VL we have. This codex and the Milan fragments,

case, it illustrates the challenge of determining the original reading and reveals the extent to which the received text can be enriched in its transmission without necessarily betraying the text closest to the original.

The other example is John 7:1. Most Greek manuscripts read καὶ μετὰ ταῦτα περιεπάτει ὁ Ἰησοῦς ἐν τῇ Γαλιλαίᾳ· οὐ γὰρ ἤθελεν ἐν τῇ Ἰουδαίᾳ περιπατεῖν, ὅτι ἐζήτουν αὐτὸν οἱ Ἰουδαῖοι ἀποκτεῖναι ("After this Jesus went about in Galilee, for he did not want to go about in Judea, because the Jews sought him to kill him"). In contrast, the Codex Washingtonianus (032) and two minuscules (196, 743) preserve the reading οὐ γὰρ εἶχεν ἐξουσίαν ("for he had no power") instead of οὐ γὰρ ἤθελεν ("for he did not want"). Being such a minority reading in Greek, it is surprising that it is nevertheless attested by five VL manuscripts, including the oldest: 3, 4, 8, 11, 14, which read *non habebat potestatem* ("he had no power"). The Curetonian Syriac version also supports the reading, and, as we shall see, so does John Chrysostom's commentary in his *Hom. Jo.* 48 on John's Gospel.[14] Is it possible that this was the original reading? It seems that we should prefer εἶχεν ἐξουσίαν as the older reading insofar as the expression ἔχειν ἐξουσίαν also appears in John (10:18; cf. 19:10), the use of ἔχειν followed by a noun is characteristic of the evangelist's style (see 3:16, 4:44, 9:41), ἐξουσία is an important concept in this gospel, and, above all, it is the *lectio difficilior* ("he did not want" is in principle less problematic than "had no power"). This option (οὐ γὰρ εἶχεν ἐξουσίαν) is confirmed by Chrysostom's testimony, which shows that he had at his disposal a Greek text with that reading. Moreover, the way he quotes that text seems to suggest that it was customary for the passage to be understood as "having no authority." In fact, the presence of this expression surprises the bishop, insofar as it appeared to question the power of Christ, confirming that it was the more difficult reading and, accordingly, the one we should prefer.[15]

---

though dating from the seventh or eighth century, come from a Gallican lectionary, so their testimony is not particularly strong (see Houghton, *Augustine's Text of John*, 75).

14. Instead, the Latin MSS 16, 6, 5, 2, 10, 13, and Vg (supported by the Syriac Sinaitic version) read *non volebat* (e: *non habebat uoluntatem*).

15. John Chrysostom, *Homiliae in Joannem* (PG 59:269). Chrysostom wonders how the evangelist could say that Jesus had no power to go to Judea and then appear in the temple, speaking before those who wanted to kill him and yet do not seize him. The bishop responds by saying that, when the evangelist mentions that Jesus "had no power," he refers to his human nature, but when he says that "he was in the midst of them and they did not seize him," he shows his divine power. And he adds: καὶ γὰρ ἔφευγεν ὡς ἄνθρωπος, καὶ ἐφαίνετο ὡς θεός ("for he fled as a man, but appears [before

The arguments, however, are not definitive. In fact, Rainer Riesner argues for the majority reading ("did not want") as *lectio difficilior*, since in his opinion "not wanting to go to Judea" could imply that Jesus feared being killed, thereby showing a weakness incompatible with his nature. For Riesner, the minority reading, "he had no power," was not the original but could be explained as a second-century textual harmonization.[16] Whatever it was, despite the fact that the VL supports the minority reading and that for many it could be the closest to the original text, modern critical editions retain the majority reading. Metzger discloses in his textual commentary that the committee for the critical edition of the Greek New Testament was too reluctant to decide on the basis of a single witness (032) and preferred to leave the majority reading.[17]

As we see, it is not easy to reach a conclusion. However, the example is meant only to illustrate how some Latin translations preserve a text that differs from the majority reading and thereby manifest the living character of the original text.

3. Modern Latin Translations

So far, the examples come from the ancient versions. However, the textual variety continues in some form in the contemporary Latin translation, as displayed in the Neo-Vulgate.[18] Two additional examples from the Fourth Gospel illustrate this.

---

them] as God"). See also Razvan Perşa, "Autenticitatea textului scripturistic in 7,1 în comentariul hrisostomic la evanghelia după Ioan, (The Authenticity of John 7,1 in the Chrysostomic Commentary to the Gospel according to John)," *StTe* 2 (2014): 153–78. On this being the preferred reading, see Burton, "Latin Version of the New Testament," 192. At any rate, it is also conceivable that οὐ γὰρ εἶχεν ἐξουσίαν did not mean here "not having authority or right" (which makes no sense in the light of what follows) but simply "not being able to." See Wieland Willker, *A Textual Commentary on the Greek Gospels*, vol. 4, *John*, 12th ed. (Bremen, 2015), https://tinyurl.com/SBL7016i. Thus, this reading could be admitted as older without necessarily revising the theology of Jesus's authority in the Fourth Gospel.

16. Rainer Riesner, "Joh 7,1: fehlender Wille oder fehlende Vollmacht Jesu?," *ZNW* 96 (2005): 259–62.

17. Metzger, *Textual Commentary*, 215–16.

18. On this version, see Antonio García-Moreno, *La Neovulgata: precedentes y actualidad*, 2nd ed. (Eunsa, 2011), and below under "The Authority of the Text."

3.1. John 8:25: "Principium quia et loquor vobis"

The first is the famous *crux interpretum* of John 8:25, Jesus's answer to the question of Jewish authorities: σὺ τίς εἶ; ("Who are you?"). As is known, the Greek text most frequently found in critical editions reads εἶπεν αὐτοῖς ὁ Ἰησοῦς· τὴν ἀρχὴν ὅ τι καὶ λαλῶ ὑμῖν.[19] But how should this answer be translated? ὅτι can be read as ὅτι ("because") or as ὅ τι ("that which") and punctuated likewise in various ways. Consequently, Jesus's words ὅ τι καὶ λαλῶ ὑμῖν can be understood as a statement ("I am what I am telling you"), a question ("What is it that I am speaking to you?"), or an exclamation ("What I am speaking to you!").[20] In addition, τὴν ἀρχήν ("the beginning") also has no clear meaning. Some fathers and ecclesiastical writers in the Eastern tradition, while finding the Greek text problematic, resolve it by understanding τὴν ἀρχήν adverbially as ὅλως (*omnino*; "absolutely" / "fundamentally") or as ἐξ ἀρχῆς ("from the beginning" / "beginning").[21] Depending on which interpretation is adopted, the Master's answer could be translated as, "Fundamentally, I am what I am telling you," or "What is it that I am speaking to you at all?" or "What I am speaking to you absolutely!" or "[I am] what I have told you from the beginning." Modern interpreters argue over which should be preferred, although the last option ("[I am] what I have told you from the beginning") is perhaps the best translation, and, for what it's worth, would be supported by Nonnus of Panopolis's interpretation. Moreover, Cyril of Alexandria also considers it a possibility.[22] In any case, equally attractive are the reading of P66, εἶπεν

---

19. In the manuscript transmission, the text presents some variants. Sinaiticus's original reading introduces ἕν ("one thing only") before λαλῶ. For its part, P66's corrector adds εἶπον ὑμῖν ("I told you") before τὴν ἀρχήν. P75 features a dot after the *omicron* and below the *tau* in ὅ τι. But it is not clear whether it is a punctuation mark or a spot. Finally, 047 omits τὴν ἀρχήν.

20. Metzger, *Textual Commentary*, 223–24.

21. This interpretation is in line with one of the two offered by Cyril of Alexandria. See Antonio Piras, "Gv 8,25 e la versione gotica della bibbia," in *Studi in onore di Vittoria Dolcetti Corazza*, ed. Carla Falluomini and Roberto Rosselli Del Turco (Edizioni dell'Orso, 2015), 152–54. Among other questions, Piras reviews the interpretations that have been made of this passage. See also Christophe Rico, "Jn 8:25 au risque de la philologie: histoire d'une expression grecque," *RB* 112 (2005): 596–627; Rico, *Le traducteur de Bethléem: Le génie interprétatif de saint Jérôme à l'aune de la linguistique* (Cerf, 2016), 137–41.

22. Following a study of the expression in Greek literature, Chrys Caragounis

αὐτοῖς ὁ Ἰησοῦς· εἶπον ὑμῖν τὴν ἀρχὴν ὅ τι καὶ λαλῶ ὑμῖν ("Jesus said to them: 'I said to you at the beginning the same thing I am speaking to you [now]'"),[23] and the translation proposed by Hans Förster based on the punctuation of Codex Bezae and Codex Basiliensis (07). According to this punctuation, τὴν ἀρχήν would depend on εἶπεν ("said"), functioning as an adverb (from a grammatical construction influenced by Hebrew), and would mean, "Jesus said to them first of all / immediately: I am telling you this" (or "I am also telling you this").[24]

If we look at the Latin versions, we see that the translators were faced with a difficult text and opted for a slavish translation.[25] The VL translation is quite uniform and translates the Greek as "Dixit eis Iesus principium quod et loquor vobis." The Vulgate version, for its part, reads, "principium quia et loquor vobis." They could be translated literally: "Jesus said to them: 'The principle that (or 'because') I also speak to you.'"[26] But precisely by translating τὴν ἀρχήν with the nominative/accusative *principium*, which has no syntactic function in Latin, the Latin versions gave rise to interpretations that go beyond the purview of the Greek text. This is the case in much of the Western tradition, which applies an anagogical exegesis of the text and interprets the principium as Christ ("[I am] the principium who also speaks to you [or because I speak to you]"), something the Greek text

---

proposes, "[I am] From the beginning!—precisely what I have been saying (speaking) to you." See Caragounis, "What Did Jesus Mean by τὴν ἀρχήν in John 8:25?," *NovT* 49 (2007): 147. He comments, "The English may translate it with '[I am] what I have been saying to you from the beginning,' but this is only a functional rendering deprived of the literary effect of the original" (147 n. 53).

23. Brown, *Gospel according to John*, 1:348.

24. Hans Förster, "Grammatik von Joh 8,25 im Lichte der handschriftlichen Überlieferung," *ZNW* 107 (2016): 1–29; Forster, "Possible Similarities in the Linguistic Structure of John 8.25b and John 8.45a," *BT* 68 (2017): 166–68.

25. Piras, "Gv 8,25 e la versione gotica della bibbia," 157. The ancient non-Latin versions do not help much either. The Syriac versions ignore the sense of *omnino* and stress that of "beginning" (Rico, *Le traducteur de Bethléem*, 140 n. 1); the Bohairic version reads, "In the beginning I also said to you," and the Sahidic, "From the beginning I speak to you." The Arabic Diatessaron translates, "If I should speak to you." See Willker, *Textual Commentary*, ad loc.

26. The most relevant variants are *initium* for *principium* in 3 (Vercellensis) and 6 (Colbertinus) and *inprimis* in 4 (Veronensis), and *quia* in 4, *quoniam* in 5 (Bezae) and *qui* in 2 (Palatino). The Clementine edition of the Vulgate reads *principium quod et loquor vobis*. See also Houghton, *Augustine's Text of John*, 264.

excludes, since the accusative τὴν ἀρχήν cannot be the predicative attribute of an implied verb εἰμί.²⁷

Probably for this reason, the Neo-Vulgate translation departs from this tradition and prefers to read, "Dixit eis Iesus: In principio: id quod et loquor vobis!" Here we have, therefore, a modern correction of the Latin translation, made from the Greek text considered the best attested today, without support in the older Latin versions. The punctuation adopted by the Neo-Vulgate involves understanding τὴν ἀρχήν as ὅλως (*omnino*) and, on the basis of the ὅ τι, seems to mean, "Above all / At the beginning, that is what I am telling you!" The translation is legitimate, though freer than that of the VL and the Vulgate, inasmuch as *in principio* would correspond to a supposed ἐν ἀρχῇ rather than to the adverbial accusative τὴν ἀρχήν.²⁸ On the other hand, it is still rather obscure and allows for a translation that is faithful to the Greek text but also affords fewer liberties than those offered by *principium* by closing the way to allegorical interpretations.

3.2. John 20:17: "Noli me tangere"

Let us now take another passage that serves as an example of how the ancient versions affect the way we understand the best-attested Greek text. This is the case of the famous words of the risen Jesus to Mary Magdalene in John 20:17: λέγει αὐτῇ Ἰησοῦς· μή μου ἅπτου.²⁹ Again, we encounter a translation challenge. Should we understand, "Jesus says to her: do not touch me," or, as it appears in many modern New Testament editions, "Jesus says to her: stop holding me / Let me go"? The Latin versions attested by both the VL and the Vulgate translate it without any variant as, "Dicit ei Iesus: noli me tangere" ("Jesus says to her: do not touch me"). However, the revisers of the Neo-Vulgate seem to have considered this Latin translation deficient, understanding, in conformity with the contemporary majority interpretation, that the negation μή followed by the present imperative is used to stop an action already begun. Consequently, bearing in mind that the prohibition in the present imperative μὴ ἅπτου μου should mean "stop holding me" in Classical Greek (rather than the apparent "don't touch me" suggested by the Latin text), the Neo-Vulgate translators corrected *noli*

---

27. Piras, "Gv 8,25 e la versione gotica della bibbia," 158–65.
28. Rico, *Le traducteur de Bethléem*, 140–41.
29. This is a reading of the Greek text, which has no noteworthy variants. Only Codex Vaticanus, changing the order of the words, reads μὴ ἅπτου μου.

me tangere to *iam noli tenere* ("do not hold me / let go of me"), a reading apparently more in keeping with the Greek and with the apparent sense of the passage but not recorded in the Latin manuscript tradition.

The option, again, is legitimate. But is it entirely satisfactory? On the one hand, we should not forget that the function of the present imperative in Koine Greek did not necessarily carry that sense of continuity that Classical Greek had. Along with the traditional sense, μή followed by a present imperative could also indicate the prohibition to initiate a process.[30] Therefore, from the Greek perspective, it could be understood as Mary Magdalene wanting to touch Jesus and that he tells her not to do so.[31] It is true that weighty exegetical reasons exist to argue that John follows classical usage here, especially if one were to compare the scene with the appearance of Thomas, where Jesus tells him to touch him, and with the statements of Matt 28:9 ("They came and embraced his feet and worshiped him") and Luke 24:39 ("Behold my hands and my feet: it is I myself. Feel me and see"). Theoretically, however, we cannot rule out that the evangelist had adopted the Hellenistic usage. In fact, there are Greek fathers and ecclesiastical writers, familiar with the usages of the language they mastered, who understand it in this sense, such as Origen, Eusebius of Caesarea, and Cyril of Alexandria.[32] Nor does the text of Nonnus of Panopolis, who, being the author of a *Paraphrase to the Gospel of John* in 3,660 dactylic hexameters and also of the *Dionysiacs*, the last and longest great poem of classical antiquity (21,286 verses distributed in 48 books, the same as the *Iliad* and the *Odyssey*), leave any doubt that he knew well

---

30. This usage occurs, for example, in Luke 10:4, 7: μὴ βαστάζετε βαλλάντιον.... μὴ μεταβαίνετε ἐξ οἰκίας εἰς οἰκίαν ("Carry no bag.... Do not go from house to house"), which the versions translate by, *Nolite portare sacculum.... Nolite transire de domo in domo.* See also Rico, *Le traducteur de Bethléem*, 149.

31. See BDF §336.5.

32. Origen, *Comm. Jo.* 6.287 (Blanc [SC 220]): "After he has destroyed his enemies by his passion, the Lord, who is mighty and strong in battle, needing purification by his human works, which have been given to him alone by his Father, prevents Mary from touching him saying: Do not touch me." Also see 6.291, 10.245, 13.180. Eusebius, *Quaest. ev.* 3 (PG 22:949): "As she began to go to him as one who goes to a teacher and not as befits God, [Jesus] avoids her and rejects her saying: *Do not touch me.*" See Rico, *Le traducteur de Bethléem*, 149–50. Cyril of Alexandria, *Comm. Jo.* 3.119 (Pusey): "How could it not be fitting that Mary should be prevented from touching his body, which was clearly holy, if she had not yet received the Spirit? For, although Christ had risen from the dead, the Father had not yet given the Spirit through him to mankind."

the various uses of the Greek language. And yet, Nonnus had no qualms about understanding this present imperative as a prohibition to initiate an action and paraphrased the text, "And God restrained the woman who was going straight to approach the immortal garment. And he said to her one word: 'Do not touch my garments, for I have not yet returned to my Father after death.'" Certainly, Nonnus's quasi-docetic tendencies could partly explain his translation. But neither does John Chrysostom escape this way of understanding the text, and he is inclined to think that Jesus prevents Mary from touching him because such an action would not be in conformity with his dignity as the Risen One.[33] Therefore, in spite of the fact that the translation that has prevailed today understands Mary to be holding Jesus, the problem is not resolved. Hence there are also those who choose a path similar to the classical one and consider it more likely that μή μου ἅπτου anticipates an attempt to do something and should be translated as, "Do not try to touch me" or "Do not come near," in line with the meaning of the verb ἅπτομαι as a verb of movement. The variant καὶ προσέδραμεν ἅψασθαι αὐτοῦ at the end of verse 16 and before λέγει αὐτῇ Ἰησοῦς—μή μου ἅπτου is in conformity with this view. It is attested in some Greek manuscripts (01[2a] 038 044 f13), in four manuscripts of the VL (29, 30, 35*, 48*) and in other versions (sy[(s).h.] geo[a.b]).[34]

That said, it is also not clear that the Latin translation of *noli me tangere* necessarily implies the usual sense of rejection that seems to be meant by

---

33. John Chrysostom, *Hom. Jo.* 86.1–2 (PG 59:469): "Correcting her, then, in her thinking and excessive freedom in speaking with Him [for we see that not even with the disciples is she seen to converse thus], he corrects her in her way of reasoning in order that she may treat Him with more reverence.... He who is to go up there and will no longer be with men, it was not fitting henceforth to treat Him in the same way as before."

34. Reimund Bieringer, "Noli me tangere and the New Testament: An Exegetical Approach," in *"Noli me tangere": Mary Magdalene; One Person, Many Images*, by Barbara Baert, Reimund Bieringer, Karlijn Demasure, and Sabine Van Den Eynde (Peeters, 2006), 13–28. Codex Sangallensis 51 (48) and Codex Moliensis (35) have this phrase crossed out. The text of 48 is more elaborate: "Rabboni, quod dicitur magister bone. Et cum occurrit ut tangeret dicit illi Iesus." For more detail, see Elizabeth Schrader and Brandon Simonson, "'Rabbouni,' Which Means Lord: Narrative Variants in John 20:16," *TC* 26 (2021): 133–54. See also Tjitze Baarda, "Jesus and Mary (John 20 16f.) in the Second Epistle on Virginity Ascribed to Clement," in *Studien zum Text und zur Ethik des Neuen Testaments: Festschrift zum 80. Geburtstag von Heinrich Greeven*, ed. Wolfgang Schrage, BZNW 47 (De Gruyter, 1986), 11–34.

the text at first glance and has given rise to classical artistic representations. Augustine seems to suggest this by interpreting Jesus's command as a mystical reference to the divinity of Christ, who can be touched only by faith, but implying that the expression did not preclude that Mary could be holding him.³⁵ This might show that in the West there were those who understood that *noli me tangere* did not imply a prohibition to initiate an action. The use of *nolo* would also confirm this. This verb in the imperative indicates not only a prohibition against doing something but also a command to stop doing something already begun. The Latin translation of John 2:16, μὴ ποιεῖτε τὸν οἶκον τοῦ πατρός μου οἶκον ἐμπορίου ("do not make my Father's house a house of business"), is, "nolite facere domum patris mei domum negotiationis," which can be understood as, "Stop making my Father's house a house of business." The same is true in John 6:43: μὴ γογγύζετε μετ' ἀλλήλων ("do not murmur among yourselves"), which the VL and Vulgate translate as *nolite murmurare invicem* (or *inter uos*). The prohibition implies that the criticism should stop, because that is in fact what they were doing. Considering the literal character of the VL and Vulgate translation and the fact that Latin does not have aspect, as Greek does, it is unsurprising that the aorist and present imperatives are sometimes translated the same way. So, neither a linguistic nor an exegetical approach precludes that the Greek present imperative in John 20:17 could indicate a prohibition to initiate a process, nor that the Latin could also have been understood as an order to stop doing something (in this passage, to release Jesus).

In any case, the Neo-Vulgate's choice to translate *iam noli me tenere*, using terminology unattested in the manuscript tradition, is a sign of the text's continuing vitality and another example of how tradition has the capacity to interpret the text. What the recent editors of the Neo-Vulgate have done is analogous to what some New Testament translators did a century after these books were written, although for different reasons in this case from those of the earlier translators.

---

35. Augustine, *Serm.* 245.2.2: "So what's 'Do not touch me; for I have not yet ascended to the Father?' Because you can see me, you think I'm only a man, you don't yet know I am equal to the Father; don't touch me as just that, don't believe in me only as a man, but understand here the Word equal to its begetter. So what's 'Do not touch me?' Don't believe. Don't believe what? That I am only what you can see." See *The Works of Saint Augustine*, trans. Edmund Hill, OP (New City, 1993), 7:101. See also Berrouard, *Oeuvres de saint Augustin 75*, 86–87; Houghton, *Augustine's Text of John*, 351.

4. Translation and Tradition

In light of these examples, Parker's comments on the *pericope adulterae*, as paradigmatic of what is generally understood as an expansion of the gospel text and which, for this reason, has been eliminated from some modern editions of the Bible, are apropos.[36] Despite all the problems the episode presents, Parker maintains that, whether we like it or not, it is impossible to dispense with it. He supports the assertion by pointing out that, just as variants often show that one textual form is influenced by others, so it is with passages considered spurious. That is to say, just as the six textual forms he detects in the Lord's Prayer contribute (in his opinion) to a better understanding of the prayer (without being able to read a supposed original text as if the other forms had not existed), so we cannot dispense with the story of the adulterous woman when reading the gospels (or even when interpreting the historical Jesus) as if it did not exist. Moreover, the story of the adulterous woman has an appeal that cannot (and will not) be renounced. The same could be said of the traditions about the number of the magi or the ox and the mule in the apocryphal infancy narratives. The oral tradition, Parker asserts, is not something that ended at a certain point in the second, third, or fourth century. The way we read the written text is part of the whole tradition that has passed from generation to generation.

In the encounter of the risen Jesus with Mary, we may think that the evangelist intended to say that Mary Magdalene should let Jesus go. However, we cannot approach that passage as if *noli me tangere* had never existed. Nor can we eliminate the many artistic representations of that scene from our collective imagination. Something similar can be said of the term *principium* in John 8:25 and the other noted cases. As Parker writes, "The sum total of all that we have received from the tradition, written and oral (not even to mention such possible curiosities as inherited memory), is a part of the way in which we build up our interpretations, regardless of our decisions about the historical value of particular items."[37]

Undoubtedly, Parker's concept of tradition is not the same as the one used when speaking of Scripture and tradition in a strictly theological context, at least from a Catholic perspective. For Parker, manuscripts and their variations are witnesses to a free way of understanding the text, as examples

---

36. Parker, *Living Text of the Gospels*, 102.
37. Parker, *Living Text of the Gospels*, 102.

of a text that is alive because it changes. From a theological perspective, however, these variants are signs of the living tradition that was present in certain communities of faith, which understood these texts in light of the whole gamut of received traditions. Variety was tolerated provided it did not infringe on the consensus of that tradition. What mattered was the message, and that message could be enriched by small variations. In this sense, one could invoke the famous words of Pope Gregory the Great: *divina eloquia cum legente crescunt*, "divine words grow with those who read them."[38] The reading of God's Word is a process that leads to spiritual growth that is always appropriate to the reader's situation.[39] Textual variants—in this case, translations—are a manifestation of this growth, as they emerge from the same root and are offshoots of the same plant. The act of translation, which is incapable of an exact transfer of what is said in one language to another, shows that the biblical text was not conceived as something untouchable, written in heaven by a divine being. Rather, translators faced a text that was capable of being understood in various ways within the limits established by the rule of faith. And these translators, scribes, and exegetes from the second century and up to the time of the Reformation understood the text to contain both a literal sense and a pluriform spiritual sense, a hermeneutical presupposition that no doubt contributed at times to decisions made when copying and correcting manuscripts.

As Antonio Piras points out, in the case of the VL, translators did not yet have the adequate resources to translate and interpret the text, so they limited themselves to a literal translation, especially in difficult cases. They left the interpretation of Scripture to those who possessed the proper gifts. They were aware that they had before them a text in which "et uerborum ordo mysterium est" ("there is a mysterious order of words") and "singula nomina habent singula sacramenta: quot enim verba, tot mysteria" ("all words possess a mystery of their own").[40] They could not sacrifice

---

38. Gregory, *Hom. Ezech.* 7.8 (CCSL 142, 140; PL 76:843D).
39. See Pier C. Bori, "Circolarità e sviluppo nell'interpretazione spiritual: 'Divina eloquia cum legente crescent,' Gregorio M., In Hiez. I, VII, 8," *ASE* 2 (1985): 263–74; Bori, "Attualità di un detto antico?, 'La sacra Scrittura cresce con chi la legge,'" *Intersezioni* 6 (1986): 15–49; Bori, *L'interpretazione infinita. L'ermeneutica cristiana e le sue trasformazioni* (Il Mulino, 1987).
40. Piras, "Gv 8,25 e la versione gotica della bibbia," 157–58. The quotations are from Jerome, *Ep.* 57; *Pamm.* 7 and *Tract. Ps.* 82.42–43. One can also add Augustine, *Ep.* 55.38: "Sacramentum, aut aliquis sermo de sacris litteris."

that mystery with risky translation proposals. Therefore, if, as we have seen in previous pages, the new way of doing textual criticism invites us to prioritize variants and avoid imprisoning them in the critical apparatus (as Cerquiglini exaggeratedly puts it),[41] then neither is it advisable in problematic cases to corset the text in a translation that sets undue limits on interpretive possibilities. This will not always be feasible, but at least it will be necessary to concede with humility that a given translation is one among other possible ones.

---

41. See above.

Early Christian Book Production and Canon

We have noted in the preceding pages that, as far as we can tell from the surviving witnesses, some Christian writings appear to have acquired an authoritative character from very early on and were copied almost exclusively in codex format.[1] We have also noted that those that would later remain outside the canon were copied mainly in rolls.[2] Thus, the question we will attempt to answer in this chapter is whether it is possible to establish a relationship between the format of a book and its perceived degree of authority by those who produced these books.

1. Codex and Canon

The link between the configuration of a closed list of authoritative Christian books and the codex, the specific format of these books, is a recurring theme in the debate on the origin and development of the canon.[3] Opinions

---

1. Only the following New Testament fragments come from rolls (and are "opisthographs"; see above, p. 24): P13 (third or fourth century, Hebrews); P18 (third or fourth century, Revelation); P98 (third century, Revelation); and perhaps P22 (third century, John).
2. See ch. 1 of this book.
3. The literature on this subject is extensive. Some recent works are Wallraff, *Kodex und Kanon*; Lee M. McDonald, *The Formation of the Biblical Canon*, vol. 2, *The New Testament: Its Authority and Canonicity* (T&T Clark, 2017), 222–64; Tomas Bokedal, *The Formation and Significance of the Christian Biblical Canon: A Study in Text, Ritual and Interpretation* (Bloomsbury T&T Clark, 2014), 125–55; Michael J. Kruger, *The Question of Canon: Challenging the Status Quo in the New Testament Debate* (IVP Academic, 2013), 79–118; Kruger, *Canon Revisited: Establishing the Origins and Authority of the New Testament Books* (Crossway, 2012), 233–59; Hans R. Seeliger, "Buchrolle, Codex, Kanon: Sachhistorische und ikonographische Aspekte und Zusammenhéinge," in *Kanon in Konstruktion und Dekonstruktion: Kanonisierungsprozesse religiöser Texte von der Antike bis zur Gegenwart, Ein Handbuch*, ed. Eve-Marie Becker and Stefan Scholz (De Gruyter, 2012), 547–76. See also Daryl D. Schmidt, "The Greek New Testa-

on the matter, however, differ. For Hans von Campenhausen, for example, the relationship between codex and canon does not exist.[4] On the other hand, many other scholars recognize, to a greater or lesser degree, that the codex format played an important role in establishing the list of books that came to form the Christian Bible, especially in the case of the New Testament; so Gamble:

> However that may be, the appearance in the fourth century of very large, multiple quire codices finally capable of containing the whole of Christian scriptures suggests that the technology of book production played a role in the delimitation of the canon, even as it did in the creation of early smaller collections. The aim of transcribing all scriptural documents in a single codex forced, in the most practical and unavoidable way, the question of precisely which books ought to be included.[5]

Nonetheless, the way the format of the book influenced the configuration of a closed list of authoritative books admits more nuanced positions. Not everyone agrees that the format had a delimiting effect on closing the canon. Some believe it played only a subordinate role. This is, for example, Elliott's view:

> Roberts and Skeat remind us that the adoption by Christians of the codex did not in itself create the fourfold Gospel canon. That observation applies to the other sections of the New Testament as well. The

---

ment as a Codex," in *The Canon Debate*, ed. Lee M. McDonald and James A. Sanders (Hendrickson, 2002), 469–84; and Eldon J. Epp, "Issues in the Interrelation of New Testament Textual Criticism and Canon," in McDonald and Sanders, *Canon Debate*, 485–515. Most of the discussion in this chapter has been published in Juan Chapa, "Early Christian Book Production and the Concept of Canon," in *Authoritative Writings in Early Judaism and Early Christianity Their Origin, Collection, and Meaning*, ed. Tobias Nicklas and Jens Schröter (Mohr Siebeck, 2020), 271–88.

4. Hans von Campenhausen, *The Formation of the Christian Bible*, trans. John A. Baker (Fortress, 1972), 173–74: "The codex form seems to have been the rule for biblical texts even as early as the second century; but these codices were, so far as we can tell, at first still small, and hardly adequate to combine four gospels at once in a single volume, which would be necessary in order to establish a 'canonical' order. That there was at first no such authentic arrangement is confirmed also by the variations in the sequence of the gospels, both at that time and later."

5. Harry Y. Gamble, "The New Testament Canon: Recent Research and the Status Quaestionis," in McDonald and Sanders, *Canon Debate*, 294.

New Testament canon was decided by Church authorities on theological and historical grounds, but canon and codex go hand in hand in the sense that the adoption of a fixed canon could be more easily controlled and promulgated when the codex was the normal means of gathering together originally separated compositions. (On the other hand, we also need to remind ourselves that the Jews had a canon but not the codex).[6]

In any case, as Robert Kraft points out, it is quite common to recognize that the codex has conditioned our understanding of the canon: "Once it was possible to produce and view (or visualize) 'the Bible' under one set of physical covers, the concept of 'canon' became concretized in a new way that shapes our thinking to the present day and makes it very difficult for us to recapture the perspectives of earlier times. 'The canon' in this sense is the product of fourth-century technological developments. Before that, it seems to me, things were less 'fixed,' and perceptions, accordingly, less concrete."[7]

In any case, the codex format must have had some influence on the process of delimiting the list of authoritative books, as this format could bring together a collection of writings by various authors. The roll, the standard format for a Greco-Roman literary work, did not have that capability. Generally speaking, each roll corresponded to one book. Of course, more than one roll was used in the case of lengthy works, and only in the case of shorter works (such as lyric poems, epigrams, and similar writings) could a single roll accommodate several independent compositions by the same author (occasionally even by several authors). If this was the usual practice, it makes sense to think that the adoption of the codex as the preferred format for Christian books indicated a significant change in the customs of the time and eclipsed the dominant tradition.

2. Single or Multiquire Codices

Although from very early on the codex became the preferred format for authoritative writings, its adoption does not necessarily mean that it was chosen from the beginning to gather writings of different authors or of

---

6. Elliott, "Manuscripts, the Codex," 111. The reference to Roberts and Skeat is *Birth of the Codex*, 65.

7. Robert A. Kraft, "The Codex and Canon Consciousness," in McDonald and Sanders, *Canon Debate*, 233.

different types.[8] Judging by the paleographic dating assigned to the extant manuscripts, the earliest New Testament papyri come from codices containing a single work. This is clear from the fact that virtually all of the earliest gospel fragments found at Oxyrhynchus (at least 16 out of a total of 18) come from codices whose size could hardly include more than one writing. As Head argues, "Although the four-Gospel canon was conceptualized at Oxyrhynchus (evidence includes knowledge of Irenaeus and the use of excerpts from four Gospels on amulets), this does not seem to have coincided with the presence of any four-Gospel codices. If on other grounds Oxyrhynchus seems to be generally representative of the textual situation in Egypt this suggests it might be reasonable to disconnect the two issues: codex construction from canonical conception."[9]

This statement seems accurate if we consider that the format of the first gospel codices made them portable (one of the advantages of the codex mentioned by Martial) and made their use more convenient for the first Christian itinerant missionaries. Of the list of 135 New Testament papyri, only seven attest to more than one book, and of these, five have been dated before the end of the fourth century.[10] The vast majority, that is, each of the remaining 128 papyri, attest to a single book.[11] This is also the general tenor of the first majuscule manuscripts. Up to the sixth century, only thirty of the 141 majuscules bear witness to more than one book.[12] In any case, the fragmentary nature of the witnesses does not allow us

---

8. On this question, see, e.g., Charles E. Hill, "A Four-Gospel Canon in the Second Century?," *EC* 4 (2013): 310–34; Juan Chapa, "Textual Transmission of Canonical and Apocryphal Writings within the Development of the New Testament Canon: Limits and Possibilities," *EC* 7 (2016): 113–33.

9. Peter M. Head, "Graham Stanton and the Four-Gospel Codex: Reconsidering the Manuscript Evidence," in *Jesus, Matthew's Gospel and Early Christianity: Studies in Memory of Graham N. Stanton*, ed. Daniel M. Gurtner, Joel Willitts, and Richard A Burridge, LNTS 435 (T&T Clark, 2011), 100. See also Kruger, "Manuscripts, Scribes, and Book Production," 18–27.

10. See Epp, "Issues in the Interrelation," 488–89. There are six more, if extended to the fifth century. For more detail, see table 6.1. P64 and P4 are not counted since there are doubts as to whether they were part of a single codex, nor are P15 and P16, which present the same doubts.

11. The following figures, updated to 2020, are based on Epp, "Issues in the Interrelation," 489. See also table 6.2 in this chapter.

12. The figures are slightly adapted from table 6.10 in Epp, "Are Early New Testament Manuscripts," 94–102. Epp also notes that, among the 201 majuscule manuscripts dated before the ninth century, only 44 contain more than one writing (22

to say with certainty whether a particular papyrus comes from a codex that originally contained one or more writings. Only on occasion can we reconstruct approximately the measurements that the original codex had and, from there, infer the possibility that it included one or several works. On other occasions, fragments with visible pagination allow us to deduce whether the codex could have contained several writings.

On the other hand, we note that of the six largest and best-preserved ancient manuscripts, four are codices containing more than one work (P45, P46, P72, P75). This is also the case of some papyri that bear witness to more than two pages: P30 (1 and 2 Thessalonians; besides, page numbers 207–10 are visible, so it is possible that the original codex brought together a larger collection of Paul's letters), P53 (Matthew and Acts), and P92 (Ephesians and 2 Thessalonians).[13] That a codex contained more than one work can also be inferred from fragments that bear witness to a single book but, as in P30, have page numbers that appear to indicate that they probably belonged to a codex with more works. This is the case of P13, P54, P126, and some ancient parchment codices (0185, 0201, 0206, 0207, 0232, 0274).[14] We note, moreover, that there are probably Christian LXX codices paleographically assigned to the second century that seem to have preserved more than one book:[15] P.Bad. 4.56b attests Exod 8 and Deut 29;

---

percent attest more than one writing, versus 78 percent containing only one) (Epp, "Are Early New Testament Manuscripts," 92–93). See table 6.3 in this chapter.

13. Third-century codices containing more than one book: P45 (four gospels + Acts: 200–250), P30 (1–2 Thessalonians: 175–225), and P46 (records all of Paul's letters except 2 Thessalonians, Philemon, and the Pastorals: 200–225). Of the third-century codices, it is impossible to know whether P75 had all four gospels or only three or only two. A separate case is P72 (Jude and 1–2 Peter: 300–350), a miscellaneous codex in which writings of different types were included. See Brent Nongbri, "The Construction of P.Bodmer VIII," *NovT* 58 (2016): 394–410; Nongbri, "Recent Progress in Understanding the Construction of the Bodmer 'Miscellaneous' or 'Composite' Codex," *Adamantius* 21 (2015): 171–72; Nongbri, *God's Library*, 195–96. See also Tommy Wasserman, "Papyrus 72 and the Bodmer Miscellaneous Codex," *NTS* 51 (2006): 137–54. For the dating, see table 1.1 in ch. 1.

14. For more detail, see Michael Dormandy, "How the Books Became the Bible: The Evidence for Canon Formation from Work-Combinations in Manuscripts," *TC* 23 (2018), https://tinyurl.com/SBL7016j.

15. Let it be said in passing that this is a point Wallraff overlooks when he argues that the Christians' choice of the codex implied that literature copied in this format was not considered sacred (*Kodex und Kanon*, 16–18). Brent Nongbri's review of Wallraff's book in *JECS* 22 (2014): 480–81 hits on the same point.

and P.Beatty 5 (pap. VI) + P.Mich. inv. 5554 attest Num 5–8, 13, 25–36, and Deut 1–7, 9–12, 18, 19, 27–33.[16] Although the evidence is fragmentary, if second-century Christians (assuming the dating is correct) copied some of Israel's sacred books into a single codex, we cannot rule out that in this or the following century they also copied several gospels or several of Paul's letters into a single codex.[17]

For these reasons, we must be cautious in assuming that an early New Testament fragment bearing witness to part of a single book comes from a codex with only one work. Even if we were to suspect that this is likely the case, we cannot rule out the possibility that some of these fragments may have belonged to codices containing more than one book.[18]

3. The Production of Books: Possibilities and Reality

It is certain that, since the codex began to be used, the techniques for book production in this format were perfected to the point of facilitating the production of codices that could accommodate large quantities of text. Origen's Hexapla (early third century, a milestone in the history of the book) is proof of this. Although we do not have direct or close witnesses that are contemporary with its production, the assumption that Origen used the codex format to produce this work appears reasonable. It is hard to fathom that he would use rolls if he had to carry out such a project, the final product of which was closer to a library than to a single work. Anthony Grafton and Megan Williams argue on the basis of later

---

16. See more information in, e.g., Mugridge, *Copying Early Christian Texts*, 172–73, 178.

17. Other LXX codices with more than one book are P.Ant. 1.8 + 3.210 (third century), which brings together several sapiential books (Prov 5–9, 19–20, Wis 11–12 with title, and Sir 45) and Freer Greek MS V (third century, although Turner dates it to the fourth century), which seems to have contained the twelve minor prophets. There is only one "opisthograph" papyrus (P.Oxy. 8.1075, 1079) that could have represented the combination of one OT and one NT book: it attests Exod 40 on the recto and Rev 1 (P18) on the verso. For a discussion of the format of this fragment, see Brent Nongbri, "Losing a Curious Christian Scroll but Gaining a Curious Christian Codex: An Oxyrhynchus Papyrus of Exodus and Revelation," *NovT* 55 (2013): 77–88; Peter Malik, "P.Oxy. VIII.1079 (P18): Closing on a 'Curious' Codex?," *NTS* 65 (2019): 94–102. See also Edwin A. Judge and Stuart R. Pickering, "Biblical Papyri Prior to Constantine: Some Cultural Implications of their Physical Form," *Prudentia* 10 (1978): 8–10.

18. Epp, "Textual Criticism in the Exegesis," 56.

fragments that the Hexapla would have occupied forty codices, each of four hundred leaves (800 pages), constituting a monumental undertaking in both magnitude and cost.[19] This is not to say that Origen invented the format and design of the Hexapla, but we can imagine that the use of multiple columns characteristic of this work, when codices with more than one column per page were rare, may have influenced the future design of other books.[20] Who knows whether the columnar arrangement of the great biblical codices of the fourth and fifth centuries, capable of bringing together more than seventy different works in a single volume, does not in fact reflect the influence of the Hexapla format or was even inspired by it.[21]

---

19. See Anthony Grafton and Megan Williams, *Christianity and the Transformation of the Book: Origen, Eusebius, and the Library of Caesarea* (Harvard University Press, 2006), 86–132, esp. 96–107. On 106 they comment, "For the *Hexapla* as we have reconstructed it, the cost of the writing alone would have been approximately 75,000 denarii. Unfortunately, the passage of the Price Edict regulating the cost of papyrus has not survived. The parchment required for a copy written on that relatively luxurious material would have cost another 75,000 denarii, for a total of approximately 150,000 denarii." In note they add, "Note that ... a copy of the *Hexapla* would have cost the same as a year's subsistence for 38 laborers, which makes each codex of the *Hexapla* equal in value to one laborer's annual subsistence" (324 n. 39). See also John S. Kloppenborg, "Literate Media in Early Christ Groups: The Creation of a Christian Book Culture," *JECS* 22 (2014): 24.

20. See Loveday Alexander, "Ancient Book-Production and the Circulation of the Gospels," in *The Gospels for All Christians: Rethinking the Gospel Audiences*, ed. Richard Bauckham (Eerdmans, 1997), 85–86: "Early Christian book technology presupposes robust and vigorous intercommunity connections across the eastern Mediterranean area. And whatever their origins, these features help to create an effect of a distinctive book style which, 'though not an esoteric code, stands out as an in-group convention that expressed a community consciousness and presumed a particular readership' (H. Y. Gamble, *Books and Readers in the Early Church*, 78)." Turner thinks that scribes who copied into a single-column papyrus codex considered it a second-class book and suggests that codices with more than one column were intended to imitate the high-quality rolls of Greek prose literature (*Typology of the Early Codex*, 35–37). See also Mugridge, *Copying Early Christian Texts*, 64–65, 486–88.

21. Elliott, "Manuscripts, the Codex," 110: "Up to the third century no surviving codex is known to have had more than 300 pages. After that the codex grew: B, Codex Vaticanus (fourth century), had 1600 pages; Sinaiticus (fourth century) 1460 pages; Codex Alexandrinus (fifth century) 1640 pages. (All these figures are minima because all three are defective at the end.) This meant that more than one section of the New Testament could be included within one set of covers."

Be that as it may, there is no doubt that the great codices of the Bible and Origen's work represent exceptional cases. Borrowing Martin Wallraff's image, it is possible to affirm that Codex Sinaiticus and Codex Vaticanus are to papyrus codices (before the beginning of the fourth century) what a sports utility vehicle is to a compact car or a basilica is to a house church.[22] Although we tend to imagine that after the appearance of these codices and the near closing of the canon that the standard format for copying and transmitting the New Testament was the codex with all twenty-seven books, the reality was quite different. The number of witnesses that have come down to us confirms this (although the figures vary, depending on whether we consider only complete manuscripts or also those with lacunae). In 1996, Elliott wrote:

> Only about 60 of our 3,000 or so surviving continuous-text Greek New Testament manuscripts were written as complete New Testaments, that is with all 27 books included. Some 150 contain the whole New Testament minus Revelation (which was looked upon with some suspicion by the church in the East for some time, before being eventually admitted into its canon). Even today the Eastern Orthodox churches do not include readings from Revelation in the lectionary. In total 2,361 manuscripts including fragmentary manuscripts contain the Gospels, 662 including fragments contain Acts and the Catholics, 792 contain Paul and 303 Revelation.[23]

Parker indicates that, apparently, the correct number of Greek manuscripts containing the entire New Testament is sixty-one, while Epp specifies fifty-three.[24] In any case, between six and eight of these contain (or contained)

---

22. See Wallraff, *Kodex und Kanon*, 23; Gamble, *Books and Readers*, 80.
23. Elliott, "Manuscripts, the Codex," 110.
24. Parker, *Introduction to the New Testament Manuscripts*, 70; Epp, "Are Early New Testament Manuscripts," 90–91 and n. 20. Epp points out that lists of New Testament manuscripts are often misleading. They sometimes list codices that are damaged as if they contained the entire New Testament (e.g., the Codex Vaticanus, often presented as complete, ends at Heb 9:14 and is missing the Pastorals, Philemon, and Revelation; also, Sinaiticus and Alexandrinus contain writings that were left out of the canon). Schmidt points out that the two oldest New Testament codices containing only the twenty-seven New Testament books and nothing else—minuscules 1424 and 175—are from the ninth/tenth and tenth/eleventh centuries ("Greek New Testament," 476).

the entire Bible. The same is true of the Latin manuscripts.[25] As Parker says about manuscripts before 800, "a complete Bible is equally rare in Greek and in Latin, and ... a complete New Testament on its own is unheard of in Greek, and in Latin is as rare as a complete Bible."[26] We do not know the reason for these data, but it is possible that they are due to the limited extant material available or otherwise reflect the prohibitive cost of parchment production.[27] In any case, they highlight the exceptional character of codices such as Sinaiticus or Vaticanus.

Setting aside extraordinary cases, we imagine that the normal practice was to copy each one of the New Testament books individually and group them in collections of medium size. The criteria by which these intermediate collections are compiled, however, do not appear to reflect a clear pattern, since we encounter great variety.[28] Even so, the groupings attested by our papyrus sources are consistent with the three collections

---

25. Parker, *Introduction to the New Testament Manuscripts*, 76. For Byzantine, Syriac, and Coptic manuscripts of the New Testament, see 77–79. The lists of papyrus and ostraca books show that no community or monastery library had a complete edition of the Bible.

26. See also Markschies, "Canon of the New Testament," 186. A complete New Testament seems to be found in only six ancient book lists (187). For lists of Christian books in the early centuries, see also Rosa Otranto, *Antiche liste di libri su papiro* (Edizioni di Storia e Letteratura, 2000), 123–44. See also Hermann Harrauer, "Bücher in Papyri," in *Flores litterarum Joanní Marte sexagenario oblate: Wissenschaft in der Bibliothek* (Böhlau,1995), 59–77; Chrysi Kotsifou, "Books and Book Production in the Monastic Communities of Byzantine Egypt," in *The Early Christian Book*, ed. William E. Klingshirn and Linda Safran (Catholic University of America Press, 2007), 48–66; Herwig Maehler, "Bücher in den frühen Klöstern Ägyptens," in *Spätantike Bibliotheken: Leben und Lesen in den frühen Klostern Ágypten* (Phoibos-Vlg, 2008), 39–47.

27. Parker, *Introduction to the New Testament Manuscripts*, 74: "Even the wonderfully fine parchment of Codex Sinaiticus runs into a number of separate volumes, and a considerable overall thickness. And the coarser parchment which typifies the later majuscule period would have made a complete Bible even more unwieldy. Thus, the abandonment of fine parchment may have rendered the one-volume Bible unviable." See also Thomas S. Pattie, "The Creation of the Great Codices," in *The Bible as Book: The Manuscript Tradition*, ed. John L. Sharpe and Kimberly van Kampen (British Library and Oak Knoll, 1998), 61–72.

28. Elliott, "Manuscripts, the Codex," 108–9. The tendency to form collections was not a novelty. Papyrus roll data from ancient libraries show that books could be sorted into groups according to genre or subject, stored in separate containers, rooms, or buildings. See George W. Houston, *Inside Roman Libraries: Book Collections and Their Management in Antiquity*, SHGR (University of North Carolina Press, 2014), 84.

found in later manuscripts: the four gospels (as in P45), the letters of Paul (as in P46), and Acts and Catholic Letters (as in P74). These three collections circulated in separate codices, although Acts could also go with the Gospels (as in P45).[29] That said, we should also add that the vast majority of manuscripts with works that became part of the New Testament canon attest only partially to these three collections (four gospels; Acts and Catholic Letters; Paul and Revelation). Some manuscripts, as indicated, contain all twenty-seven New Testament books, and others, all but Revelation. Most had only the gospels. And within these collections, the order of the books attested is also quite varied, possibly contingent on canonical considerations. For example, Codex Vaticanus has the same order as Athanasius's list, although its presumed canonical understanding is not necessarily that of Egypt (it is more likely that the codex was copied in Caesarea).[30] In any case, the fluctuation is great at this point. As Aland and Aland underscore, "The only characteristic common to the whole manuscript tradition (extending also to canon lists, patristic references, and other sources which allude to the sequence of the writings) is that the Gospels stand at the beginning and Revelation at the end."[31]

In short, the fact that the New Testament books continued to be transmitted in groups within smaller collections, despite the existence of the great codices of the fourth and fifth centuries, shows that the role of the codex in canon formation cannot be reduced to its physical capacity to contain particular writings between two covers.[32] If the large codices of the fourth and fifth centuries were the exception, it is clear that the authority of those books that were delimited by the canon was not based on the mere fact that a certain number of works could be integrated into a single volume. Undoubtedly, other factors must have played a role.

---

29. Epp, "Textual Criticism in the Exegesis," 56. We should note that, given the variety of collections, we cannot be sure that fragmentary majuscule manuscripts attesting to a single writing can be adduced as evidence for standard collections (see Elliott, "Manuscripts, the Codex," 109–11).

30. See Epp, "Issues in the Interrelation," 505–8.

31. Aland and Aland, *Text of the New Testament*, 79.

32. Elliott is of the opinion that the codex helped to limit the number of gospels ("Manuscripts, the Codex," 107). On the one hand, he argues, we do not preserve codices with canonical and noncanonical gospels, and, on the other hand, the fact that the codex had a limiting factor (in the sense that it involves planning how much text fits within a quire) helped to fix the canon.

4. The Canon as a Reference Table

The work of Eusebius of Caesarea (ca. 265–ca. 339/340), who, in continuity with Origen and Pamphilus, has been called the "Christian impresario of the codex," may shed light on the subject.[33] Wallraff has stressed the importance of Eusebius's use of the word *canon* to mean "table" or "synopsis."[34] This usage predates the application of κανών to Scripture and was employed primarily in a technical-geometrical sense to refer to the Πτολεμαίου πρόχειροι κανόνες, that is, to the astronomical tables of Ptolemy (second century), designed to calculate the positions of the sun, moon, planets, and so on and intended to be consulted easily (πρόχειροι, "were at hand").[35] Eusebius resorts to this meaning of canon as table in the second part of his *Chronicon*, in which he presents a chronicle of universal history (at least since Abraham), collecting in tables arranged in parallel columns (canons) the lists of rulers and the most outstanding facts of the nineteen kingdoms (from the Assyrians to the Romans) he had dealt with in several chapters of book 1 of the *Chronicon*. It is quite possible that Origen's use of columns in the Hexapla would have allowed him to compare texts word for word, while the codex's double-page format allowed Eusebius to present the history of the different kingdoms synchronically.[36]

Eusebius also made use of this same method for the lesser-known tables of the Psalms, in which the system of canons functioned as a way of establishing a reciprocal relationship between the text and the table, between the reference and the referent. Again, it was a system that was facilitated by the codex, since it is difficult to imagine that a roll was used for this purpose.[37]

---

33. Grafton and Williams, *Christianity and the Transformation*, 178–232.

34. See Wallraff, *Kodex und Kanon*, 28–29.

35. Wallraff, *Kodex und Kanon*, 28–29. The use of κανών as "rule" in a geometrical or mathematical sense appears also in Plutarch, *Soll. an.* 974F, 979C. For more details, see the more recent works of Matthew R. Crawford, *The Eusebian Canon Tables: Ordering Textual Knowledge in Late Antiquity* (Oxford University Press, 2019), esp. 43–55; Jeremiah Coogan, *Eusebius the Evangelist: Rewriting the Fourfold Gospel in Late Antiquity* (Oxford University Press, 2022), esp. 28–58, 166, 172–73.

36. Grafton and Williams, *Christianity and the Transformation*, 169. Wallraff points out that through this system the canon not only became an ordering principle to provide a clearer presentation of history but also had the extra value of being a history in the singular (*Kodex und Kanon*, 30–31).

37. Eusebius classified the Psalms in seven numbered columns (1, 2, 3, etc.). In the first he put the psalms of David, in the second those of Solomon, in the third

This method is also found in the canons of the four gospels that Eusebius designed to show at a glance when one gospel coincides with the others. Since the use of columns was impractical for relating similar passages, insofar as it would have implied rupturing the unity of the text,[38] he solved the problem by dividing the text of the gospels into numbered sections and arranging those numbers in ten columns at the beginning of the codex. With each of these columns Eusebius indicated which sections were common to the four evangelists, which to the three, which to two, and which were specific to each one (the reference numbers that were written next to the text had a red number underneath to indicate in which of the ten tables that reference was found). With this system, the canons at the beginning of the volume allowed the reader to quickly locate parallel passages in the four gospels.

But these canons also had another function. They allowed the four narratives to relate to each other and, as it were, become a single gospel. As Wallraff imagines, following the etymological relationship between text and fabric (>*texere*), the *textus* appears as an interweaving of four *rows* (the threads of each gospel text) through this ingenious system of canons. The four gospels, then, are united in an interwoven structure by means of cross-references, forming part of a network that appears visible with symbols at the beginning of the book in the tables of the canon.[39] Wallraff's conclusion relates to the meaning of the term *canon*. He deduces from Eusebius's usage that it would be inappropriate to pay too much attention to the word *canon* as a *regula fidei* and abandon the meaning of *canon* as "list." The understanding of canon as a catalog or list would be as impor-

---

the *anepigraphoi* (untitled), in the fourth those of the sons of Korah, etc. See Wallraff, *Kodex und Kanon*, 31; Martin Wallraff, "The Canon Tables of the Psalms: An Unknown Work of Eusebius of Caesarea," *DOP* 67 (2013): 1–14.

38. Wallraff, *Kodex und Kanon*, 32–33. In fact, as Grafton and Williams point out, Ammonius had taken extracts from the Gospels of Mark, Luke and John and placed them alongside the parallel texts of Matthew (*Christianity and the Transformation*, 195). Eusebius complains in his letter to Carpianus that this system broke the integrity of the texts because it ruined the sequential thread of the other three gospels, preventing a continuous reading (see *Ep. Carp.* 1–10, in NA[26], 41*).

39. Wallraff, *Kodex und Kanon*, 35. Also Grafton and Williams, *Christianity and the Transformation of the Book*, 199: "They enabled readers not simply to rely on memory or to use rearranged texts of the Bible, but to turn the four Gospels into a single web of cross-commentary—to move from text to text as easily as one could move from kingdom to kingdom in the Canon."

tant as that of rule, thereby underscoring the canon's practical character without excluding its literary features.⁴⁰

We can reasonably suppose, then, that the use of the word κανών shows the importance of having at one's fingertips information one wishes to consult, while also being able to cross-reference the various writings collected in a single codex, as the tables indicate. That is to say, the tables, the κανόνες, are not valuable in themselves but only insofar as they refer to texts that are related to each other. The technical use of the term κανών supports this idea, as it appears in the aforementioned astronomical books and connects the canon and the codex with each other. Most of the astronomical almanacs preserved on papyrus are codices, some of which were copied in the first (P.Laur. 144) and second centuries, that is, prior to the Christian codices. And within works of this type, there is a clear preference for the codex for texts containing the πρόχειροι κανόνες and similar sets of tables. The codex format facilitated quick reference to different tables for calculations. As Alexander Jones points out, it would have been quite cumbersome to have to refer frequently to scattered parts of a large compilation of tables if these had been copied onto a roll.⁴¹

In other words, the codex's practicality and ease of reference made it the appropriate format to bring together related texts.⁴² The included books were to be read as a unitary corpus. This again suggests that the selection of a number of books in a codex was not determined by the format's physical characteristics but by the possibility and the need to relate to each other a set of texts that were similar or useful for a particular purpose. Echoing Eusebius's words to Carpianus, the canon made it possible to find τὰ παραπλήσια, the "similarity" between the various writings.⁴³ The codex thus became the specific means of establishing homogeneity within diversity, a fundamental characteristic of the biblical canon.

---

40. Wallraff states, "The theological consequences are not insignificant: Scripture is then not measure, but norm; not a testimony of faith, but a rule of faith (*regula fidei*), not a prescribed but a prescriptive truth; ultimately: *norma normans, non normata*" (*Kodex und Kanon*, 35).

41. Jones, *Astronomical Papyri from Oxyrhynchus*, 1:61. But most of the almanacs with entries for each sign of the zodiac are later than 161 CE. It appears that ephemerides continued to be used on the rolls until the fifth century. Primary tables relating to arithmetical astronomy were written on rolls on the back of other documents.

42. This point is also underscored by Crawford, *Eusebian Canon Tables*, 74–75 and n. 56.

43. *Ep. Carp.* 1–10, 33–45, in NA²⁶, 42*.

This circumstance, however, does not imply that all the writings had to be homogeneous in their content to be included in a codex. That there were miscellaneous codices or codices composed of very diverse works at the time demonstrates that this was not the case.[44] It is unlikely that those who compiled heterogeneous texts into a single volume necessarily saw a collection of authoritative writings governed by a unifying principle in the final product. The various attempts to find a common underlying theme in the various works of the celebrated Bodmer Papyri, "Miscellaneous" or "Composite," show how difficult and subjective this task can be.[45] It is perhaps easier to imagine that codices with heterogenous content were intended for private use, perhaps suitable for use in schools or for private teaching, with no common denominator among them.[46] It follows, then, that although the codex can contribute to the appearance of a certain unity between different kinds of writings, the artifact as such is insufficient to confer authority to the writings it contains. That is to say, the fact that books are bound between two covers does not necessarily indicate a closed canon.

5. Textual Relationships, Authority, and Models

As indicated, one of the codex's main characteristics is the capacity to facilitate relationships between different texts. Here, it may be useful to consider Trobisch's proposal on the formation of the New Testament.[47] Leaving aside the difficulties of his approach and its conclusions, what he states about how the New Testament was given its final canonical form in the second century is worth highlighting.[48] For Trobisch, the way the

---

44. On the miscellaneous codices, see Edoardo Crisci, "I più antichi codici miscellanei greci," in *Il codice miscellaneo. Tipologie e fanzioni. Atti del Convegno internazionale (Cassino 14–17 maggio 2003)*, ed. Crisci and Oronzo Pecere (Universitá degli Studi di Cassino, 2004), 109–44; Armando Petrucci, "Del libro unitario al libro misceláneo," in *Libros, escrituras y bibliotecas* (Ediciones Universidad de Salamanca, 2011), 249–76.

45. See, e.g., Dormandy, "How the Books Became," 19.

46. As Turner notes, behind the "composite" title given to some codices is the suspicion that scribes did not want to waste material to write on and wished to fill the pages left free at the end of a codex (*Typology of the Early Codex*, 81).

47. Trobisch, *First Edition of the New Testament*.

48. It is certainly difficult to prove that a canonical edition existed at that early time. See Parker, "Review: *The First Edition of the New Testament*"; Jason T. Larson,

nomina sacra were written, the codex format, the uniform arrangement and number of writings of the manuscript tradition, the way the titles were written, and the data indicating that the collection was called "New Testament" from the beginning demonstrate that there was a careful final redaction: "These editorial features did not originate with the authors of the individual writings. They serve to combine disparate material into a collection and to create the impression of a cohesive literary unit for readers of the work. Furthermore, these elements are so idiosyncratic that they cannot be credited to several independently operating editors but must be the work of a single editorial entity."[49] According to Trobisch, those who produced this canonical edition of the New Testament considered three elements: the perspective of the reader, the macrostructure of the edition ("the user interface") that was to serve as a guide for readers, and the traditional material that did not fit well into the whole. These three elements are especially evident in the titles of the various books, in which the editors added names of a number of apostolic figures:

> The naming of authors in the titles of specific writings is another editorial feature that illuminates the editorial concept. From the readers' perspective these famous names seem to guarantee the reliability of the Canonical Edition. As far as the macrostructure is concerned, the authoritative names are part of a carefully woven web holding together the disparate parts of the New Testament. And seen from the perspective of the traditional material, the Fourth Gospel clearly did not intend to disclose the name of the "beloved disciple." The final editors, however, presented it as the work of John. All three perspectives therefore display a strong editorial interest in conveying the names of the prominent authors to the readers. This concern demonstrates another element of the editorial concept.[50]

---

review of *The First Edition of the New Testament*, by David Trobisch, *TC* 6 (2001). One might add to these the observations of Michael W. Holmes, who points out that the significant differences in both the content and arrangement of the books so evident in the codices Vaticanus, Sinaiticus, and Alexandrinus are strong testimony against Trobisch's hypothesis that the mid-second-century editors of his so-called canonical edition made the LXX features standard and placed the NT books in a specific order. See Holmes, "The Biblical Canon," in *The Oxford Handbook of Early Christian Studies*, ed. Susan Ashbrook Harvey and David G. Hunter (Oxford University Press, 2008), 421 n. 3.

49. Trobisch, *First Edition of the New Testament*, 44.
50. Trobisch, *First Edition of the New Testament*, 46.

In light of these elements, Trobisch argues that the titles of the different books implicit in some of the writings gave way to a collection of twenty-seven books attributed to eight authors: Matthew, Mark, Luke, John, Paul, James, Peter, and Jude.[51] For Trobisch, the possibility of cross-referencing the various books linked to these apostolic figures was fundamental. Therefore, John 21 (as an editorial note added to the final edition of the four gospels and the entire collection), Acts (especially 15:1–19), 2 Timothy, and 2 Peter occupied a fundamental role in that edition.[52] As noted, Trobisch believes that the codex, and with it the *nomina sacra*, would have played an essential role in this editorial activity, since it allowed disparate material to be brought together into a single collection. This gave the impression of a coherent literary unity—a unity that allowed for authoritative editing, making it so that none of the writings (especially the shorter ones) were left out. At the same time, it helped to differentiate it from the Jewish community, which used the roll.[53]

Many of Trobisch's conclusions are problematic, and some quite improbable. And yet, a number of his ideas are interesting for their exploration of the intersection of canon and codex. This is especially clear in how they highlight the important role that the author to whom a book is attributed plays in a canonical collection. All the New Testament writings are attributed explicitly, implicitly, or by tradition to apostolic figures, that is, to some of Jesus's direct disciples or others who were close to them. Thus, the canon is not only a list of books attributed to persons whose authority is reflected in some writings but also a list of *authorities recognized* in particular books that have been preserved and transmitted by tradition. In other words, the texts could not be separated from the authors to whom

---

51. Trobisch, *First Edition of the New Testament*, 59. "The titles, with their carefully constructed cross-references between authors and specific text passages, connect the collection units and function as the user interface of the edition. They are the result of a deliberate redactional effort typical for anthologies to direct the interest of the readers to what the editors feel is the central message of the collection."

52. Trobisch, *First Edition of the New Testament*, 79–101.

53. Trobisch, *First Edition of the New Testament*, 73–77. See also Larson, review of *First Edition of the New Testament*: "From an editorial perspective, the codex was more profitable to the publisher when produced in larger numbers, and, coupled with the missionary activity of early Christians, this was certainly an important factor. The codex could also hold more texts than a roll, and its form of binding could ensure the integrity of the collection: very short writings benefited from the protection of other larger works surrounding them" (n. 12).

they were attributed.⁵⁴ This is an important literary feature that is inseparable from the concept of canon and functions regardless of who was the actual author of a book in question. The feature is linked to the concept of literary authority as understood in antiquity.

It is well known that in classical times there were authorities whose recognition was based on the weight that scholarly tradition had given their works. Homer was clearly the authority par excellence among the Greeks, as indicated by the large number of papyri of the *Iliad* and the *Odyssey* discovered in Egypt (Mertens-Pack³ lists more than 3,000).⁵⁵ Naturally, Homer was not the only authority. The fragments found in the land of the Nile also attest to other figures who enjoyed authority in various literary genres: Apollonius of Rhodes in Greek epic; Aeschylus, Sophocles, and especially Euripides in tragedy; Aristophanes and Menander in comedy; Pindar, Alcaeus, Sappho, and Bacchylides in lyric poetry; Theocritus in the pastoral poetry genre. Thucydides, Herodotus, and Xenophon should be added for history; Plato and Aristotle in philosophy, and Demosthenes and Isocrates in rhetoric. The archaeological evidence shows that there was a tendency in antiquity to read mainly literary works that were handed down from century to century. This is likely due to the educational system since schools taught mainly Homer, Hesiod, Aeschylus, Sophocles, Euripides, Aristophanes, and Menander.⁵⁶ These were taught not so much because of the interest in their works per se but because of the figures who had written them. That is to say, the authorities were the authors themselves, not the works they had written. This is demonstrated by the fact that, when literary critics disapproved of a work, they were not attacking that text but its author.⁵⁷

---

54. On the canonicity of the book rather than the text, see Lee M. McDonald, "Wherein Lies Authority: A Discussion of Books, Texts, and Translations," in *Exploring the Origins of the Bible: Canon Formation in Historical, Literary, and Theological Perspective*, ed. Craig A. Evans and Emanuel Tov, ASBT 6 (Baker Academic, 2008), 203–39; Eugene Ulrich, "The Notion and Definition of Canon," in McDonald and Sanders, *Canon Debate*, 30–32.

55. See Mertens-Pack³, *Catalogue des papyrus littéraires grecs et latins*, http://www.cedopalmp3.uliege.be/.

56. See, among others, Cribiore, *Writing, Teaching, Students*; Raffaella Cribiore, "Higher Education in Early Byzantine Egypt: Rhetoric, Latin, and the Law," in *Egypt in the Byzantine World, 300–700*, ed. Roger S. Bagnall (Cambridge University Press, 2007), 47–66; Parsons, *City of the Sharp-Nosed Fish*, 137–58.

57. Robert M. Grant, "Literary Criticism and the New Testament Canon," *JSNT* 16 (1982): 24–44.

This concept is also interesting for understanding the type of authority reflected in the idea of canon. As is well known, the Greek word κανών originally designated a "straight object"; later, it was also used to mean "rule or measure that acquires the status of a model."[58] In the Hellenistic period, a time when all kinds of lists were in vogue, we also find lists of κανόνες, that is, of writers who were considered exemplary or models. The Greek expression for selecting these authors was ἐγκρίνειν, "to include in a list" (ἐκκρίνειν was used to mean "to remove from [a list]"), so that those writers who were κανόνες were sometimes called ἐγκριθέντες, "those who were considered to be inside." That is, they were those "registered" in the selective list of authors (the word gave way to the Roman expression *classici*: writers *primae classis*). These authors became πραττόμενοι, those who were studied, that is, chosen to be the object of philological treatment, and therefore edited, commented on, and so on. Their writings were thus copied over and over again, to be read and studied in schools and among the educated public, so that, while the ἐκκριθέντες perished into oblivion, the ἐγκριθέντες remained for posterity.[59] These lists of authors, which in antiquity were often attributed to Aristophanes of Byzantium and/or Aristarchus, were probably born in a scholarly context and followed a criterion of inclusion rather than exclusion, since they contained more names of authors than were generally read. But they were not official lists. Rather, they were an expression of common opinions, a response to the need to select and establish the models that had to be read, studied, and imitated.[60] This is how the canon of the three tragic authors, the nine lyric poets, the three comic poets, or the ten orators originated.[61] Only in the eighteenth century, under the influence of the biblical use of the word *canon*, were these lists of authors called canons. But originally the κανόνες were the authors, not the lists.[62]

---

58. See José B. Torres Guerra, "Literatura Griega: las bases del canon," *RFC* (2012): 23–24.

59. Pfeiffer, *History of Classical Scholarship*, 206–8.

60. Grant, "Literary Criticism," 25–28; Torres Guerra, "Literatura griega," 24.

61. Torres Guerra, "Literatura griega," 25 n. 16: Three tragic authors: Aeschylus, Sophocles, and Euripides. Nine lyric poets: Alcman, Alcaeus, Sappho, Stesichorus, Píndar, Bacchylides, Íbycus, Anacreon, and Simonides. Three comedians: Eupolis, Cratinus, and Aristophanes (see Horace, *Sat.* 1.4.1). Ten orators: Antiphon, Androcides, Lysias, Isocrates, Isaeus, Aeschines, Lycurgus, Demosthenes, Hypereides, and Dinarchus.

62. Pfeiffer notes that this characteristic use of the canon was suggested by Ruhnken in his 1768 work (Pfeiffer, *History of Classical Scholarship*, 207). See David

In short, the κανόνες were the ones to be imitated, as specifically mentioned by Quintilian in *Inst.* 10.1.46-131 (where he compiles the list of authors that anyone wishing to become a *rhetor* had to know), or Dion of Prusa in his discourse 18.6-19 (when he presents the list of writers that had to be read by those who aspired to enter politics).[63] Surely this was also the case for philosophy, since we know that the works of Plato and Aristotle occupied a special place in the Academy and in the Peripatos, where the books of these authors had to be read in a particular sequence. But all this suggests that what was taught in the schools about literary criticism, at a time when forgeries were the order of the day, also played an important role.[64] In the face of the schools' influence, book lists were of relative value. The collective judgment on authorities was more important than the list.

In other words, this collective judgment about the authorities, which took shape by consensus and was transmitted from one generation to the next, may also have contributed to the production of the canonical list of the Bible. When it was necessary to define the identity of the Christian group, this list of authorities and their writings may have been more decisive than the decision to establish the specific list of canonical books by a single person or a particular group. And it may also have been more conclusive than the need to establish a canon as a response to a crisis that arose in the second century, specifically as a response to the canon established by Marcion.[65]

This digression has no other purpose than to highlight some factors—in this case the role of the authorities—that can determine what is copied and included in a codex and what is left out of it. The peculiarity of the Christian codex of the Bible is that it not only brings together works by a single author (like a roll), but, in the style of an anthology, it also compiles the works of several authorities, facilitates mutual references between the various books, and allows them to be recognized as a unity, with a beginning and an end.

Ruhnken, *Historia critica oratorum Graecorum* (1768), 386. See also Otto Kroehnert, *Canonesne poetarum scriptorum artificum per antiquitatem fuerunt?* (1897); Lee M. McDonald, "Hellenism and the Biblical Canons: Is There a Connection?," in Porter and Pitts, *Christian Origins and Greco-Roman Culture*, 25.

63. Torres Guerra, "Literatura Griega," 24.

64. Grant, "Literary Criticism," 44.

65. See Markschies, "Canon of the New Testament," 175-82; Holmes, "Biblical Canon," 416-18.

6. The Authority of the Codex

It has occasionally been said that in the beginning there were as many canons as there were communities.[66] Along with the rule of faith, some communities kept a specific number of writings considered authoritative, while others had a greater or lesser number of such writings.[67] Whatever the case may have been, each collection implied a living canon created by tradition; at the beginning and for several ensuing centuries, the need to define it in a list was not felt. Only in the fourth century (because it was possible to gather all the canonical books in a single volume) did numerous ecclesiastical authorities begin to establish the Old Testament and New Testament canons as a strictly delimited list composed exclusively of authorized or sacred books to which nothing could be added or subtracted. In the Catholic tradition, the definitive decision came only with the Council of Trent.

The codex format helped to determine these limits, insofar as it circumscribes its collection by means of two covers that separate the writings included in the codex from others that remain outside it. The format facilitates the mutual relationship between authors and writings, so that it gives the impression of a uniform book. The format is particularly suitable for compiling, as in an anthology, the writings of various authorities and for presenting them as a unit. In such a volume, the index reflects the synchronic character of the whole work, as the use of the word *canon* in the sense of table suggests, and unifies the diverse information conveyed in each of the writings collected in the codex. As Wallraff notes regarding the Eusebian canons: the tables, the divisions into chapters, and the covers and illustrations of the sacred book of Christians have

---

66. James A. Sanders, "Scripture as Canon for Post-modern Times," *BTB* 25 (1995): 58, quoted in Schmidt, "Greek New Testament," 479.

67. See Holmes, "Biblical Canon," 419. After pointing out the decisive role played by Irenaeus in the process of selecting the books that would be canonical, Holmes comments that, in any case, with him the matter was not settled: "During the period between Irenaeus and Athanasius at least nineteen books formed a part of the floating penumbra around the relatively stable core group: not just 2–3 John, 2 Peter, Jude, James, Hebrews, and Revelation, but also the Gospel of the Hebrews, Gospel of the Egyptians, Acts of Paul, Acts of Peter, 3 Corinthians, Letter to the Laodiceans, Apocalypse of Peter, Didache, 1 Clement, 2 Clement, Letter of Barnabas, and Shepherd of Hermas—all of which were considered by someone sometime as scripture."

the same stabilizing function as the codex.[68] They grant the text an aura of immutability and untouchability. As such, the canon as a closed and harmonious list of catalogs is by no means a simple formal description but also has an authoritative and normative function. The two meanings of κανών as "list" and "rule" are quite similar.[69] But the authority each of the writings collected in a codex has is given by the whole, insofar as that whole is defined by an external entity.

In other words, the content of the codex is still a collection, not *the* collection. And as a collection, it can exert only an indirect influence on the canon. Any collection is always partial, unless there is an external authority to close it. An expert or a group of experts can compile an anthology of the fifty best novels written by Nobel Prize winners. But that anthology will have a different authority from the one compiled by the Swedish Academy. The production of particular books in specific formats reflects part of reality, just as a photograph discloses only a partial view of things. Certainly, the codex contributed to defining the limits of the collection by selecting some writings and setting others aside. But the material format does not offer a panoramic view that reflects every possibility or historical contingency.[70] The use of authoritative writings depends on the locus of authority.[71] We will deal with this in the next chapter.

---

68. Crawford's comprehensive introduction to the Eusebian canons and their use in late antiquity and the Middle Ages appeared after the original Spanish publication of this work in 2020. Applying the concept of hypertextuality as a mode of reading, he arrives at a conclusion similar to Wallraff's: "What the Eusebian canons are saying to the reader is that each of the gospels in a fourfold gospel codex no longer has the same meaning it would have if it were housed in a single coterminous codex with a single-membered canon. Rather, this juxtaposition of four texts between two covers, understood as constituting a closed canon of sacred literature, now has a new meaning as a result of this editorial process" (Crawford, *Eusebian Canon Tables*, 104).

69. Wallraff, *Kodex und Kanon*, 48.

70. See the considerations of Francis Watson, *Gospel Writing: A Canonical Perspective* (Eerdmans, 2013), 604–19, esp. 616–19.

71. It is true that in certain circumstances the biblical codex was considered to embody the presence of Christ as the Word of God, but the holiness of the divine Logos in book form is ultimately defined by authority, as shown by the Quinisextus Council of 692, which threatened with excommunication anyone who destroyed the books of the Old Testament and New Testament. See Claudia Rapp, "Holy Texts, Holy Men and Holy Scribes," in Klingshirn and Safran, *Early Christian Book*, 196–200.

Table 6.1. Papyrus codices up to the fourth/fifth century that attest to more than one New Testament writing[72]

More than one gospel	*P45*: Four Gospels + Acts
	P75: Luke + John
One or two gospels + other writings	*P45*: Four Gospels + Acts
	P53: Matthew + Acts
Acts + other writings	*P45*: Four Gospels + Acts
	P53: Matthew + Acts
Two or more Catholic letters	P72: 1–2 Peter + Jude
Two or more Pauline letters	P30: 1–2 Thessalonians
	P46: Romans + Acts + 1–2 Corinthians + Ephesians + Galatians + Philippians + Colossians + 1 Thessalonians
	P92: Ephesians + 2 Thessalonians

Table 6.2. Papyri up to the third/fourth centuries that attest to a single New Testament writing[73]

Part of one gospel only: 37 papyri	Matthew: P1, P37, P64, (P62), P70, (P71), P77+P103?, (P86), P101, P102, P104, P110
	Mark: (P88), P137
	Luke: P4?, P7, P69, P111, P138
	John: P5, P22, P28, P39, P52, P66, P90, P95, P106, P107, P108, P109, P119, (P120), P121, P134, P141
Part of Acts only: 7 papyri	P8, P29, P38, (P48), (P50), P91, P127

---

72. Those in more than one group are indicated in italics.
73. For dating, see ch. 1, table 1.1. Manuscripts whose dating is in doubt are indicated in parentheses.

Part of a Catholic letter exclusively: 8 papyri	James: P20, P23, P100
	1 Peter: (P81), (P89), (P82), P125
	1 John: P9
Part of a Pauline letter exclusively: 18 papyri	Romans: P10, P27, P40, *P46*, P113, P118, P131
	1 Corinthians: P15, P123
	2 Corinthians: (P117), P124
	Ephesians: P49, P132
	Philippians: P16
	1 Thessalonians: P65
	Titus: P32
	Philemon: P87, P139
Part of Hebrews exclusively: 6 papyri	P12, P13, P17, P114, P116, P126
Part of Revelation exclusively: 5 papyri	P18, (P24), P47, P98, P115

Table 6.3. Majuscule parchment codices up to the sixth century with more than one book of the New Testament[74]

Second/third centuries	0171: Matthew and Luke
Fourth century	Codex Sinaiticus (01) and Codex Vaticanus (03): New Testament
	0171: Matthew and Luke
Fourth/fifth centuries	Codex Washingtonianus (032): Gospels

---

74. For more details, see Dormandy, "How the Books Became," 24–25. Their contents are noted generically. Most of these codices have gaps.

Fifth century	Codex Alexandrinus (02): New Testament (except Catholic Letters)
	Codex Ephraemi Rescriptus (04): New Testament
	Codex Bezae (05): Gospels and Acts
	Codex Freerianus (016): from 1 Corinthians to Philemon
	Codex Guelferbytanus (026) and Codex Borgianus (029): Luke and John
	048: Acts, most Pauline letters, and Catholic Letters
	067: Matthew and Mark
	0166: Acts and James
	0208: Colossians and 1 Thessalonians
	0240: 1 Timothy and Titus
	0289: Romans and 1 Corinthians
Fifth/sixth centuries	088: 1 Corinthians and Titus
	0247: 1 and 2 Peter
	0251: 3 John and Jude
Sixth century	Twelve manuscripts containing more than one New Testament book

The Question of the Authoritative Text

The study of the text of the Bible in Catholic treatises on Sacred Scripture does not usually occupy a prominent place. Until the 1990s, it was common to include it in the general introduction to Scripture, once the canon had been studied and before engaging questions of biblical hermeneutics.[1] Inspiration is linked to the canon and precedes it; and this, in turn, brings with it the study of the text's transmission. The underlying purpose of this approach is to show that the canonical books have been faithfully transmitted and should be considered trustworthy.[2] The focus on textual criticism meets the need to have the text as close as possible to the one written by its authors. To this end, ancient manuscripts and the way in which the text has been transmitted in these copies are studied.

In more recent textbooks on Scripture, however, it is common to consider the study of the text as a preliminary step to the treatises on inspiration, canon, and hermeneutics. The text is considered an element linked to the transmission of the Word, or as one of the preliminary questions to the theological study of Scripture, together with biblical geography,

---

1. See, e.g., Gaetano M. Perrella, *Introducción general a la Sagrada Escritura*, trans. Juan Prado (Perpetuo Socorro, 1954), 193–277. The same distribution appears in, among others, John E. Steinmueller, *Introducción general a la Sagrada Escritura*, trans. José Alfredo Jolly (Desclée de Brouwer, 1947), 149–246; and E. Martín Nieto, *Introducción general a la Sagrada Escritura* (Casa de la Biblia, 1966), 223–69. See also Carlo M. Martini and Pietro Bonati, *Il messaggio della Salvezza*, CCSB 1 (Elledici, Leumann, 1987), 154–223. In any case, this disposition continues in recent manuals: for example, Miguel Ángel Tábet, *Introducción general a la Biblia* (Palabra, 2004), 33–297; Giovanni Deiana, *Introduzione alla Sacra Scrittura alla luce Della "Dei Verbum"* (Urbaniana University Press, 2009), 99–116.

2. Perrella, *Introducción general*, 12: "The history of the text, both in its original language and in the versions ... proves that the inspired text has come down to us, at least substantially, intact."

archaeology, and biblical history.³ The text is studied as a presupposition of theological analysis.⁴

The traditional model prioritizes the faithful transmission of the text, since it is considered to have come from the hand of authors through whom God has spoken. Being linked to the treatise on inspiration and the problem of the canon, the study of the text underscores the importance of understanding that the texts of the Bible are God's Word *in* the church. In more recent models, although there is a wide variety of approaches to Scripture, a more text-centered perspective predominates. This is an approach in which we can appreciate the influence of biblical renewal and the weight of exegesis that originated in Protestant traditions. In line with advances in the historical-critical method and the influence of the theology of the Word, the text's importance is emphasized as the foundation and result of God's communication with humankind. The existence of writings that contain and witness to God's Word is presupposed. First come the texts as documents of the past and then the theological implications that derive from them. Considerable importance is given to the original text and to the way it can be accessed through textual criticism within this framework. Little consideration is given, however, to the possible theological implications that follow from the fact that most of the Bible's books are the result of a lengthy process of composition and that we do not preserve any original copies of these books. In other words, readers seldom recognize that we do not know with certainty what the text of the Bible is and that we should be speaking of *texts* rather than *a text* of the Bible.

---

3. For example, Valerio Manucci, *La Biblia como palabra de Dios: Introducción general a la Sagrada Escritura* (Desclée, 1988), 95–108; Rinaldo Fabris, *Introduzione generale alla Bibbia*, LCSB 1 (Elledici, Leumann, 1994), 291–372. The latter treats the text within the philological section devoted to the Bible as literature. In Raymond E. Brown, Joseph A. Fitzmyer, and Roland E. Murphy, questions of the text are covered in the articles that follow inspiration and canonicity, but separated from these two topics by an article devoted to the Apocrypha, Dead Sea manuscripts, and other Jewish books, following the same arrangement of the original edition. See Brown, Fitzmyer, and Murphy, eds., *The New Jerome Biblical Commentary* (Prentice Hall, 1990), 1083–1112.

4. See Ignacio Carbajosa, Joaquin González Echegaray, and Francisco Varo, *La Biblia en su entorno*, IEB 1 (Verbo Divino, 1992), 433–574. This approach is kept in the new edition of Carbajosa, González Echegaray, and Varo, *La Biblia en su entorno* (Editorial Verbo Divina, 2013), 411–652.

This being the case, it is timely to ask to what extent the need to determine the integrity and original wording of the texts transmitted in these books (such as, for example, whether there were several editions of Mark's Gospel or what exactly was the Lord's Prayer taught by Jesus) is relevant to the understanding of Scripture, since their integrity and exact wording (or lack thereof) raise questions about the nature of revelation. Is it critical to understanding Scripture and consequently revelation that the Bible is composed of texts that, to put it crudely, we do not know what they were like when written, nor are we absolutely certain that they were all intended to be read as Scripture by their authors? How relevant to understanding revelation is it that there is no agreement on the exact wording of the texts of these books? Is it important to recognize that there are no originals and that ultimately the biblical text is, so to speak, a fluid text?

It is clear that there are neither simple nor definitive answers for these and other similar questions. Neither is this the place to attempt to offer them. On the other hand, the difference between the composition of Old Testament books and those of the New Testament is remarkable. We nonetheless have an opportunity to highlight some of the theological implications that the current way of approaching the New Testament's original text and its authoritative character have for the understanding of Scripture. Mutatis mutandis, these implications are also applicable to the Old Testament text.

1. The Authoritative Text

We reviewed a relatively recent approach to textual criticism above (see ch. 4), especially by textual critics associated with narrative textual criticism. Generally speaking, these scholars are engaged in textual criticism and explore the theological implications of their textual analyses only indirectly or occasionally. Ehrman has regularly pointed out, mostly in books marketed to the general public, the importance of a knowledge of ancient manuscripts for the faith. His assessments, however, are often polemically charged. They are designed to provoke negative reactions to literal interpretations of the Bible, but they do so from an understanding of Christianity as a religion of the book, with no other criterion of authority than the biblical text.[5] Epp is far more cautious and rarely alludes to the

---

5. See, e.g., Ehrman, *Misquoting Jesus*, 1–15.

theological consequences of textual criticism. Parker, on the other hand, has reflected on the theological implications of his understanding of the text in several articles, almost all of which are collected in his *Manuscripts, Text, Theology*. Space limitations prevent a detailed discussion of Parker's proposals, but it appears that some of his assertions, perhaps motivated by a desire to question positions assumed or generally accepted by common readers of Scripture, grant insufficient consideration to the question at hand, while other proposals require greater precision. Here we will consider only the implications of his reluctance to identify a printed text with the authoritative text, something already mentioned (see ch. 4). Parker's approach is commendable insofar as it prevents us from being drawn into naive forms of fundamentalism. However, his approach can also affect one's understanding of the biblical text's authority.[6] The following words capture the implications (for Parker) of regarding the New Testament text as a living text: "Any 'authoritative' text is formed by selecting readings from this reservoir or bank of variant readings. If we set aside the citations [in early Christian writers], which are of a different nature, we have a collection of witnesses, the manuscripts."[7]

These words beg the question. If we only have manuscripts, what do we understand by the "authoritative text"? The answer is not simple. As with the concept of the original text, "authoritative text" allows for several meanings. Parker notes that the definition of *authority* depends on the nature of the textual tradition under consideration and how an editor understands their role in editing a book. To illustrate, he draws on the concepts of authority articulated by Peter Shillingsburg, an expert on editorial matters in nineteenth-century Victorian literature.[8] According to Shillingsburg, we must position the authority that controls the text before speaking of authoritative texts. This is necessary since there is no uniformity when it comes to understanding whose text it is. For some it belongs

---

6. Incidentally, one is unlikely to find any theologian who is unaware that the text of a critical edition is not the text that came from the hand of the author to whom it is attributed. However, it is also true that, in practice, it is possible that such a theologian may act and use it as if it were the text that came directly from the author's hand. This is a real danger.

7. David C. Parker, "Textual Criticism and Theology," *ExpTim* 118 (2007): 588.

8. Parker, *Introduction to the New Testament Manuscripts*, 188–89. Parker refers to Peter L. Shillingsburg, *Scholarly Editing in the Computer Age: Theory and Practice* (University of Michigan Press, 1996), 5–23.

to the reader; for others it is autonomous or the property of the social institution that includes proofreaders and editors; for others it belongs to the author alone. Moreover, the way in which the text is published may carry with it a different authority depending on the orientation chosen by the scholarly editor. This authority may be historical, aesthetic, authorial, or sociological. For each of these, the editor of an authoritative text pursues different criteria.

Parker applies these orientations to the New Testament. So, if authority is presumed to reside in a historical document (a historical orientation), the conception of New Testament authority would be based on manuscript copies. If authority is fixed in the author or editor's artistic forms (an aesthetic orientation), the idea of New Testament authority would be based on the selected text in a carefully produced edition that offers the text of a particular period. If authority resides in the author (an author-derived orientation), New Testament authority would be what is closest to that which is traditionally held by New Testament readers, who are not textual critics and tend to consider the text of the printed edition that which Matthew, Paul, and other New Testament authors produced. The author-derived orientation would be the closest to "the traditional ascription of authority of the texts to the divine inspiration (or even dictation)." Finally, if authority is found in the author or editor's institutional unit (a sociological orientation), the idea of authority would be based on a text that is considered the result of a copying process with a mixture of intentional and unintentional textual changes; the text is seen not as the product of an author but as a consequence of a process of reading and rewriting.

Parker believes that textual critics use all of these types of textual authority and argues that the various theories about the best method of editing a text should be built on proven historical-critical research. In his view, these approaches serve to test the value of concepts of textual authority and defend against fundamentalism and bibliolatry.[9]

In light of the enumerated orientations, Parker's rejection of an authoritative text identified with a specific edition is understandable. Starting from the contested theory of the original fluidity of the gospel texts, Parker forcefully asserts that "the quest for a single authoritative

---

9. See Parker, *Introduction to the New Testament Manuscripts*, 189. He continues: "Textual criticism and the discipline of textual editing is a basic requirement of research and reflection. It has nothing to say directly in the world of philosophical and theological reflection, but there is a great deal to be learned from it."

text is in itself a distortion of the tradition."[10] And, as we have seen, this is precisely what has happened, in Parker's opinion, with the invention of the printing press and the production of an edition of a specific text. The printed text has become identified with a single authoritative text, so that the gospel has lost its original character as a living text. In the end, the Word of God has been identified with a text that never existed: "The uniformity that is the essence of the printed book masked the difference between authoritative books and authoritative copies, so that what could not be claimed on behalf of any individual manuscript could be claimed for an edition.... The ability to produce a huge number of identical copies of the Greek New Testament led to a new concept of the text as authoritative. The difference between the text itself and the printed copy became obliterated."[11]

We have already highlighted some of the limitations of Parker's ideas. They contain a measure of truth and cohere with his perspective, but the relationship he proposes between the original and the authoritative text is a departure from how a good part of the ecclesiastical tradition understands it and could prove problematic. For this reason, we should clarify what we mean by the authoritative text vis-à-vis the so-called original text without resigning ourselves to a meaning that fluctuates depending on the adopted perspective of each editor.

2. The Authority of the Text

Traditionally speaking, Christians have considered the New Testament text authoritative in one form or another. The challenge is how to determine what confers authority on a text and what should be understood by an "authoritative text." In this sense, textual criticism's failure to reach an original text highlights the weakness of the concept of authority embraced by various Christian groups when the authoritative text is identified with the original text. If we do not have the original text, how do we know God speaks

---

10. Parker, *Living Text of the Gospels*, 202.
11. Parker, *Living Text of the Gospels*, 189. Further on, he writes: "It is thus possible to show, by comparison with other traditions, what kind of text that of the Gospels is not. It is harder to find a suitable language to describe what it is. The terminology which I adopt here is to characterise the text of the Gospels as a free, or perhaps as a living, text" (200).

in a particular edition?[12] Naturally, in this area, although not uniformly, this question is debated more intensely, since there is a greater tendency to equate both texts.[13] In any case, as Holmes points out, there are Protestant groups that reject the authority of the original text and are inclined to grant the status of authoritative text to the majority text, or even to the putative Greek text that underlies the King James Version.[14] In that sense, according to Holmes, these groups would be close to the Orthodox tradition, for which the authoritative text is the Byzantine text, or to the Catholic tradition, for which, after Trent, the authoritative text would be the Vulgate.[15]

To clarify the variety of ways the expression "authoritative text" is understood, it may be useful to turn precisely to the Vulgate, the Bible version explicitly granted that status by the Council of Trent (in a decree that, we should remember, is exclusive to the Latin Catholic Church and is disciplinary and not dogmatic in nature). In declaring the Vulgate authentic, the Council sought only to confer on it the status of a text suitable for public use and for use in controversies:

> [The] same sacred Council, considering that it would be of no small advantage to the Church of God if, of all the Latin editions of the sacred

---

12. See, e.g., the statements of Ehrman in speaking of his process of "conversion" from being a "born-again Christian," with a literalist understanding of the Bible, to other, more agnostic positions (*Misquoting Jesus*, 1–15). Here is an example: "How does it help us to say that the Bible is the inerrant word of God if in fact we don't have the words that God inerrantly inspired, but only the words copied by the scribes—sometimes correctly but sometimes (many times!) incorrectly? What good is it to say that the autographs (i.e., the originals) were inspired? We don't have the originals! We have only error-ridden copies, and the vast majority of these are centuries removed from the originals and different from them, evidently, in thousands of ways" (7).

13. The implications of this problem for the principle of *sola Scriptura* can be seen in the section "Theological Impact: Toward a Transformation of *Sola Scriptura* in Christian Theology," in Clivaz, "New Testament in the Time," 52–55; and in Xavier Gravend-Tirole, "From Sola Scriptura to Pluralibus Scripturis," in Clivaz and Zumstein, *Reading New Testament Papyri*, 355–81. See also Juan Chapa, "De la letra al Espíritu pasando por la historia," *CTeo* 43 (2018): 73–96.

14. Holmes, "From 'Original Text,'" 642–43.

15. Holmes, "From 'Original Text,'" 642. We should point out, however, that the authority to which Holmes refers currently rests, at least for liturgical use, in the text of the Neo-Vulgate. However, as will be seen below, the concept of authority Holmes attributes to the Vulgate is not exactly the same as that given to a particular text in other confessions.

books that are in use, it were to make known which should be considered authentic, establishes and declares that this same ancient and Vulgate edition, which is approved by the long use of so many centuries in the Church itself, be considered authentic in public lessons, disputations, preaching and expositions, and that no one, for any pretext whatsoever, should dare or presume to reject it.[16]

The meaning of *authentic* used by the decree refers to that which is "worthy of faith," "guaranteed," "authorized," "authoritative," "reliable," and which, when applied to a document, means that, because of its incontestable validity, it is fit to bear witness in a trial. It does not have the critical sense by which a book is said to have been truly written by the author attributed to it or, in the case of a version, to be in conformity with the original.[17] As Pius XII puts it in his encyclical *Divino afflante Spiritu*, this kind of authenticity is not understood in a critical sense but in a juridical one:

> Hence this special authority or as they say, *authenticity* of the Vulgate was not affirmed by the Council particularly for critical reasons, but rather because of its legitimate use in the Churches throughout so many centuries; by which use indeed the same is shown, in the sense in which the Church has understood and understands it, to be free from any error whatsoever in matters of faith and morals; so that, as the Church herself testifies and affirms, it may be quoted safely and without fear of error in disputations, in lectures and in preaching; and so its *authenticity* is not specified primarily as *critical*, but rather as juridical (*atque adeo eiusmodi authentia non primario nomine critica, sed iuridica potius vocatu*).[18]

---

16. Council of Trent, session 4, April 8, 1546: "Insuper eadem sacrosancta Synodus considerans, non parum utilitatis accedere posse Ecclesiae Dei, si ex omnibus latinis editionibus, quae circumferuntur sacrorum librorum, quaenam pro authentica habenda sit, innotescat: statuit et declarat, ut haec ipsa vetus et vulgata editio, quae longo tot saeculorum usu in ipsa Ecclesia probata est, in publicis lectionibus, disputationibus praedicationibus et expositionibus pro authentica habeatur et quod nemo illam reicere quovis praetextu audeat vel praesumat" (DH 1506; *EnchB*. n. 61). See Jacques M. Vosté, "The Vulgate and the Council of Trent," *CBQ* 9 (1947): 9–25.

17. Perrella, *Introducción general*, §§232, 259. See also Martini and Bonati, *Il messaggio della Salvezza*, 205–9.

18. Pius XII, *Divino afflante Spiritu*, n. 21: "Haec igitur praecellens Vulgatae auctoritas seu, ut aiunt, authentia non ob criticas praesertim rationes a Concilio statuta est, sed ob illius potius legitimum in Ecclesiis usum, per tol saeculorum decursum habitum ; quo quidem usu demonstratur eamdem, prout intellexit et intellegit Eccle-

The juridical character is confirmed by the definition of *authentic* attributed to Salvianus Julianus, a jurist of the second century CE, which is taken up by the decree of Trent with very similar words: "authenticum est scriptum aliquod, quod ex se fidem facit in iudicio et supremae est auctoritatis, ut a nullo reiici vel in quaestionem vocari debeat" ("a writing is authentic, because by itself it makes faith in judgment and enjoys such supreme authority that no one should reject or doubt it").[19]

With the decree, the council was not referring to the value of the original texts and non-Latin translations, nor did it wish to prohibit their use, nor to eliminate the LXX or other versions.[20] As has been said, its purpose was to counter abuses. What it declared was that, in the Church of the Latin Rite, the Vulgate was for public use and that this text should be followed in controversies, since its use throughout the centuries guaranteed that it contained no error in matters of faith and morals. The Vulgate's critical authenticity, its substantial conformity to the original text, was assumed but not affirmed. Pius XII also recalled that the Council of Trent wanted the Latin versions and, as far as possible, the Hebrew and Greek editions to be revised and did not prohibit the study of older texts or translations into other vulgar languages.[21] John Paul II continued this same line

---

sia, in rebus fidei ac morum ab omni prorsus esse errore immunem; ita ut, ipsa Ecclesia testante et confirmante, in disputationibus, lectionibus concionibusque tuto ac sine errandi periculo, proferri possit; atque adeo eiusmodi authentia non primario nomine critica, sed iuridica potius vocatur" (DH 3825; *EnchB.* n. 549).

19. According to Briani Walton, these words are attributed to Julian, in his treatise *De fide instrumentorum*, but I have not been able to confirm this. See Walton, *Biblia Polyglotta prolegomena* (Weygandianis, 1777), 248. See also Edmund F. Sutcliffe, "The Council of Trent on the 'Authentia' of the Vulgate?," *JTS* 49 (1948): 35–42.

20. Stephen D. Ryan quotes Richard Simon's words on the ancient versions of the Bible: "The Roman Church receives all those nations with their Bibles." See Ryan, "The Word of God and the Textual Pluriformity of the Old Testament," in *Verbum Domini and the Complementarity of Exegesis and Faith: Catholic Theological Formation*, ed. Scott Carl (Eerdmans, 2014), 131; Simon, *Réponse au livre intitulé Défense des sentiments*, taken from Dominique Barthélemy, "L'enchevêtrement de l'histoire textuelle et de l'histoire littéraire dans les relations entre la Septante et le texte massorétique," in *De Septuaginta: Studies in Honor of John William Wevers on His Sixty-Fifth Birthday*, ed. Albert Pietersma and Claude Cox (Benben, 1984), 37.

21. Pius XII, n. 14, who quotes in n. 25 (*EnchB.* n. 549) the *Decretum de editione et usu Sacrorum Librorum: Concilium Tridentinum*, ed. Societas Goerresiana, 10:471; cf. 5:29, 59, 65; 10:446–47. See also Ryan, "Word of God," 132.

in promulgating the apostolic constitution *Scripturarum thesaurus* on the new edition of the Vulgate (Neo-Vulgate).[22]

The decree of Trent partially illustrates the authoritative character of a text, in this case the Vulgate, and determines its concrete value within the Latin Church. However, the council was not referring to the true authority of the sacred text with the words of the decree. For Trent, the authority of the biblical text lies in its status as an inspired and true witness to the Word of God and not in the fact that it is purportedly closer to an original writing. Although the church has established a canon of sacred books, it has never canonized the putative original text of those books. And while the Council of Trent explicitly determines the canonicity of all the passages included in the Vulgate by proclaiming that the canon is made up of "libros ipsos integros cum omnibus suis partibus, prout in ecclesia catholica legi consueverunt et in veteri Vulgata Latina editione habentur" ("the books themselves integral with all their parts, as they have been accustomed to be read in the Catholic Church and are contained in the ancient Latin Vulgate edition"), it is not advocating the untouchability of the Vulgate's text.[23] It is referring, instead, to the canonicity of some parts of specific books, such as the Greek fragments of Daniel, the long ending of Mark, the passage of the adulterous woman, or the bloodlike sweat of Jesus in Luke, whose originality was questioned from the textual point of view and was discussed by the council fathers but which were not mentioned in the decree to avoid confusion.[24] Yet, when Trent states that the canon is determined by the way in which particular books, "with all their parts," have been read in the church and are found in the Vulgate, it is not referring to the canon being delimited by two distinct realities—the reading in the church and the texts of the Vulgate—but by a single reality: the praxis of the church, that is, the use she makes of a book or a passage.[25] In

---

22. John Paul II, *Address to Members of the Pontifical Commission for the New Vulgate*, 27 April 1979: "The new linguistic and exegetical knowledge confer on the new version a stamp of reliability certainly not inferior to St Jerome's version, which stood the test of a millennium and a half of history." See also García-Moreno, *La Neovulgata*, 257–322.

23. *EnchB*. n. 60.

24. See Juan C. Ossandón Widow, *Introduzione generale alla Sacra Scrittura* (EDUSC, 2018), 186, with reference to Peter G. Duncker, "De singulis S. Scripturae libris controversis in Concilio Tridentino," in *Miscellanea biblica et orientalia Athanasio Miller completis LXX annis oblata*, ed. Adalberti Metzinger (Herder, 1951), 66–93.

25. Perrella mentions that the two phrases, those referring to the reading in the

other words, behind the consideration of a text as authoritative, there are hermeneutical options that do not depend on a supposedly neutral critical analysis but are prior to it.[26]

That particular texts were not canonized as purportedly original is a fact, but one that is seldom given due attention. It is important because if one considers the Christian faith from the perspective of a religion of the book, the fact that a particular text is not available could call into question the normative character of the books of the Bible. Yet, in order to avoid indifference to the text and to prevent it from losing its normative character (by being dissolved in a myriad of manuscripts and plagued by questions about its wording), the church establishes a standard text to serve as a reference point for the many other possible texts and to guarantee its authority in liturgical celebrations and official teachings. That authoritative text with that specific function was the Vulgate for the Catholic Church of Latin Rite, and in a sense it is now the Neo-Vulgate. However, the text's authority does not derive from the edition itself but from its status as a witness to God's Word. Certainly, the church encourages seeking the text that is closest to the originals, but whatever it may be, that does not qualify it as normative.

When the church does not canonize a particular form of the text, it does nothing more than continue the same attitude early Christian communities had toward sacred texts. The Christians of the first generations did not adopt only the Hebrew Scriptures of Israel as normative or authoritative writings but also made use of the various extant Greek translations. They were therefore apparently unaware of the need to be subject to the exact wording of a specific text, which could not be altered because it was sacred (or "because it defiled the hands" according to the rabbinic formula). With this they indicated that the text was not untouchable and that it was not required to be faithful to the original wording (as is the case with Jewish translations subsequent to the LXX) but that it was a matter of understanding the text in the light of a higher doctrine that goes back to Moses and

---

church and to the Vulgate, are to be understood in a unitive and not a disjunctive sense (*Introducción general*, 161 n. 149).

26. Ignacio Carbajosa, *De la fe nace la exegesis: La interpretación de la Escritura a la luz de la historia de la investigación sobre el Antiguo Testamento*, EstBib 43 (Verbo Divino, 2011), 184. See also Carbajosa, *Hebraica veritas versus Septuaginta auctoritatem: Does a Canonical Text of the Old Testament Exist?*, trans. Paul Stevenson (Pickwick, 2024), chs. 7–8.

that accompanies the letter from its birth.[27] Basically, they understood that the written legislation was ambiguous because it was just a written text. The letter itself is not enough. It needs to be interpreted. And although these early Christians also recognized that the original text was the Hebrew, they understood that the Greek translation fulfilled the function of discovering the depth of that text over and above the story alone.[28]

3. Text, Canon, and the Rule of Faith

It seems quite clear then that there is no concern for the canonization of a given form of the text in the earliest Jewish and Christian traditions. In any case, it is clear that the selection of a text goes through the choice of a canon. As we have seen in connection with the codex format and the canon, the process of canonization requires the intervention of an authority external to the text. Even if one defends the presence of elements that show the coherence of the criteria by which the canonical books are selected, the church's intervention in the selection of books for the canon is beyond dispute. It is only after a long discernment process within the context of ecclesial communion that the church establishes the canonicity of particular books.[29] But it does not make assertions about the original text (or proximity thereto) of these canonical books. In fact, the fathers were not concerned with establishing a single normative text of the Old Testament. They were aware of textual plurality and of errors in Scripture, but they accepted variants for the interpretation of texts that could advance the gospel without being scrupulously attached to the letter:

---

27. So Hilary of Poitiers, *In Psalmum* 2.2 (CSEL 22:39). See Ignacio Carbajosa, "La vida de los manuscritos bíblicos: Cuando la tradición de lectura se hace Escritura," *EstBib* 71 (2013): 191–93. Regarding Jewish translations subsequent to the LXX, this is the traditional theory regarding the translations of Aquila, Symmachus, and Theodotion, although today the position is more nuanced. See, e.g., Natalio Fernández Marcos, *The Septuagint in Context: Introduction to the Greek Version of the Bible* (Brill Academic, 2001), 109–73; Timothy M. Law, "Kaige, Aquila, and Jewish Revision," in *Greek Scripture and the Rabbis*, ed. Law and Alison Salvesen (Peeters, 2012), 39–64.

28. As is the tendency of Augustine of Hippo, *Civ.* 18.43–44 (CCSL 48:638–41). See Carbajosa, "La vida de los manuscritos bíblicos," 193–94.

29. See Gonzalo Aranda, "Il problema teologico del canone biblico," in *La Sacra Scrittura anima della teologia: Pontificia Università della Santa Croce. Facoltà di Teologia; Atti del IV Simposio Internazionale della Facoltà di Teologia*, ed. Miguel Ángel Tábet (Librería Editrice Vaticana, 1999), 13–35.

In their way of doing exegesis, the fathers did not seem to be concerned with establishing a text considered the only good, original and authentic, normative text, to the exclusion of divergent forms considered noncanonical. Keeping the text of the Septuagint is the usual norm.... But often, in the presence of several forms of the same text, the fathers accept this plurality with serenity: they quote a verse in one form or another. Sometimes the form that the verse received in the New Testament is preferred. When Origen's Hexapla makes more widely known the differences that separate the Septuagint from the other Jewish versions, the fathers take advantage of these variants, they use them from time to time for their interpretation. Their exegesis is not burdened with excessive scrupulosity regarding "the letter."[30]

For the fathers, Scripture exists simultaneously in various canonical forms. This is how Origen, Augustine, and Jerome (for whom the use of the Greek and Hebrew forms of the Old Testament by Jesus, the apostles, and the early church was normative) considered it.[31] Something analogous can be asserted about the New Testament texts.

Therefore, the text's authority cannot be separated from the church's decision on the canon, regardless of whether the text was more or less close to the so-called original.[32] Certainly, as a means of approaching

---

30. Marguerite Harl, "La Septante et la Pluralité textuelle des Écritures: Le Témoignage des Peres Grecs," in *Naissance de la Méthode critique* (Cerf, 1992), 231: "Dans leur pratique exégétique, les Pères ne semblaient pas s'être préoccupés d'établir un texte considéré comme seul bon texte, original et authentique, normatif, avec exclusion de formes divergentes jugées non canoniques. Le maintien du texte de la Septante est la règle.... Mais le plus souvent, en présence de plusieurs formes d'un même texte, les Pères acceptent avec sérénité cette pluralité: ils citent un verset sous une forme ou sous une autre. Parfois le privilège est accordé à la forme que le verset a reçue dans le Nouveau Testament. Lorsque les Hexaples d'Origène feront connaître plus largement les différences qui séparent la Septante des autres versions juives, les Pères tireront profit de ces variantes, ils les utiliseront à l'occasion pour leur interprétation. Leur exégèse ne s'encombre pas d'un excès de scrupules à l'égard de "la lettre."

31. See Adrian Schenker, "L'Écriture sainte subsiste en plusieurs formes canoniques simultanées," in *L'interpretazione della Bibbia nella Chiesa: Atti del Simposio promosso dalla Congregazione per la Dottrina della Fede* (Libreria Editrice Vaticana, 2001), 183; Ryan, "Word of God," 129; Carbajosa, *Hebraica veritas versus Septuaginta auctoritatem*.

32. In this regard, it is worth recalling how *Dei Verbum* teaches that the Bible was not given by God to any particular person but to the church (n. 11). The Pontifical Biblical Commission, for its part, in the document *The Interpretation of the Bible in the*

and interpreting texts, the church promotes textual criticism, since this is part of the historical method.[33] Proof of this is the presence of Catholics on the United Bible Societies committee preparing future editions of the Nestle-Aland (Carlo Martini and Stephen Pisano were members of this committee) and the enormous effort made by the committee of experts to update the Vulgate, taking as a basis the Biblia Hebraica Stuttgartensia for the Old Testament and the Nestle-Aland for the New Testament, which culminated in the Neo-Vulgate. But the church does not make the authority of the text dependent on the greater or lesser probability that the text is closer to the autograph.[34] As Epp states: "The text-critical discipline per se carries with it no normative implications and imposes no theological overlay onto such a text or variant.... Some (perhaps many) textual critics may be seeking an authoritative 'original' New Testament text and may choose to identify it with an authoritative 'canon,' but such a goal is neither intrinsic to textual criticism as a historical-critical discipline, nor is it within the domain of textual criticism to place a theological overlay on either its purposes or its results."[35] For this reason, according to the Catholic tradition, the church has not assumed any particular critical edition of the New Testament as authoritative. As noted, not even the Vulgate canonizes a particular form of the text. As Ignacio Carbajosa rightly points out and Parker underscores in a different way and with a different meaning, the church does not own the text, just as it does not own Christ.[36]

Church, states: "Guided by the Holy Spirit and in the light of the living tradition which it has received, the Church has discerned the writings which should be regarded as sacred Scripture.... The discernment of a 'canon' of sacred Scripture was the result of a long process... [These] texts ceased to be merely the expression of a particular author's inspiration; they became the common property of the whole people of God" (III, B. 1).

33. *Divino afflante Spiritu*, nn. 12–13 (*EnchB*. n. 548); Pontifical Biblical Commission, *The Interpretation of the Bible in the Church*, III, B. 3 and IV, B; cf. *Verbum Domini*, n. 115.

34. The relationship between original text and authoritative text is historical and/or theological but "not intrinsic" (Holmes, "From 'Original Text,'" 642).

35. Epp, "Multivalence of the Term," 279.

36. Ignacio Carbajosa, "El texto de la Biblia y la crítica textual," in Carbajosa, González Echegaray, and Varo, *La Biblia en su entorno* (2013), 415, 419. Cf. Parker, "Scripture Is Tradition," 16: "The fact that the recovery of the original text is a task that remains beyond all of us sets a question mark against any claim that we can in any sense 'possess' the text—literally or metaphorically."

For this very reason and with all the more reason, textual criticism cannot provide the last word on the text's authority, especially when it proves incapable of determining with complete certainty what the original text is. If textual authority were dependent on textual criticism, passages such as Mark's long ending or the adulterous woman should cease to be authoritative because they are most likely later additions to our oldest extant manuscripts. And what about the actual text of many Old Testament books that have such a complex textual history?[37] In a situation in which the original texts have been progressively enriched and have undergone variations, there must be an external element that can determine the authority of particular texts, analogous to what happens with the canonization of biblical books. For example, can we say that the story of the adulterous woman is God's inspired Word when textual criticism concludes it is a later addition?[38] When a Christian community in the East read the Fourth Gospel without the passage of the adulterous woman in its liturgical celebration and another in the West read it as part of John's Gospel, should we understand that the second community was not following the right tradition and treating as authoritative (and therefore inspired) a text that was not?[39] The same could apply to the various Hebrew and Greek texts of the Old Testament and, similarly, to the use of the versions.[40] There exists a multiplicity of texts, and we do not know which of them is the original. It is clear that inspiration does not depend on the autographic condition of the sacred book. But if not, then what is its relationship to the text? Certainly, there is a nucleus that is substantially the same, but if we take things to the extreme, it is legitimate to ask which text, with all its parts, is the canonical one, or, similarly, which text is inspired and therefore has authority.

The answer to this question does not lie in the selection of a particular text, nor even in the affirmation that all textual forms are inspired and

---

37. See Schenker, "L'Écriture sainte subsiste," 178–86.
38. See Breed, *Nomadic Text*, 119, who considers the reception of the biblical text "an open-ended process": "A biblical text has no moment of purity, origin, finality, or true meaning that could constitute a necessary, universally valid boundary between the text and its later receptions." For other approaches to the text as a process, see Keith, *Gospel as Manuscript*, 39–64.
39. See Knust and Wasserman, *To Cast the First Stone*, 64, 95.
40. See, e.g., what is pointed out by Ryan, "Word," 134 n. 31, on the discussion by Conleth Kearns, Maurice Gilbert, and Louis F. Hartman concerning the inspiration of the additions to the book of Sirach.

canonical, but precisely in an external factor: the rule of faith that governs the community reading those texts. The difficulties presented lead to the logical conclusion that, once the church has determined which books make up the canon, then the authoritative and therefore inspired text must be the one that conforms to the *regula fidei* received by tradition.[41]

The degree to which those who embraced the faith in the first decades of the early Christian movement were encouraged to follow teachings contained in books is unclear. At the very least, it did not appear to be a priority. The Didache, for instance, makes no reference to books or texts but rather reflects oral instruction. Of course, the Scriptures of Israel played a fundamental role, but these were primarily aimed at demonstrating the fulfillment of Scripture in Christ. What we do know is that, through baptismal faith, early followers entered a community that transmitted what they had received from the witnesses of the Risen One. Faith preceded the written text. First there were the formulas of baptismal faith, which were concise expressions of a rule of faith on which the various ecclesial communities based their consensus.[42] Irenaeus calls this *regula fidei* or *regula veritatis* ("rule of faith" or "rule of truth"),[43] which he considered "a well-founded system," or "a harmonious melody," which could only be perceived from faith (*Haer.* 2.27.1, 2.28.3). For the church fathers it was evident that Christ was the ultimate norm of faith. But there was also the conviction that Christ himself had given a rule of what was to be believed. The concrete words with which this rule was expressed were an expansion of the core of the gospel message, considering its expression a develop-

---

41. A good synthesis on the formation of the biblical canon and the role played in it by the rule of faith can be found in Holmes, "Biblical Canon," 418–19.

42. See Juan Chapa, "La Biblia en la formulación y la comprensión de la fe," in *La Sagrada Escritura*, ed. Juan Luis Caballero (Palabra actual, 2005), 268–78.

43. The idea and the way of expressing it first appears in Irenaeus, *Haer.* 1.10.1, 3.4.2, 4.33.7, 5.20.1, and later in Tertullian, *Praescr.* 13; *Prax.* 2; *Virg.* 1.3. Other examples can be found in Hippolytus, Cyprian, Novatian, Origen, Dionysius of Alexandria, Eusebius, etc. See Richard P. C. Hanson, *Tradition in the Early Church* (Westminster, 1962), 75–129; Vittorino Grossi, "Regula fidei," in *Encyclopedia of Ancient Christianity*, ed. Angelo di Berardino (IVP Academic, 2014). See also Prosper Grech, "The Regula fidei as Hermeneutical Principle in Patristic Exegesis," in *The Interpretation of the Bible: International Symposium on the interpretation of the Bible, Ljubljana 1996*, ed. Jože Krasovec (Sheffield Academic, 1998), 589–602; Grech, "The 'Regula fidei' as Hermeneutical Principle Yesterday and Today," in *L'interpretazione della Bibbia nella Chiesa*, 208–24.

ment of the baptismal formula. For this reason, the phrase "rule of faith" could be applied to the whole of this body of doctrine.[44] It indicated both the norm that delimited the scope of the Christian search for truth[45] and "*that which* the apostles, having received it from Jesus Christ, have handed down and that which the church, receiving it from them, continues to transmit *because this is normative for faith.*"[46]

The texts of apostolic origin, then, become like a music score.[47] They become the written notes of a musical composition that, interpreted according to the apostolic rule of faith, permit the harmonious melody of which Irenaeus speaks. The voice of Scripture could only be heard clearly if its text was interpreted correctly and rationally according to the *regula fidei*. The rule of faith was prior to Scripture, so much so that the baptismal confessions that are at the origins of the *regula fidei* could have been handed down as a creed even if we had not had a Bible.[48] Irenaeus himself points out that, if the apostles had not bequeathed us any writings, Christians would have to follow "the rule of faith which they handed down to the leaders of the Church" (*Haer.* 3.4.1).

God's Word is witnessed in various manuscripts, which in turn become witnesses themselves. There is neither a manuscript nor an edition

---

44. See Jaroslav Pelikan, *The Christian Tradition: A History of the Development of Doctrine*, vol. 1, *The Emergence of the Catholic Tradition (100–600)* (University of Chicago Press, 1971), 117: "The term 'rule of faith' or 'rule of truth' did not always refer to such creeds and confessions, and seems sometimes to have meant the 'tradition,' sometimes the Scriptures, sometimes the message of the gospel." See also Frances M. Young, *Biblical Exegesis and the Formation of Christian Culture* (Cambridge University Press, 1997), 18–21.

45. See Grossi, "Regula fidei," 3:387.

46. See Yves M. J. Congar, *La tradition et les traditions* (Artheme Fayard, 1960–1963). See also Damien van den Eynde, *Les normes de l'enseignement chrétien dans la littérature patristique des trois premiers siècles* (Gabalda, 1933); César Izquierdo, "El dogma y las fórmulas dogmáticas," in *Teología fundamental: Temas y propuestas para el nuevo milenio* (Desclée de Brouwer, 1999), 672–73.

47. See Chapa, "La Biblia en la formulación," 269. In relation to the Old Testament, Schenker also speaks of a polyphonic text: "Since Scripture presents an irreducible textual diversity, it is necessary to understand the textual form of Scripture not as a one-voice song, but a polyphonic song." ("Puisque l'Écriture présente une certaine diversité textuelle irréductible il faut comprendre la forme textuelle de l'Écriture non pas comme un chant à une voix, mais polyphonique"; "L'Écriture sainte subsiste," 189).

48. Prosper Grech, "Alle origini di un'ermeneutica biblica," in Tábet, *La Sacra Scrittura anima*, 107.

that contains the original text in toto. In a certain sense, the editions bear witness to *books* and not to texts. But what matters is that these texts are interpreted in accordance with the faith of the community that transmitted the books. If the text's authority is based on its status as an autographic text, then it is reasonable to question that authority, since we do not know which text the author wrote. If, on the other hand, we understand that these books were composed in a community of faith (Israel and the church) that existed before the books were produced, the authority is guaranteed by the faith of that community of believers. That is to say, the existence of a canon presupposes a community for whom it is canonical.

Theoretically, a third-century manuscript of John's Gospel found in the trash heaps of Oxyrhynchus could have been bought and read or used by a gnostic or a pagan without the need to conform to the rule of faith. The text had no authority *in se* or was limited to a subjective authority. On the other hand, for a Christian of a church in communion with other churches of the apostolic tradition, that same book (with or without the passage of the adulterous woman, with or without variants that deviate from the "original") was read as a text that came from the hands of the author to whom it was attributed and therefore had the authority of an original text. In other words, we can say that there is a relationship between the original text and the authoritative text, provided that we understand that this original text does not exist in a particular manuscript. In fact, for modern readers of a Bible version, the text before them functions as the original text when read *in ecclesia*. The authority is conferred by the community of faith that interprets that text in continuity with the original apostolic community.

It is possible to assert, therefore, that the score (the apostolic texts) is always original when interpreted by the rule of faith. As Benedict XVI points out in the apostolic exhortation *Verbum Domini*, "the Book is the very voice of the pilgrim People of God, and only within the faith of this People are we, so to speak, attuned to understand sacred Scripture."[49] The text's authority is recognized by the interpreter when the interpreter reads it with the church and in the spirit in which it was written.[50] In this sense it

---

49. Benedict XVI, *Apostolic Exhortation Verbum Domini*, n. 30.

50. Benedict XVI, *Apostolic Exhortation Verbum Domini*: "Saint Jerome recalls that we can never read Scripture simply on our own. We come up against too many closed doors and we slip too easily into error. The Bible was written by the People of God for the People of God, under the inspiration of the Holy Spirit. Only in this com-

is true that the text is a living text. The authoritative text of the Bible is not identified with a single text but is a living text in numerous manuscripts. That text in a particular manuscript is authoritative when it conforms with the apostolic community's standard of truth. It functions with the authority that corresponds to the autographic text because it makes present the apostolic figure to whom that text is attributed.

---

munion with the People of God can we truly enter as a 'we' into the heart of the truth that God himself wishes to convey to us.... An authentic interpretation of the Bible must always be in harmony with the faith of the Catholic Church." See also Second Vatican Council, Dogmatic Constitution *Dei Verbum*, n. 12.

Conclusion: The Text in the Church

We opened with a discussion of the oldest extant New Testament witnesses and underscored how their physical characteristics appear to suggest a connection to their public reading. The numerous corrections and the fact that many of these manuscripts were found in trash heaps also suggest that their readers did not have a particular veneration for the materiality of the book as a transmitter of sacred teachings. The features of the ancient codices lead us to believe that their texts were undoubtedly of value for private or catechetical reading, but for the most part they had a public function. They were conceived, above all, to be read publicly in liturgical celebrations.

1. Texts Subordinate to Orality

In a certain sense, it seems that the earliest codices represented an attempt to continue the function of the earliest Christian texts of which we have evidence, namely, to serve as a substitute for the individual. Paul's letters substituted in some way for the person of the apostle. The ancient epistolary rhetorical rule, which maintained that a letter's purpose was to make the sender present among the recipients to whom it was addressed, suggests this. The letter served as a substitute for a conversation.[1] The apostle was heard through the letters as if he were present

---

1. See, e.g., Pseudo-Libanius, Ἐπιστολιμαῖοι Χααρακτῆρες 2, in Abraham J. Malherbe, *Ancient Epistolary Theorists*, SBLSBS 19 (Scholars Press, 1998), 67. On this subject, see also Hans-Josef Klauck, *Ancient Letters and the New Testament: A Guide to Context and Exegesis* (Baylor University Press, 2006), 183–227. On the oral-performative aspect of Paul's letters, see Phil J. Botha, "The Verbal Art of the Pauline Letters," in *Rhetoric and the New Testament: Essays from the 1992 Heidelberg Conference*, ed. Stanley E. Porter and Thomas H. Olbricht, JSNTSup 90 (Sheffield University Press, 1993), 409–28.

where they were read. Analogously, we may think that the memoirs of the apostles (the use of the term ἀπομνημονεύματα in Justin's *1 Apol.* 67 appears to connote this) that were read in liturgical celebrations made the apostolic preaching present. Similarly, early Christian codices continued to give primacy to orality. The character of the written text was necessary, but it could not be dissociated from the oral origins to which it was linked.[2]

We must also consider that most people did not know how to read.[3] The texts were not for a select audience, however. The text's authority was recognized when the community listened to it. This explains why apparent discrepancies could coexist among the texts. Variants were not really serious because they were subsumed by the text as a whole (if the professional reader did not correct them on the fly).[4] Moreover, the reading required skill. It was a proclamation, an "oral performance of the text, and the

---

2. In continuity with the emphasis pointed out by Birger Gerhardsson more than four decades ago, there has been a growing interest in orality and its relationship to early Christian texts. See, e.g., Keith, *Gospel as Manuscript*, 1–14 and passim; Haines-Eitzen, "Social History," 481. Also see Eric Eve, *Writing the Gospels: Composition and Memory* (SPCK, 2016); Rafael Rodriguez, *Structuring Early Christian Memory: Jesus in Tradition, Performance and Text* (T&T Clark, 2010), 39–113; Samuel Byrskog, *Story as History—History as Story: The Gospel Tradition in the Context of Ancient Oral History*, WUNT 123 (Mohr Siebeck, 2002), 93–175; Jack Goody, *The Interface between the Written and the Oral* (Cambridge University Press, 1987).

3. Literacy in antiquity has been widely discussed. For a recent overview, see Peter Arzt-Grabner, John S. Kloppenborg, and Christina M. Kreinecker, *More Light from the Ancient East: Understanding the New Testament through Papyri* (Brill, 2023), 69–118. See also William V. Harris, *Ancient Literacy* (Harvard University Press, 1989); John H. Humphrey, *Literacy in the Roman World*, JRASup (University of Michigan Press, 1991); Alan K. Bowman and Greg Woolf, *Literacy and Power in the Ancient World* (Cambridge University Press, 1994); Alan R. Millard, *Reading and Writing at the Time of Jesus* (Sheffield University Press, 2000). Although the majority of the population could not read, there was a great interaction between orality and written text. Texts were read aloud for a variety of reasons and on different occasions so that people from all walks of life had relative access to them. The texts were written by their authors more for the ear than for the eye (see Gamble, "Literacy, Liturgy, and the Shaping," 29–30). See also Paul J. Achtemeier, "Omne Verbum Sonat: The New Testament and the Oral Environment of Late Western Antiquity," *JBL* 109 (1990): 3–27; Gamble, *Books and Readers*, 30; Keith, *Gospel as Manuscript*, 161–232.

4. See Aland, "Significance of the Chester Beatty Papyri," 117–18. It does not necessarily follow that from the fluidity of the text attested in the first two centuries, there is a fluidity of doctrine.

Conclusion: The Text in the Church

text served as the 'score.'"[5] The individual words had value in the overall framework of the passage being read. Herein lay their effectiveness. At the same time, the community determined the passage's correct meaning and declared which variants could be of importance. The community acted as the text's custodian.

An incident documented in the correspondence between Augustine and Jerome is illustrative.[6] In 403, Augustine wrote to Jerome about an upheaval that occurred during the liturgical celebration of the Christian community of Oea (present-day Tripoli, Libya). It all started when the local bishop had Jerome's new Latin translation of the book of Jonah read rather than the traditional VL version. Augustine tells Jerome that, when a word was read that was not the one that "had long been familiar to the senses and memory of all [the worshipers]" nor the one that "had been sung for so many generations in the church," there was an uproar, especially among the Greek-speaking faithful. The outcry was such that the bishop had to consult local Jews to verify the accuracy of the translation. They confirmed that the Hebrew words had been translated correctly into Greek and Latin, so, Augustine continues, the bishop had to correct Jerome's version so as not to be left without a community.

The tumult arose not because of an argument of great dogmatic weight but because of the translation of the word for the bush that shielded Jonah (Jonah 4:6–10). The Hebrew read קיקיון (*qiqiyon*), which had been translated as κολόκυνθα in the LXX and as *cucurbita* in the VL, both of which mean "gourd" and which was the reading to which Augustine's readers were accustomed. Jerome's translation in the Vulgate, however, was *hedera*, "ivy." As can be seen, the word in question did not have the slightest theological importance but caused a stir just the same, since it was not the one that had always been heard.

---

5. Gamble, "Literacy, Liturgy, and the Shaping," 35. Gamble stresses the importance of liturgical usage for establishing the canon of sacred books: "In this sense we can say with full justice that the formation of the canon of scripture was nothing other than the church's retrospective recognition of its own reading habits, whereby the *de facto* tradition was finally made *de iure*" (35). In what is stated below, I follow Gamble.

6. Augustine, *Ep.* 71A.3.5 (CCSL 31A:253); see also *Ep.* 75 (CCSL 31A:280–324). The episode is mentioned in Gamble, "Literacy, Liturgy, and the Shaping," 37–38, and in Joseph A. Fitzmyer, "A Recent Roman Scriptural Controversy," *TS* 22 (1961): 426–27.

Although the incident occurred in the early fifth century and at a time when the texts were already largely fixed, the episode illustrates the implications of the public reading of Scripture in a liturgical context. We must remember that the reading of Jonah was comparatively limited. The gospels were much better known. But the listeners had become so familiar with the passage about the plant that provided shade to the prophet that they knew it by heart and considered it untouchable. Faced with an unexpected change in what they were accustomed to hearing, the bishop, as Augustine relates, had to act "so as not to be left without people."[7]

The event demonstrates that the text's liturgical use implies repeatedly listening to the same text without devaluing its words. The Christian community of Tripoli wanted to hear the same familiar words, which shows that the role of liturgical reading is based more on the ability it has to inspire than to instruct (even if it does in fact instruct). The reading of texts that were considered normative was meant to form and reinforce the self-understanding of Christian communities. The public reading of Scripture was not about the past but also and equally about the present, to the extent that listeners understood themselves in terms of the history of Scripture.[8] That is to say, the biblical texts read in liturgical celebrations had the capacity not only to make present the event narrated in those books but also to establish continuity with the first recipients of those texts. Listening to what had long been familiar to the senses and memory of all the worshipers guaranteed the effectiveness of the word read because it put the listeners in contact with the authors who had written it and with the community that used these texts for the first time. At the same time, the episode demonstrates that the community exercised influence over the text. The scribes did not enjoy complete freedom to change texts, at least not if they intended for them to be received by the community that was to proclaim them in the liturgy.

Thus, the analysis of the oldest extant Christian manuscripts suggests (with due caution and a healthy dose of skepticism on account of methodological limitations) that during the first centuries these texts were to a

---

7. The story does not prove that the community authorized the text. It simply illustrates the power of the liturgical use of Scripture and shows that tradition and Scripture form a single deposit of the word of God entrusted to the church, where pastors and the faithful collaborate to preserve, live, and profess the faith (see Vatican II, *Dei Verbum*, n. 10).

8. Gamble, "Literacy, Liturgy, and the Shaping," 38–39.

large extent subordinate to (or circumscribed by) oral tradition and to the community that proclaimed them, since they were texts fundamentally to be read in liturgical settings.[9]

In a certain sense, Guy Stroumsa's representation of the Christian religion can be recalled here: by using codices that had a popular character and reached an enormous diffusion, Christianity is not a religion of the book but of the *paperback*.[10] The image is illustrative of the function that books had and have in Christianity, but it does not go far enough. We ought to recognize that the Christian religion is not a religion of the book, nor of the *paperback*, but a religion of the living text, of the Word incarnated and proclaimed.[11] And any private reading was mediated by public reading.

2. Community Texts

We have also seen that some of the variants in the different papyri and other ancient manuscripts are not simply the result of scribal copying errors but also of the oral or textual influences of other writings or even of

---

9. This does not signify the devaluation of the written text. As indicated by Keith, "*What Christians did with manuscripts of the Gospels* was an articulation of early Christian identity separately from, though ultimately in conjunction with, the narrative content of those manuscripts. The reading of the Gospels alongside, or in rotation with, Jewish Scripture in assembly reflected a Christ-oriented reading culture that continued and developed the Jewish practice of reading sacred texts in community, but was simultaneously distinct from that of Jews for whom the gospel narratives of Jesus of Nazareth did not function in an authoritative capacity. The public reading of the Gospels was thus a key social arena in which their authoritative status came to be actualized" (*Gospel as Manuscript*, 230, italics original).

10. Guy G. Stroumsa, "Early Christianity: A Religion of the Book?," in Finkelberg and Stroumsa, *Homer, the Bible, and Beyond*, 173. See also Stroumsa, *The End of Sacrifice: Religious Transformations in Late Antiquity*, trans. Susan Emanuel (University of Chicago Press, 2009), 43.

11. See Benedict XVI, *Apostolic Exhortation Verbum Domini*, n. 7, who quotes Saint Bernard of Clairvaux, *Hom. sup.* 4.11 (PL 183:86B). In his sermon, the saint places these words on the lips of the Virgin Mary: "And let Him not become for me a written and silent word, but a Word incarnate and living: that is to say, not a word inscribed in dumb characters upon dead parchment, but the Word of God in human form impressed upon the living page of my chaste bosom, impressed, I say, not by the agency of mortal hand, but by the operation of the Holy Spirit." Trans. *St. Bernard's Sermons for the Seasons and Principal Festivals of the Year*, ed. a priest of Mount Melleray (Carroll, 1950), 131. See also 4 n. 7.

a diversity of traditions existing in the communities to which the copyists of those texts belonged. Given that texts were altered as they were copied, it seems implausible to hold that there was not some kind of control over them. We have already seen what happened in Tripoli as a result of such an apparently irrelevant change. It is difficult to imagine that scribes or copyists decided on their own to delete or add a long passage or a relevant expression without the backing of a community (this does not mean, of course, that there could not be cases of a total lack of control). In this sense, Ehrman has a point. Manuscripts are witnesses to the lives of scribes who inhabit a particular social world. But the copyists were also part of a community that was engaging writings that furnished the reason for its identity with oral traditions about faith, worship, and praxis (not to say that these traditions were always uniform). In other words, texts were not the sole guarantor of what was to be believed and lived. There were contrasting traditions (of the oral type) that could be at their same level and which conditioned how the texts were copied.[12]

The various textual variants, especially those with more or less clear theological implications, show that respect for the text coexists with the need to adapt it to the lived community's circumstances at a given moment. The same variants, however, show that a large part of the changes stem from harmonization not with any text but with texts that were equally authoritative as the one being copied.[13] As we have seen with the gospels, the oldest papyri betray the influence of the other gospels, especially Matthew. Even the earliest witnesses to preserve noncanonical gospels show the influence of the one gospel that was manifested in the four canonical ones.[14] In a certain sense, the phenomenon of harmonization shows that

---

12. See Roli Dela Cruz, "Allegory, Mimesis and the Text: Theological Moulding of the Lukan Parables in Codex Bezae Cantabrigiensis" (PhD diss., University of Birmingham, 2004), 283–84: "For the 'textual tradition' is not only understood as a transmission of the 'letters' of the 'text' understood within the context of a language—the general working assumption of philological approach—but rather as a 'tradition' that could only be passed on with the accepted 'interpretation.'"

13. Theoretically we do not know the type of Christian community reflected in each manuscript. We have no data to discern which papyri were copied and transmitted in some kind of marginal group.

14. Think, for example, of noncanonical gospel texts such as P.Egerton 2 or the Secret Gospel of Mark or the Gospel of Peter, in spite of some proposals—without much foundation—that believe these to be earlier and to have influenced the canonical ones (see, e.g., Koester, *Ancient Christian Gospels*).

the gospel that was copied was the one tetramorphic gospel (i.e., the gospel in four forms).

It is true that what has been said by the authors discussed above can be applied to a certain degree to what was happening at the end of the second or beginning of the third century. However, would this have been the case prior to the second-century threshold? Is it not possible that previously there was no control whatsoever and that the gospels, for example, did not have their present form but would have been a mixture of magmatic and malleable texts in keeping with the tastes of the different scribes or communities? And if we admit this possibility, should we be content with affirming that the only thing that can be known of the text of the gospels or of other New Testament writings is found in the scarce and not very precise quotations of the fathers and ecclesiastical writers of the second century?[15]

It is true that from the end of the first century and almost all of the second century we have no evidence that the gospels existed in a form that more or less corresponds with or is even close to what they are today. What we do know is that a particular gospel text did not come from the hand of the first author as we have it today in our critical editions, a fact that any literary, exegetical, or theological interpretation of the gospels must consider.[16] This does not mean, of course, that one should adopt a radically skeptical attitude. It is true that, following the example of the gospels, we do not know exactly how these texts, which have come down to us as a single gospel according to four testimonies attributed to relevant figures in apostolic times, originated. But it does seem possible to assert, from the transmitted manuscripts, that the evidence favors texts whose original forms (in general terms) must not have been too different from the text we currently possess. This does not preclude that they could have been reedited and modified by their authors or by their disciples some years after their original composition or that, in certain cases, after a longer period of time, they underwent retouches and additions. What seems likely is that

---

15. For the treatment of quotations in the fathers, see. Hill, "'In These Very Words,'" 261–81. Among other things, he suggests that the various quotations from the gospels (and especially the harmonizations) need not necessarily reflect an uncontrolled text but a text revered as authoritative (270–72).

16. In this sense, the implications of textual criticism for history, literary criticism, exegesis, and theology mentioned in previous chapters are illustrative (see Parker, *Introduction to the New Testament Manuscripts*, 181–89).

they must have soon adopted the form of a book similar to the present one and were accordingly copied with the care with which other books of their time were copied, a task that certainly admitted varying degrees of professionalism and fidelity.

In the first centuries of our era, books were not copied with the exact fidelity that subsequently prevailed in Western culture. Besides exposure to the usual dangers that Origen and other ancient ecclesiastical writers identified (i.e., inaccurate transcription, revisions with omissions or additions, error in attributing their paternity, etc.), the apostolic texts were not always revised and corrected, or duly revised and duly corrected, comparing what was copied with other manuscripts of the same work. Not even the assumption that these writings were considered sacred guaranteed that they could not be modified.[17] In any case, it is unlikely that the correction of a text was purely the result of an educated guess.[18]

The data suggest that the texts that later entered the canon were copied, like many other texts of their time. The gospels, however, which pagans would likely have understood as a Life of Jesus, were not subject to continuous rewriting, as was the case with the Life of Aesop, for example. Nor do they present the kind of wide variations found in other books, as was the case in a manual of rhetoric attributed to Aelius Aristides or in the acts of pagan or Christian martyrs. It is possible that in some cases the scribes' lack of professionalism is responsible for remarkable textual variation.[19] But the gospel papyri do not show a greater lack of care than is

---

17. See Michael J. Kruger, "Early Christian Attitudes toward the Reproduction of Texts," in Hill and Kruger, *Early Text of the New Testament*, 64–66.

18. Harry Y. Gamble further notes, "To this end the methods of textual, philological, and literary criticism developed mainly by the Alexandrian grammarians began to be employed by educated Christians as early as the 2nd cent." See Gamble, "The Book Trade in the Roman Empire," in Hill and Kruger, *Early Text of the New Testament*, 36 n. 43. Turner, *Greek Manuscripts of the Ancient World*, 108: "The writers of these early papyri felt no compulsion to copy accurately because they did not regard the exact expression (especially the order of words) of the author as sacred.... In the Roman period, on the other hand, there is a steady respect for the authority of the text. It is hard not to ascribe a large share of the credit for this change to the scholars of Alexandria."

19. Parsons, "People of the Book?," 52. Moreover, they were not textbooks used in school. And in times of persecution they might have had to be hidden. Perhaps they were spread by chain transmission for particular uses, and in this process it is easy for variants to be introduced (see Haines-Eitzen, *Guardians of Letters*, 77–104).

found, for example, in the papyri of Demosthenes.[20] It is a copy of a copy, wherein diverse readings were introduced simultaneously with new ones. Each papyrus then potentially offers the possibility of an original reading. Peter Parsons's image is illustrative: several dishes can be served from the same bowl of minestrone; each dish will have a unique texture, even if they all come from the same pot.[21] Further research is therefore necessary to determine whether the oldest Christian literary texts were transmitted in a manner different from other texts of the time or whether they simply represent a particular case within the general phenomenon whereby each copy is different from the other due to scribal error or intervention.

Nevertheless, what we can say is that what differentiates the most ancient papyri of the books that eventually formed the New Testament from manuscripts of literary works of the time is that the former were read in communities that were not simply governed by those texts. Rather, the faith traditions of those communities, which were similar to the traditions of other Christian communities, were inseparable from their texts and even interacted with them.[22] In that sense, each individual text (with or without Mark's long ending, with or without the pericope of the adulterous woman, with varying degrees of variation) constituted the original text of a gospel when read according to those traditions.[23] On the other hand, it is hypothetically possible that some of the gospel papyri that have come down to us belonged to learned pagans who read them with curiosity, as they might read a novel by Achilles Tatius.[24] In such cases, a reference to the original is irrelevant. That particular writing functions as a more or less exact text to an earlier copy. It does not need to be measured against or read in light of a rule of faith by the learned pagan. But if the copy of a gospel, with many or few additions, changes, or omissions, is to be understood as a writing that is part of a tradition that goes beyond particular texts and is not limited to them, the character of original text is,

---

20. Parsons, "People of the Book?," 53.

21. Parsons, "People of the Book?," 53–54.

22. For communication between different communities, see Stephen R. Llewelyn, "The Conveyance of Letters," *NewDocs* 7:1–57; Llewelyn, "Sending Letters in the Ancient World," *TynBul* 46 (1995): 337–56; Epp, "New Testament Papyrus Manuscripts," 43–51.

23. See above under "Text, Canon, and Rule of Faith."

24. This genre of romance literature has also appeared among the Oxyrhynchus trash: P.Oxy. 56.3836; 10.1250 (Achilles Tatius); 41.2948; 7.1019 (Chariton, *Chereas and Callirroe*); 3.416, 417; etc.

so to speak, guaranteed. It is endorsed by the faith professed by the reader within the community that has given rise to these books.

3. The *Kenosis* of the Word Made Ink and Papyrus

In the previous discussion of theologically motivated variants, we alluded to the *Ecce homo* passage from John's Gospel and how Bultmann saw the scandal of the incarnation in this outraged man. The Word of God has condescended to unimaginable extremes. This self-abasement, however, is not limited to the incarnation. As attested in antiquity, it also occurs in Scripture. The colophon of a twelfth-century Armenian gospel, for example, appears to imply that the Word has also "become incarnate" in the text. The scribe responsible for the colophon claims "to have changed the words of Him, who is Spirit and Life, into a body."[25] In this case, the body is the book that he has copied. The identification of the written word with Christ's body transforms the codex into the bearer of the "Word incarnate" and, as such, a sacred object worthy of veneration.[26] Now, when the scribe of this copy affirms that the codex materializes and incarnates the Word of God (to the point of becoming tangible in a text), the scribe may be reflecting a textual monophysitism consistent with the christological perspectives that prevailed in the manuscript's provenance. That is to say, the colophon may be understood to say that the eternal Word has been absorbed—identified with that concrete text—to the point of justifying that text's absolutization in its wording.

Parker rightly reacts against this danger. Establishing an analogy with the incarnation, Parker also excludes what he dubs "text-critical docetism," which is another way of describing the Armenian scribe's text-critical monophysitism. The Word of God, Parker affirms, does not exist without the materiality of each manuscript's ink and papyrus.[27] Indeed, if the text is

---

25. Quoted in Wallraff, *Kodex und Kanon*, 53.
26. See John Lowden, "The Word Made Visible," in Klingshirn and Safran, *Early Christian Book*, 13–47. See also Luijendijk, "Sacred Scriptures as Trash," 232–33.
27. David C. Parker, "Et incarnatus est," in *Manuscripts, Texts, Theology*, 314: "The incarnation provides a precise analogy to the Gospels which exist only as manuscripts, as ink and papyrus. God is not behind or beyond the Word made flesh, but the Word made flesh is God. In the same way, the text of the Gospels is not beyond the manuscripts. It is not the surviving manuscripts that are meant here, though for us perhaps it might as well be, but all those manuscripts, lost or extant, in which the Gospels have

Conclusion: The Text in the Church

a manifestation of the Word of God's *kenosis*, we cannot elevate it to the category of a divine text and endow it with an absolute value free of cultural or historical conditioning.[28] The exegete and the theologian cannot dispense with this reality. But if, in fact, we must discard all text-critical docetism and monophysitism, then (expanding Parker's analogy) we should also reject a text-critical adoptionism that reduces the Word to a text, that is, a text identified with the materiality of a concrete codex but elevated to divine status by the sublimity of its message. God's Word is not simply or only a text. Although the Word of God has condescended to the point of becoming a text, it is not reduced to ink and papyrus. God has become incarnate in human language, taking on the properties of units of meaning within human language so that God may be understood.[29] That Word converted into a text cannot be dissociated from the meaning given to it by the author or authors of that text, nor from the meaning given to it by the community from which it emerged. It is the living Word of God that becomes present to a people, both in the Eucharist and in the sacred writings. The Scriptures, insofar as they bear witness to the Spirit, are inseparably linked to the place where God's Word is at work. As Benedict XVI states in the prologue to his first volume on Jesus of Nazareth, "The Scripture emerged from within the heart of a living subject—the pilgrim People of God—and lives within this same subject.... [Its authors] form part of a collective subject, the 'People of God,' from within whose heart and to whom they speak. Hence, this subject is actually the deeper 'author' of the Scriptures. And yet likewise, this people does not exist alone; rather, it knows that it is led, and spoken to, by God himself, who—through men and their humanity—is at the deepest

---

ever existed. Text-critical docetism is quite out of order. The Gospels exist, we might say, as *real* ink and papyrus" (italics original).

28. See John Paul II, *Address to the Pontifical Biblical Commission*, 23 April 1993, n. 8.

29. This is what *Dei Verbum*, n. 13, teaches: "In Sacred Scripture ... while the truth and holiness of God always remains intact, the marvelous 'condescension' of eternal wisdom is clearly shown, 'that we may learn the gentle kindness of God, which words cannot express, and how far He has gone in adapting His language with thoughtful concern for our weak human nature.' (St. John Chrysostom, *In Genesis* 3, 8 [Homily 17, 1]: PG 53, 134; *Attemperatio* [in English 'Suitable adjustment'] in Greek *synkatabasis*.) For the words of God, expressed in human language, have been made like human discourse, just as the word of the eternal Father, when He took to Himself the flesh of human weakness, was in every way made like men." Paul VI, *Dei Verbum*, 18 November 1965, https://tinyurl.com/SBL7016l.

level the one speaking."[30] The papyri that transmit the New Testament texts, more than bearers of a living text, bear witness to the Word that is both alive and life giving. They bear witness to the fact that Scripture cannot be simultaneously a divine and static text. That biblical texts presumed to be authoritative were translated into other languages from the earliest stages demonstrates the living character of Scripture. They were incapable of becoming a crystallized text in gilded letters.

It is likely that most readers of the versions did not question whether their text was *the* perfect and authoritative translation.[31] Translated texts could not be separated from the original matrix (i.e., the church). The Word of God is *attested* by various manuscripts, none of which guarantee transmitting the text as it came from the holy author's hand. And yet, since the Bible's human authors are also part of a living community of believers (Israel for the Hebrew Scriptures and the church for the New Testament), that community serves as the text's true interpreter and establisher of its authoritative status. The community is an interpretative community. And the Bible's early translations demonstrate that that community's text could be updated in the living community of faith. The ancient translator considered the text to be translated as the original text because it was read *in ecclesia*.[32]

The text-critical problems that appear in the manuscript tradition and that, as we have seen, are also attested in translations highlight once again the important role of oral tradition in interpreting Scripture. This is an

---

30. Ratzinger, *Jesus of Nazareth*, xx–xxi.

31. This is not to say that there were not those who did take care to ensure that the translation was faithful, at least in later times. See, e.g., Augustine, *Doctr. chr.* 2.13.19: "But since we do not clearly see what the actual thought is which the several translators endeavor to express, each according to his own ability and judgment, unless we examine it in the language which they translate; and since the translator, if he be not a very learned man, often departs from the meaning of his author, we must either endeavor to get a knowledge of those languages from which the Scriptures are translated into Latin, or we must get hold of the translations of those who keep rather close to the letter of the original, not because these are sufficient, but because we may use them to correct the freedom or the error of others, who in their translations have chosen to follow the sense quite as much as the words" (trans. *NPNF* 1/2:541).

32. See Chapa, "Texto autoritativo y crítica textual," 170–76. See also the observations of Vicente Balaguer on how historical studies "show that what is transmitted is not so much Scripture as an object but Scripture interpreted" ("La Sagrada Escritura *una cum Sacra Traditione* ante el reto de la *sola Scriptura*," *ScrTh* 49 [2017]: 192).

essential feature of Christian origins, but it has never ceased to be present in the interpretation of the biblical text. The subject of the tradition, that is, the church, as a depository of faith contained in the apostolic tradition[33] and Scripture, lives from particular texts and is continually renewed by those texts, but it also maintains its vitality through that same tradition as the guarantor of interpretation in the church. The written text and the living tradition are inseparable. They coexist in tension and are interdependent. Cardinal Ratzinger's words are illustrative:

> In the process of critical exegesis on the nature of the biblical Word ... we have become aware that the biblical Word, at the moment of its written fixation, has already undergone a more or less long process of oral configuration, and that, when it was put into writing, it did not remain solidified, but entered into new processes of interpretation—*relectures*—, which further developed its hidden potentialities. The extension, therefore, of the meaning of the Word cannot be reduced to the thought of a singular author of a given historical moment. Moreover, the Word does not belong to a single author, but lives in a history that progresses, and possesses, therefore, an extension and a depth towards the past and towards the future that are finally lost in the unforeseeable.[34]

The church cannot dispense with the study of the Bible since it must remain informed about what God and the human authors have said. Textual criticism allows us to get to know the text of particular books in substance, as they were composed and received by the faith community from which they came. But the discipline will never be entirely certain that its text was the one written by the author. Major and/or minor alterations will have occurred at the earliest stages of transmission. The original text is accordingly an elusive ideal, one to which textual critics may aspire but can never satisfactorily attain. In fact, the very presence of variants cautions against treating the text as a procrustean bed for theological speculation without considering the dynamics and richness of its transmission history.

At the same time, the text's emergence from and indebtedness to the church (its original matrix) commends the rule of faith as the neces-

---

33. The apostolic tradition has its origin in the historical fact of Jesus and presupposes a paradosis linked to the apostolic succession, constitutive of the *regula fidei*, or "rule of faith."

34. Joseph Ratzinger, "Discurso en la Investidura de Doctor 'Honoris Causa' del Cardenal Joseph Ratzinger en la Universidad de Navarra," *ScrTh* 30 (1998): 390.

sary and proper advocate of the authority of the text. The rule of faith's endorsement of the text's authority allows us to understand inspiration as inseparably linked to the church's faith, the guarantor of a given text's inspiration. That is to say, if the inspired character of a text were dependent on a textual reconstruction based on historical-critical criteria, the inspiration of particular passages or words would always remain in doubt. On the other hand, when the text is linked to the faith community that produced it and is read in communion with the church, we have the certainty that God has spoken and continues speaks through and in that text.

Textual criticism cannot have the final word on the question of textual authority. Textual critics should therefore consider it one of a number of tools in the study of Scripture rather than assume that philological and historical methods provide the ultimate understanding of the Bible. Textual scholars ought to concede that textual authority derives ultimately from the church, which recognizes that God speaks in those texts. An understanding of Scripture in the church should therefore situate the study of the text after the study of inspiration and canon. The move signals that the Bible's authority as God's Word depends on the church's recognition that that text is indeed the Word of God. This does not mean that the Bible submits to the church. Rather, because the Bible is born and grows in her, the church does not diminish Scripture by circumscribing it to a hypothetical text, but rather the church lets Scripture be what it is and have the authority it has.

Bibliography

Achtemeier, Paul J. "Omne Verbum Sonat: The New Testament and the Oral Environment of Late Western Antiquity." *JBL* 109 (1990): 3–27.

Aland, Barbara. "The Significance of the Chester Beatty Papyri in Early Church History." Pages 108–21 in *The Earliest Gospels: The Origins and Transmission of the Earliest Christian Gospels; The Contribution of the Chester Beatty Gospel Codex P45*. Edited by Charles Horton. JSNTSup 258. T&T Clark, 2004.

Aland, Kurt. "Über die Möglichkeit der Identifikation kleiner Fragmente neutestamentlicher Handschriften mit Hilfe des Computers." Pages 14–38 in *Studies in New Testament Language and Text: Essays in Honour of George D. Kilpatrick on the Occasion of His Sixty-Fifth Birthday*. Edited by J. Keith Elliott. NovTSup 44. Brill, 1976.

Aland, Kurt, and Barbara Aland. *The Text of the New Testament: An Introduction to the Critical Editions and to the Theory and Practice of Modern Textual Criticism*. 2nd ed. Translated by Erroll F. Rhodes. Eerdmans, 1989.

Alexander, Loveday. "Ancient Book-Production and the Circulation of the Gospels." Pages 71–111 in *The Gospels for All Christians: Rethinking the Gospel Audiences*. Edited by Richard Bauckham. Eerdmans, 1997.

American and British Committees of the International Greek New Testament Project, eds. *The New Testament in Greek: The Gospel according to St. Luke*. 2 vols. Oxford University Press, 1984–1987.

Aranda, Gonzalo. "Il problema teologico del canone biblico." Pages 13–35 in *La Sacra Scrittura anima della teologia: Pontificia Università della Santa Croce; Facoltà di Teologia. Atti del IV Simposio Internazionale della Facoltà di Teologia*. Edited by Miguel Ángel Tábet. Librería Editrice Vaticana, 1999.

Arzt-Grabner, Peter, John S. Kloppenborg, and Christina M. Kreinecker. *More Light from the Ancient East: Understanding the New Testament through Papyri*. Brill, 2023.

Askeland, Christian. "A Coptic Papyrus without John 21?" Pages 93–108 in *The New Testament in Antiquity and Byzantium: A Festschrift for Klaus Wachtel*. Edited by Hugh A. G. Houghton, David C. Parker, and Holger Strutwolf. ANTF 52. De Gruyter, 2020.

Augustine. *The Works of Saint Augustine*. Vol. 7. Translated by Edmund Hill, OP. New City, 1993.

"Ausblick: Nestle-Aland 29." Deutsche Bibel Gesellschaft. https://tinyurl.com/SBL7016d.

Baarda, Tjitze. "Jesus and Mary (John 20 16f.) in the Second Epistle on Virginity Ascribed to Clement." Pages 11–34 in *Studien zum Text und zur Ethik des Neuen Testaments: Festschrift zum 80. Geburtstag von Heinrich Greeven*. Edited by Wolfgang Schrage. BZNW 47. De Gruyter, 1986.

———. "Mk 1:41: ὀργισθείς: A Reading Attested for Mar Ephraem, the Diatessaron, or Tatian." *ZNW* 103 (2012): 291–95.

Bagnall, Roger S. *Early Christian Books in Egypt*. Princeton University Press, 2009.

Balaguer, Vicente. "La economía de la Palabra de Dios: A los 40 años de la Constitución dogmática Dei Verbum." *ScrTh* 37 (2005): 407–39.

———. "La Sagrada Escritura *una cum Sacra Traditione* ante el reto de la *sola Scriptura*." *ScrTh* 37 (2017): 171–92.

Barker, Don C. "The Dating of New Testament Papyri." *NTS* 57 (2011): 571–82.

Barrett, Charles K. "Is There a Theological Tendency in Codex Bezae?" Pages 15–27 in *Text and Interpretation: Studies in the New Testament Presented to Matthew Black*. Edited by Ernest Best and Robert McL. Wilson. Cambridge University Press, 1979.

Barthélemy, Dominique. "L'enchevêtrement de l'histoire textuelle et de l'histoire littéraire dans les relations entre la Septante et le texte massorétique." Pages 21–40 in *De Septuaginta: Studies in Honor of John William Wevers on His Sixty-Fifth Birthday*. Edited by Albert Pietersma and Claude Cox. Benben, 1984.

Barton, John. *The Spirit and the Letter*. SPCK, 1997.

Batovici, Dan. "Reading Aids in Early Christian Papyri." Pages 35–50 in *From Scrolls to Scrolling: Sacred Texts, Materiality and Dynamic Media Cultures*. Edited by Bradford A. Anderson. De Gruyter, 2020.

Benedict XVI. *Apostolic Exhortation Verbum Domini*. September 30, 2010. https://tinyurl.com/SBL7016a.

Berrouard, Marie-François. *Oeuvres de saint Augustin. Homélies sur l'Evangile de saint Jean LV–LXXIX: Traduction, introduction et notes.* BA 74a. Institut des Études Augustiniennes, 1993.

Beutler, Johannes. *A Commentary on the Gospel of John.* Eerdmans, 2017.

Bieringer, Reimund. "Noli me tangere and the New Testament: An Exegetical Approach." Pages 13–28 in *"Noli me tangere": Mary Magdalene; One Person, Many Images.* By Barbara Baert, Reimund Bieringer, Karlijn Demasure, and Sabine Van Den Eynde. Peeters, 2006.

Black, David A., and Jacob N. Cerone, eds. *The Pericope of the Adulteress in Contemporary Research.* Bloomsbury, 2016.

Blanchard, Alain, ed. *Les débuts du codex.* Brepols, 1989.

Blumell, Lincoln H. *Lettered Christians: Christians, Letters, and Late Antique Oxyrhynchus.* NTTSD 39. Brill, 2012.

Blumell, Lincoln H., and Thomas A. Wayment, eds. *Christian Oxyrhynchus: Texts, Documents, and Sources.* Baylor University Press, 2015.

Boismard, Marie-Émile. "Le chapitre XXI de saint Jean: essai de critique littéraire." *RB* 54 (1947): 473–501.

Bokedal, Tomas. *The Formation and Significance of the Christian Biblical Canon: A Study in Text, Ritual and Interpretation.* Bloomsbury T&T Clark, 2014.

Bori, Pier C. "Attualità di un detto antico?, 'La sacra Scrittura cresce con chi la legge.'" *Intersezioni* 6 (1986): 15–49.

———. "Circolarità e sviluppo nell'interpretazione spiritual: 'Divina eloquia cum legente crescent,' Gregorio M., In Hiez. I, VII, 8." *ASE* 2 (1985): 263–74.

———. *L'interpretazione infinita. L'ermeneutica cristiana e le sue trasformazioni.* Il Mulino, 1987.

Botha, Phil J. "The Verbal Art of the Pauline Letters." Pages 409–28 in *Rhetoric and the New Testament: Essays from the 1992 Heidelberg Conference.* Edited by Stanley E. Porter and Thomas H. Olbricht. JSNTSup 90. Sheffield University Press, 1993.

Bowman, Alan K., Revel A. Coles, Nick Gonis, Dirk Obbink, and Peter J. Parsons, eds. *Oxyrhynchus: A City and Its Texts.* Egyptian Exploration Society, 2007.

Bowman, Alan K., and Greg Woolf. *Literacy and Power in the Ancient World.* Cambridge University Press, 1994.

Breed, Brennan W. *Nomadic Text: A Theory of Biblical Reception History.* Indiana University Press, 2014.

———. "What Can a Text Do? Reception History as an Ethology of the Biblical Text." Pages 95–109 in *Reception History and Biblical Studies: Theory and Practice*. Edited by Emma England and William J. Lyons. Bloomsbury, 2015.

Brown, Raymond E. *I–XII*. Vol. 1 of *The Gospel according to John*. Yale University Press, 1995.

Brown, Raymond E., Joseph A. Fitzmyer, and Roland E. Murphy, eds. *The New Jerome Biblical Commentary*. Prentice Hall, 1990.

Bryant, John. *The Fluid Text: A Theory of Revision and Editing for Book and Screen*. University of Michigan Press, 2002.

Bultmann, Rudolf. *The Gospel of John: A Commentary*. Translated by George R. Beasley-Murray. Basil Blackwell, 1971.

———. *Theology of the New Testament*. Vol. 2. Translated by Kendrick Grobel. SCM, 1965.

Burton, Philip. "The Latin Version of the New Testament." Pages 167–200 in *The Text of the New Testament in Contemporary Research*. 2nd rev. ed. Edited by Bart D. Ehrman and Michael W. Holmes. NTTSD 42. Brill, 2013.

Byrskog, Samuel. *Story as History—History as Story: The Gospel Tradition in the Context of Ancient Oral History*. WUNT 123. Mohr Siebeck, 2002.

Campenhausen, Hans von. *The Formation of the Christian Bible*. Translated by John A. Baker. Fortress, 1972.

Caragounis, Chrys. "What Did Jesus Mean by τὴν ἀρχήν in John 8:25?." *NovT* 49 (2007): 129–47.

Carbajosa, Ignacio. *De la fe nace la exegesis: La interpretación de la Escritura a la luz de la historia de la investigación sobre el Antiguo Testamento*. EstBib 43. Verbo Divino, 2011.

———. "El texto de la Biblia y la crítica textual." Pages 411–652 in *La Biblia en su entorno*. By Ignacio Carbajosa, Joaquin González Echegaray, and Francisco Varo. 2nd ed. Editorial Verbo Divina, 2013.

———. *Hebraica veritas versus Septuaginta auctoritatem: Does a Canonical Text of the Old Testament Exist?* Translated by Paul Stevenson. Pickwick, 2024.

———. "La vida de los manuscritos bíblicos: Cuando la tradición de lectura se hace Escritura." *EstBib* 71 (2013): 169–99.

Carbajosa, Ignacio, Joaquin González Echegaray, and Francisco Varo. *La Biblia en su entorno*. IEB 1. Verbo Divino, 1992.

———. *La Biblia en su entorno*. 2nd ed. Editorial Verbo Divina, 2013.

Cavallo, Guglielmo. "Between Volume and Codex: Reading in the Roman World." Pages 64–89 in *A History of Reading in the West*. Edited by Cavallo and Roger Chartier. Polity, 1999.

Cerquiglini, Bernard. *Éloge de la variante: Historire critique de la philologie*. Seuil, 1989.

Chapa, Juan. "Book Format, Patterns of Reading, and the Bible: The Impact of the Codex." *Segno & Testo* 16 (2018): 131–53.

———. "The Contribution of Papyrology in the Interpretation of the Gospels." Pages 128–40 in *The Gospels: History and Christology. The Search of Joseph Ratzinger—Benedict XVI*. Edited by Bernardo Estrada, Ermenegildo Manicardi, and Armand Puig i Tàrrech. Libreri a Edítrice Vaticana, 2013.

———. "De la letra al Espíritu pasando por la historia." *CTeo* 43 (2018): 73–96.

———. "Early Christian Book Production and the Concept of Canon." Pages 271–88 in *Authoritative Writings in Early Judaism and Early Christianity Their Origin, Collection, and Meaning*. Edited by Tobias Nicklas and Jens Schröter. Mohr Siebeck, 2020.

———. "The Early Text of John." Pages 140–56 in *The Early Text of the New Testament*. Edited by Charles E. Hill and Michael J. Kruger. Oxford University Press, 2012.

———. "The 'Jewish' LXX Papyri from Oxyrhynchus: Witnesses of Ways That Did Not Part?" *SJOT* 35 (2021): 207–29.

———. "La Biblia en la formulación y la comprensión de la fe." Pages 263–94 in *La Sagrada Escritura, Palabra actual*. Edited by Juan Luis Caballero. Palabra actual, 2005.

———. "La materialidad de la Palabra." *EstBib* 69 (2011): 9–37.

———. "Texto autoritativo y crítica textual: Implicaciones teológicas del concepto 'texto original' del Nuevo Testamento." Pages 153–76 in *Revelación, Escritura, Interpretación: Estudios en honor del Prof. D. Gonzalo Aranda Pérez*. Edited by Fernando Milán. Eunsa, 2014.

———. "Textual Transmission of Canonical and Apocryphal Writings within the Development of the New Testament Canon: Limits and Possibilities." *EC* 7 (2016): 113–33.

Charlesworth, Scott D. *Early Christian Gospels*. PF 47. Edizioni Gonnelli, 2016.

———. "Indicators of 'Catholicity' in Early Gospel Manuscripts." Pages 37–48 in *The Early Text of the New Testament*. Edited by Charles E. Hill and Michael J. Kruger. Oxford University Press, 2012.

———. "Public and Private: Second- and Third-Century Gospel Manuscripts." Pages 148–75 in *Jewish and Christian Scripture as Artifact and Canon*. Edited by Craig A. Evans and H. Daniel Zacharias. LSTS 70. T&T Clark, 2009.

———. "T. C. Skeat, P64, P67 and P4, and the Problem of Fibre Orientation in Codicological Reconstruction." *NTS* 53 (2007): 582–604.

Clivaz, Claire. "The Angel and the Sweat Like 'Drops of Blood' (Lk 22:43–44): 𝔓⁶⁹ and f^{13}." *HTR* 98 (2005): 419–40.

———. *L'ange et la sueur de sange (Lc 22, 43–44) ou comment on pourrait bien encore écrire l'histoire*. BTS 7. Peeters, 2010.

———. "The New Testament in the Time of the Egyptian Papyri: Reflections Based on P12, P75 and P126 (P.Amh. 3B, P.Bod. XIV–XV and PSI 1497)." Pages 17–55 in *Reading the New Testament Papyri in Context: Lire les papyrus du Nouveau Testament dans leur context*. Edited by Claire Clivaz and Jean Zumstein. BETL 242. Peeters, 2011.

Colwell, Ernest C. "Method in Evaluating Scribal Habits: A Study of P45, P66, P75." Pages 106–24 in *Studies in Methodology in Textual Criticism of the New Testament*. NTTS 9. Eerdmans, 1969.

Congar, Yves M. J. *La tradition et les traditions*. Artheme Fayard, 1960–1963.

Coogan, Jeremiah. *Eusebius the Evangelist: Rewriting the Fourfold Gospel in Late Antiquity*. Oxford University Press, 2022.

———. "Gospel as Recipe Book: Nonlinear Reading and Practical Texts in Late Antiquity." *EC* 12 (2021): 40–60.

———. "Rethinking Adoptionism: An Argument for Dismantling a Dubious Category." *SJT* 76 (2023): 1–13.

Cosaert, Carl P. "Clement of Alexandria's Gospel Citations." Pages 393–413 in *The Early Text of the New Testament*. Edited by Charles E. Hill and Michael J. Kruger. Oxford University Press, 2012

Crawford, Matthew R. *The Eusebian Canon Tables: Ordering Textual Knowledge in Late Antiquity*. Oxford University Press, 2019.

Crawford, Sidnie White. *Rewriting Scripture in Second Temple Times*. Eerdmans, 2008.

Cribiore, Raffaella. "Higher Education in Early Byzantine Egypt: Rhetoric, Latin, and the Law." Pages 47–66 in *Egypt in the Byzantine World, 300–700*. Edited by Roger S. Bagnall. Cambridge University Press, 2007.

———. *Writing, Teachers, and Students in Graeco-Roman Egypt*. ASP 36. Scholars Press, 1996.

Crisci, Edoardo. "I più antichi codici miscellanei greci." Pages 109–44 in *Il codice miscellaneo. Tipologie e fanzioni. Atti del Convegno internazionale (Cassino 14–17 maggio 2003)*. Edited by Crisci and Oronzo Pecere. Universitá degli Studi di Cassino, 2004.

Crisp, Simon. "Eugene Nida and the UBS Greek New Testament." Pages 89–105 in *Βιβλικές μεταφράσεις – Ιστορία και πράξη: Επετειακός επιστημονικός τόμος για τα διακόσια χρόνια της Ελληνικής Βιβλικής Εταιρίας*. Edited by Maria Schick and Kostas Tsiknakis. Athens, 2021.

Cromwell, Jennifer. "Following in Father's Footsteps: The Question of Father-Son Training in Eighth Century Thebes." Pages 149–57 in *Actes du 26e Congrès international de papyrologie. Genève, 16–21 août 2010*. Edited by Paul Schubert. University of Geneva Press, 2012.

Cyril of Alexandria. *Commentary on the Gospel according to S. John*. Translated by Philip E. Pusey. LFHCC 1. Parker, 1874.

Daniel, Robert W. "Palaeography and Gerontology: The Subscriptions of Hermas Son of Ptolemaios." *ZPE* 167 (2008): 151–52.

Deiana, Giovanni. *Introduzione alla Sacra Scrittura alla luce Della "Dei Verbum."* Urbaniana University Press, 2009.

Dela Cruz, Roli. "Allegory, Mimesis and the Text: Theological Moulding of the Lukan Parables in Codex Bezae Cantabrigiensis." PhD diss., University of Birmingham, 2004.

Dormandy, Michael. "How the Books Became the Bible: The Evidence for Canon Formation from Work-Combinations in Manuscripts." *TC* 23 (2018). https://tinyurl.com/SBL7016j.

Duncker, Peter G. "De singulis S. Scripturae libris controversis in Concilio Tridentino." Pages 66–93 in *Miscellanea biblica et orientalia Athanasio Miller completis LXX annis oblata*. Edited by Adalberti Metzinger. Herder, 1951.

Ehrman, Bart D. "Jesus and the Adulteress." *NTS* 34 (1988): 24–44.

———. *Misquoting Jesus: The Story behind Who Changed the Bible and Why*. HarperCollins, 2005.

———. "Origen and the Text of the New Testament." Pages 1–20 in *The Text of the Fourth Gospel in the Writings of Origen*. Edited by Bart D. Ehrman, Gordon D. Fee, and Michael W. Holmes. NTGF 3. Scholars Press, 1992.

———. *The Orthodox Corruption of Scripture: The Effect of Early Christological Controversies on the Text of the New Testament*. Oxford University Press, 2011.

———. "Text and Interpretation: The Exegetical Significance of the 'Original' Text." Pages 307–24 in *Studies in the Textual Criticism of the New Testament*. NTTSD 33. Brill, 2006.

———. "Text and Transmission: The Historical Significance of the 'Altered' Text" Pages 325–42 in *Studies in the Textual Criticism of the New Testament*. NTTSD 33. Brill, 2006.

———. "The Text as Window: New Testament Manuscripts and the Social History of Early Christianity." Pages 803–30 in *The Text of the New Testament in Contemporary Research*. 2nd rev. ed. Edited by Bart D. Ehrman and Michael W. Holmes. NTTSD 42. Brill, 2013.

———. "The Use and Significance of Patristic Evidence for NT Textual Criticism." Pages 118–35 in *New Testament Textual Criticism, Exegesis and Church History: A Discussion of Methods*. Edited by Barbara Aland and Joel Delobel. Pharos, 1994.

———. "The Use of the Church Fathers in New Testament Textual Criticism." Pages 155–65 in *The Bible as Book: The Transmission of the Greek Text*. Edited by Scot McKendrick and Orlaith A. O'Sullivan. Oak Knoll and British Library, 2003.

"An Electronic Edition of the Gospel According to John in the Byzantine Tradition." Electronic Editions of the Gospel according to John in Greek, Latin, Syriac and Coptic. Last revised July 2014. http://www.iohannes.com/byzantine/index.html.

Elliott, J. Keith. "Manuscripts, the Codex and the Canon." *JSNT* 63 (1997): 105–23.

Elliott, William J., and David C. Parker, eds. *The Papyri*. Vol. 1 of *The New Testament in Greek IV: The Gospel according to St John*. NTTS 20. Brill, 1995.

Emmel, Stephen. "The Christian Book in Egypt: Innovation and the Coptic Tradition." Pages 35–43 in *The Bible as Book: The Manuscript Tradition*. Edited by John L. Sharpe and Kimberly van Kampen. British Library and Oak Knoll, 1998.

Epp, Eldon J. "Anti-Judaic Tendencies in the D-Text of Acts: Forty Years of Conversation." Pages 111–46 in *The Book of Acts as Church History: Apostelgeschichte als Kirchengeschichte*. Edited by Tobias Nicklas and Michael Tilly. BZNW 120. De Gruyter, 2003.

———. "Are Early New Testament Manuscripts Truly Abundant?" Pages 77–117 in *Israel's God and Rebecca's Children: Christology and Community in Early Judaism and Christianity; Essays in Honor of Larry W. Hurtado and Alan F. Segal*. Edited by David B. Capes, April D.

DeConick, Helen K. Bond, and Troy Miller. Baylor University Press, 2007.

———. "The Ascension in the Textual Tradition of Luke-Acts." Pages 131–45 in *New Testament Textual Criticism: Its Significance for Exegesis; Essays in Honour of Bruce M. Metzger*. Edited by Eldon J. Epp and Gordon D. Fee. Oxford University Press, 1998.

———. "The Codex and Literacy in Early Christianity and at Oxyrhynchus: Issues Raised by Harry Y. Gamble's *Books and Readers in the Early Church*." *CRBR* 11 (1998): 15–37.

———. "Critical Editions and the Development of Text-Critical Methods: Part 2: From Lachmann (1831) to the Present." Pages 13–48 in *From 1750 to the Present*. Vol. 4 of *The New Cambridge History of the Bible*. Edited by John Riches. Cambridge University Press, 2015.

———. "Issues in the Interrelation of New Testament Textual Criticism and Canon." Pages 485–515 in *The Canon Debate*. Edited by Lee M. McDonald and James A. Sanders. Hendrickson, 2002.

———. "It's All about Variants: A Variant-Conscious Approach to New Testament Textual Criticism." *HTR* 100 (2007): 275–308.

———. "The Multivalence of the Term 'Original Text' in New Testament Textual Criticism." *HTR* 92 (1999): 245–81.

———. "The New Testament Papyri at Oxyrhynchus in Their Social and Intellectual Context." Pages 47–68 in *Sayings of Jesus: Canonical and Non-canonical*. Edited by William L. Petersen. NovTSup 89. Brill, 1997.

———. "New Testament Papyrus Manuscripts and Letter-Carrying in Greco-Roman Times." Pages 35–56 in *The Future of Early Christianity: Essays in Honor of Helmut Koester*. Edited by Birger A. Pearson. Fortress, 1991.

———. "The New Testament Papyrus Manuscripts in Historical Perspective." Pages 261–88 in *To Touch the Text: Biblical and Related Studies in Honor of Joseph A. Fitzmyer, S.J.* Edited by Maurya P. Horgan and Paul J. Kobelski. Crossroad, 1989.

———. "The Oxyrhynchus New Testament Papyri: 'Not without Honor except in Their Hometown'?" *JBL* 123 (2004): 5–55.

———. "The Papyrus Manuscripts of the New Testament." Pages 1–39 in *The Text of the New Testament in Contemporary Research*. 2nd rev. ed. Edited by Bart D. Ehrman and Michael W. Holmes. NTTSD 42. Brill, 2013.

———. *Perspectives on New Testament Textual Criticism: Collected Essays, 1962-2004.* Vol. 1. Brill, 2005.
———. "The Significance of the Papyri for Determining the Nature of the New Testament Text in the Second Century: A Dynamic View of Textual Transmission." Pages 71–103 in *The Gospel Traditions in the Second Century.* Edited by William L. Petersen. University of Notre Dame Press, 1989.
———. "Textual Criticism in the Exegesis of the New Testament with an Excursus on Canon." Pages 45–97 in *Handbook to Exegesis of the New Testament.* Edited by Stanley E. Porter. NTTS 25. Brill, 1999.
———. *The Theological Tendency of Codex Bezae Cantabrigiensis in Acts.* Cambridge University Press, 1966.
———. "Traditional 'Canons' of New Testament Textual Criticism: Their Value, Validity, and Viability—or Lack Thereof." Pages 79–127 in *The Textual History of the Greek New Testament: Changing Views in Contemporary Research.* Edited by Klaus Wachtel and Michael W. Holmes. Society of Biblical Literature, 2011.
Eve, Eric. *Writing the Gospels: Composition and Memory.* SPCK, 2016.
Eynde, Damien van den. *Les normes de l'enseignement chrétien dans la littérature patristique des trois premiers siècles.* Gabalda, 1933.
Fabris, Rinaldo. *Introduzione generale alla Bibbia.* LCSB 1. Elledici, Leumann, 1994.
Farstad, Arthur L., and Zane C. Hodges. *The Greek New Testament according to the Majority Text: English and Greek Edition.* 2nd ed. Nelson Reference and Electronic, 1985.
Fee, Gordon D. "The Use of the Greek Fathers." Pages 191–207 in *New Testament Textual Criticism: Its Significance for Exegesis; Essays in Honour of Bruce M. Metzger.* Edited by Eldon J. Epp and Gordon D. Fee. Oxford University Press, 1998.
Fernández Marcos, Natalio. *The Septuagint in Context: Introduction to the Greek Version of the Bible.* Brill Academic, 2001.
Fitzmyer, Joseph A. "A Recent Roman Scriptural Controversy." *TS* 22 (1961): 426–44.
Förster, Hans. "Grammatik von Joh 8,25 im Lichte der handschriftlichen Überlieferung." *ZNW* 107 (2016): 1–29.
———. "Possible Similarities in the Linguistic Structure of John 8.25b and John 8.45a." *BT* 68 (2017): 164–78.
Gamble, Harry Y. "The Book Trade in the Roman Empire." Pages 23–36

in *The Early Text of the New Testament*. Edited by Charles E. Hill and Michael J. Kruger. Oxford University Press, 2012.

———. *Books and Readers in the Early Church: A History of Early Christian Texts*. Yale University Press, 1997.

———. "Literacy, Liturgy, and the Shaping of the New Testament Canon." Pages 27–39 in *The Earliest Gospels: The Origins and Transmission of the Earliest Christian Gospels; The Contributions of the Chester Beatty Codex P45*. JSNTSup 258. T&T Clark, 2004.

———. "The New Testament Canon: Recent Research and the Status Quaestionis." Pages 267–94 in *The Canon Debate*. Edited by Lee M. McDonald and James A. Sanders. Hendrickson, 2002.

García-Moreno, Antonio. *La Neovulgata: precedents y actualidad*. 2nd ed. Eunsa, 2011.

Gathercole, Simon. "The Earliest Manuscript Title of Matthew's Gospel (BnF Suppl. gr. 1120 ii 3 / P4)." *NovT* 54 (2012): 209–35.

Goodman, Martin. "Sacred Scripture and 'Defiling the Hands.'" *JTS* 41 (1990): 99–107.

Goody, Jack. *The Interface between the Written and the Oral*. Cambridge University Press, 1987.

Grafton, Anthony, and Megan Williams. *Christianity and the Transformation of the Book: Origen, Eusebius, and the Library of Caesarea*. Harvard University Press, 2006.

Grant, Robert M. "Literary Criticism and the New Testament Canon." *JSNT* 16 (1982): 24–44.

Gravend-Tirole, Xavier. "From Sola Scriptura to Pluralibus Scripturis." Pages 355–81 in *Reading New Testament Papyri in Context—Lire les papyrus du Nouveau Testament dans leur contexte. Actes du colloque des 22–24 octobre 2009 à l'Université de Lausanne*. Edited by Claire Clivaz and Jean Zumstein. BETL 242. Peeters, 2011.

Grech, Prosper. "Alle origini di un'ermeneutica biblica." Pages 101–14 in *La Sacra Scrittura anima della teologia: Pontificia Università della Santa Croce; Facoltà di Teologia; Atti del IV Simposio Internazionale della Facoltà di Teologia*. Edited by Miguel Ángel Tábet. Librería Editrice Vaticana, 1999.

———. "The Regula fidei as Hermeneutical Principle in Patristic Exegesis." Pages 589–602 in *The Interpretation of the Bible. International Symposium on the interpretation of the Bible, Ljubljana 1996*. Edited by Jože Krasovec. Sheffield Academic, 1998.

———. "The 'Regula fidei' as Hermeneutical Principle Yesterday and Today." Pages 208–24 in *L'interpretazione della Bibbia nella Chiesa: Atti del Simposio promosso dalla Congregazione per la Dottrina della Fede*. Libreria Editrice Vaticana, 2001.

Grossi, Vittorino. "Regula fidei." Page 387 in *Encyclopedia of Ancient Christianity*. Edited by Angelo di Berardino. 3 vols. IVP Academic, 2014.

Guijarro, Santiago, and Jorge Blunda. "Desafíos de la crítica textual a la exégesis, la teología y la pastoral." *ScrTh* 54 (2022): 121–48.

Habermann, Abraham M. "Genizah." *EncJud* 7:460.

Haines-Eitzen, Kim. *Guardians of Letters: Literacy, Power, and the Transmitters of Early Christian Literature*. Oxford University Press, 2000.

———. "The Social History of Early Christian Scribes." Pages 479–95 in *The Text of the New Testament in Contemporary Research*. 2nd rev. ed. Edited by Bart D. Ehrman and Michael W. Holmes. NTTSD 42. Brill, 2013.

Hanson, Richard P. C. "The Ideology of Codex Bezae in Acts." *NTS* 14 (1968): 282–86.

———. *Tradition in the Early Church*. Westminster, 1962.

Harl, Marguerite. "La Septante et la Pluralité textuelle des Écritures: Le Témoignage des Peres Grecs." Pages 231–43 in *Naissance de la Méthode critique*. Cerf, 1992.

Harrauer, Hermann. "Bücher in Papyri." Pages 59–77 in *Flores litterarum Joanní Marte sexagenario oblate: Wissenschaft in der Bibliothek*. Böhlau, 1995.

Harris, J. Rendel. "New Points of View in Textual Criticism." *Expositor* 7 (1914): 316–34.

Harris, William V. *Ancient Literacy*. Harvard University Press, 1989.

Head, Peter M. "The Early Text of Mark." Pages 108–20 in *The Early Text of the New Testament*. Edited by Charles E. Hill and Michael J. Kruger. Oxford University Press, 2012.

———. "Graham Stanton and the Four-Gospel Codex: Reconsidering the Manuscript Evidence." Pages 93–101 in *Jesus, Matthew's Gospel and Early Christianity: Studies in Memory of Graham N. Stanton*. Edited by Daniel M. Gurtner, Joel Willitts, and Richard A Burridge. LNTS 435. T&T Clark, 2011.

———. "The Habits of New Testament Copyists: Singular Readings in the Early Fragmentary Papyri of John." *Bib* 85 (2004): 399–408.

———. "Is P4, P64, and P67 the Oldest Manuscript of the Four Gospels? A Response to T. C. Skeat." *NTS* 51 (2005): 450–57.

———. "Observations on Early Papyri of the Synoptic Gospels, Especially on the 'Scribal Habits.'" *Bib* (1990): 240–47.

———. "Scribal Behaviour and Theological Tendencies in Singular Readings in P. Bodmer II (P66)." Pages 55–74 in *Textual Variation: Theological and Social Tendencies?* Edited by Hugh A. G. Houghton and David C. Parker. Gorgias, 2008.

Heath, Jane. "'Textual Communities': Brian Stock's Concept and Recent Scholarship on Antiquity." Pages 5–35 in *Scriptural Interpretation at the Interface between Education and Religion: In Memory of Hanz Conzelmann*. TBN 22. Brill, 2018.

Heilmann, Jan. "Reading Early New Testament Manuscripts: *Scriptio continua*, 'Reading Aids' and Other Characteristic Features." Pages 177–96 in *Material Aspects of Reading in Ancient and Medieval Cultures: Materiality, Presence and Performance*. Edited by Anna Krauß, Jonas Leipziger, and Friederike Schücking-Jungblut. De Gruyter, 2020.

Hendel, Ronald. "The Oxford Hebrew Bible: Prologue to a New Critical Edition." *VT* 58 (2008): 324–51.

Hernández, Juan, Jr. "Codex Sinaiticus: An Early Christian Commentary on the Apocalypse?" Pages 107–26 in *Codex Sinaiticus: New Perspectives on the Ancient Biblical Manuscript*. Edited by Scot McKendrick, David Parker, Amy Myrshall, and Cillian O'Hogan. British Library, 2015.

———. "The Early Text of Luke." Pages 121–39 in *The Early Text of the New Testament*. Edited by Charles E. Hill and Michael J. Kruger. Oxford University Press, 2012.

———. "Modern Critical Editions." Pages 689–710 in *The Text of the New Testament in Contemporary Research*. 2nd rev. ed. Edited by Bart D. Ehrman and Michael W. Holmes. NTTSD 42. Brill, 2013.

———. *Scribal Habits and Theological Influences in the Apocalypse: The Singular Readings of Sinaiticus, Alexandrinus, and Ephraemi*. WUNT 2/218. Mohr Siebeck, 2006.

Hill, Charles E. "A Four-Gospel Canon in the Second Century?" *EC* 4 (2013): 310–34.

———. "'In These Very Words': Methods and Standards of Literary Borrowing in the Second Century." Pages 261–81 in *The Early Text of the New Testament*. Edited by Charles E. Hill and Michael J. Kruger. Oxford University Press, 2012.

———. "Intersections of Jewish and Christian Scribal Culture." Pages 75–91 in *Among Jews, Gentiles, and Christians in Antiquity and the*

Middle Ages: Studies in Honour of Professor Oskar Skarsaune on His Sixty-Fifth Birthday. Tapir Academic, 2011.

Hill, Charles E., and Michael J. Kruger. "Introduction: In Search of the Earliest Text of the New Testament." Pages 1–19 in *The Early Text of the New Testament*. Edited by Charles E. Hill and Michael J. Kruger. Oxford University Press, 2012.

Hixson, Elijah. "Dating Myths 1: How We Determine the Ages of Manuscripts." Pages 90–109 in *Myths and Mistakes in New Testament Textual Criticism*. Edited by Hixson and Peter Gurry. IVP Academic, 2019.

———. *Scribal Habits in Greek Purple Codices*. NTTSD 61. Brill, 2019.

Holmes, Michael W. "The Biblical Canon." Pages 406–26 in *The Oxford Handbook of Early Christian Studies*. Edited by Susan Ashbrook Harvey and David G. Hunter. Oxford University Press, 2008.

———. "The Case for Reasoned Eclecticism." Pages 77–100 in *Rethinking New Testament Textual Criticism*. Edited by David A. Black. Baker, 2002.

———. "Codex Bezae as a Recension of the Gospels." Pages 123–60 in *Codex Bezae: Studies from the Lunel Colloquum, June 1994*. Edited by David C. Parker and Christian-Bernard Amphoux. Brill, 1996.

———. "From 'Original Text' to 'Initial Text.'" Pages 637–88 in *The Text of the New Testament in Contemporary Research*. 2nd rev. ed. Edited by Bart D. Ehrman and Michael W. Holmes. NTTSD 42. Brill, 2013.

———. "Text and Transmission." Pages 61–79 in *The Reliability of the New Testament*. Edited by Robert B. Stewart. Fortress, 2011.

Horsley, Gregory H. R. "Classical Manuscripts in Australia and New Zealand and the Early History of the Codex." *Antichthon* 27 (1993): 60–85.

Houghton, Hugh A. G. *Augustine's Text of John: Patristic Citations and Latin Gospel Manuscripts*. Oxford University Press, 2008.

———. *The Latin New Testament: A Guide to Its Early History, Texts, and Manuscripts*. Oxford University Press, 2008.

Houston, George W. *Inside Roman Libraries: Book Collections and Their Management in Antiquity*. SHGR. University of North Carolina Press, 2014.

Howard, George. "Tetragrammaton in the New Testament." *ABD* 6:392–93.

Hughes, Kyle R. "Lukan Special Material and the Tradition History of the *Pericope Adulterae*." *NovT* 55 (2013): 232–51.

Humphrey, John H. *Literacy in the Roman World*. JRASup. University of Michigan Press, 1991.

Hurtado, Larry W. *The Earliest Christian Artifacts: Manuscripts and Christian Origins*. Eerdmans, 2006.

———. "The Earliest Evidence of an Emerging Christian Material and Visual Culture: The Codex, the Nomina Sacra, and the Staurogram." Pages 271–88 in *Text and Artifact in the Religions of Mediterranean Antiquity: Essays in Honour of Peter Richardson*. Edited by Stephen G. Wilson and Michel Desjardins. SCJ 9. Wilfrid Laurier University Press, 2000.

———. "A Fresh Analysis of P.Oxyrhynchus 1228 (P22) as Artefact." Pages 206–16 in *Studies on the Text of the New Testament and Early Christianity: Studies in Honour of Michael W. Holmes*. Edited by Daniel Gurtner, Juan Hernández Jr., and Paul Foster. NTTSD 50. Brill, 2015.

———. *Lord Jesus Christ: Devotion to Jesus in Earliest Christianity*. Eerdmans, 2003.

———. "Manuscripts and the Sociology of Early Christian Reading." Pages 49–62 in *The Early Text of the New Testament*. Edited by Charles E. Hill and Michael J. Kruger. Oxford University Press, 2012.

———. "The New Testament in the Second Century: Text, Collections and Canon." Pages 3–27 in *Transmission and Reception: New Testament Text-Critical and Exegetical Studies*. Edited by Jeff W. Childers and David C. Parker. Gorgias, 2006.

Izquierdo, César. "El dogma y las fórmulas dogmáticas." Pages 667–714 in *Teología fundamental: Temas y propuestas para el nuevo milenio*. Desclée de Brouwer, 1999.

Johnson, William A. "The Ancient Book." Pages 256–81 in *The Oxford Handbook of Papyrology*. Edited by Roger S. Bagnall. Oxford University Press, 2009.

———. *Bookrolls and Scribes in Oxyrhynchus*. University of Toronto Press, 2004.

———. *Readers and Reading Culture in the High Roman Empire: A Study of Elite Communities*. Oxford University Press, 2010.

———. "Towards a Sociology of Reading in Classical Antiquity." *AJP* 121 (2000): 593–627.

Jones, Alexander. *Astronomical Papyri from Oxyrhynchus (P.Oxy. 4133–4300a)*. Vol. 1. American Philosophical Society, 1999.

Jones, Brice C. *New Testament Texts on Greek Amulets from Late Antiquity*. LNTS 554. T&T Clark, 2016.

Jongkind, Dirk. *Scribal Habits of Codex Sinaiticus*. Gorgias, 2007.

Judge, Edwin A., and Stuart R. Pickering. "Biblical Papyri Prior to Constantine: Some Cultural Implications of their Physical Form." *Prudentia* 10 (1978): 1–13.
Kannaday, Wayne C. *Apologetic Discourse and the Scribal Tradition*. TCS 5. Society of Biblical Literature, 2004.
Keith, Chris. *The Gospel as Manuscript: An Early History of the Jesus Tradition as Material Artifact*. Oxford University Press, 2020.
———. *The Pericope Adulterae, the Gospel of John, and the Literacy of Jesus*. NTTSD 38. Brill, 2009.
Kelhoffer, James A. *Miracle and Mission: The Authentication of Missionaries and Their Message in the Longer Ending of Mark*. WUNT 2/112. Mohr Siebeck, 2000.
Klauck, Hans-Josef. *Ancient Letters and the New Testament: A Guide to Context and Exegesis*. Baylor University Press, 2006.
Kloppenborg, John S. "Literate Media in Early Christ Groups: The Creation of a Christian Book Culture." *JECS* 22 (2014): 21–59.
Knust, Jennifer, and Tommy Wasserman. *To Cast the First Stone: The Transmission of a Gospel Story*. Princeton University Press, 2019.
Koester, Helmut. *Ancient Christian Gospels: Their History and Development*. SCM, 1990.
———. "The Text of the Synoptic Gospels in the Second Century." Pages 19–37 in *The Gospel Traditions in the Second Century*. Edited by William L. Petersen. University of Notre Dame Press, 1989.
Kotsifou, Chrysi. "Books and Book Production in the Monastic Communities of Byzantine Egypt." Pages 48–66 in *The Early Christian Book*. Edited by William E. Klingshirn and Linda Safran. Catholic University of America Press, 2007.
Kraft, Robert A. "The Codex and Canon Consciousness." Pages 229–33 in *The Canon Debate*. Edited by Lee M. McDonald and James A. Sanders. Hendrickson, 2002.
Kroehnert, Otto *Canonesne poetarum scriptorum artificum per antiquitatem fuerunt?* 1897.
Kruger, Michael J. *Canon Revisited: Establishing the Origins and Authority of the New Testament Books*. Crossway, 2012.
———. "Early Christian Attitudes toward the Reproduction of Texts." Pages 63–80 in *The Early Text of the New Testament*. Edited by Charles E. Hill and Michael J. Kruger. Oxford University Press, 2012.
———. "Manuscripts, Scribes, and Book Production within Early Christianity." Pages 15–40 in *Christian Origins and Greco-Roman Culture:*

Social and Literary Contexts for the New Testament. Edited by Stanley E. Porter and Andrew W. Pitts. TENTS 9. Brill, 2013.

———. *The Question of Canon: Challenging the Status Quo in the New Testament Debate*. IVP Academic, 2013.

Lake, Kirsopp. *The Influence of Textual Criticism on the Exegesis of the New Testament*. Parker & Son, 1904.

Lampe, Geoffrey W. H., ed. *The West, from the Fathers to the Reformation*. CHB 2. Cambridge University Press, 1969.

Lanier, Gregory R., and J. Nicholas Reid, eds. *Studies on the Intersection of Text, Paratext, and Reception: A Festschrift in Honor of Charles E. Hill*. Brill, 2021.

Larsen, Matthew D. C. *Gospels before the Book*. Oxford University Press, 2018.

Larsen, Matthew D. C., and Mark Letteney. "Christians and the Codex: Generic Materiality and Early Gospel Traditions." *JECS* 27 (2019): 383–415.

Larson, Jason T. Review of *The First Edition of the New Testament*, by David Trobisch. *TC* 6 (2001).

Law, Timothy M. "Kaige, Aquila, and Jewish Revision." Pages 39–64 in *Greek Scripture and the Rabbis*. Edited by Law and Alison Salvesen. Peeters, 2012.

Leggett, Katie, and Greg Paulson. "How Many Greek New Testament Manuscripts Are There REALLY? The Latest Numbers." *INTF Blog*, 29 September 2023.

Lied, Liv I., and Hugo Lundhaug. "Studying Snapshots: On Manuscript Culture, Textual Fluidity, and New Philology." Pages 1–19 in *Snapshots of Evolving Traditions: Jewish and Christian Manuscript Culture, Textual Fluidity, and New Philology*. Edited by Lied and Lundhaug. TUGAL 175. De Gruyter, 2019.

Lim, Timothy H. "The Defilement of the Hands as a Principle Determining the Holiness of Scripture." *JTS* 61 (2010): 501–15.

Llewelyn, Stephen R. "The Conveyance of Letters." *NewDocs* 7:1–57.

———. "The Development of the Codex." *NewDocs* 7:249–56.

———. "Sending Letters in the Ancient World." *TynBul* 46 (1995): 337–56.

Lorenz, Peter. "Counting Witnesses for the Angry Jesus in Mark 1:41: Interdependence and Insularity in the Latin Tradition." *TynBul* 67 (2016): 183–216.

Lowden, John. "The Word Made Visible." Pages 13–47 in *The Early Chris-*

tian Book. Edited by William E. Klingshirn and Linda Safran. Catholic University of America Press, 2007.

Luijendijk, Annemarie. *Greetings in the Lord: Early Christians and the Oxyrhynchus Papyri*. HTS 60. Harvard University Press, 2008.

———. "Reading the Gospel of Thomas in the Third Century: Three Oxyrhynchus Papyri and Origen's Homilies." Pages 241–67 in *Reading New Testament Papyri in Context—Lire les papyrus du Nouveau Testament dans leur contexte; Actes du colloque des 22–24 octobre 2009 à l'Université de Lausanne*. Edited by Claire Clivaz and Jean Zumstein. BETL 242. Peeters, 2011.

———. "Sacred Scriptures as Trash: Biblical Papyri from Oxyrhynchus." *VC* 64 (2010): 217–54.

Maas, Paul. *Textual Criticism*. Clarendon, 1958.

Maehler, Herwig. "Bücher in den frühen Klöstern Ägyptens." Pages 39–47 in *Spätantike Bibliotheken: Leben und Lesen in den frühen Klostern Ägypten*. Phoibos-Vlg, 2008.

Malherbe, Abraham J. *Ancient Epistolary Theorists*. SBLSBS 19. Scholars Press, 1998.

Malik, Peter. *P.Beatty III (P47): The Codex, Its Scribe, and Its Text*. NTTSD 52. Brill, 2017.

———. "P.Oxy. VIII.1079 (P18): Closing on a 'Curious' Codex?" *NTS* 65 (2019): 94–102.

Manucci, Valerio. *La Biblia como palabra de Dios: Introducción general a la Sagrada Escritura*. Desclée, 1988.

Markschies, Christoph. "The Canon of the New Testament in Antiquity: Some New Horizons for Future Research." Pages 175–94 in *Homer, the Bible, and Beyond: Literary and Religious Canons in the Ancient World*. Edited by Margalit Finkelberg and Guy G. Stroumsa. JSRC 2. Brill, 2003.

Martini, Carlo M., and Pietro Bonati. *Il messaggio della Salvezza*. CCSB 1. Elledici, Leumann, 1987.

"Matthew Inscriptio." New Testament Transcripts Prototype.

McCormick, Michael "The Birth of the Codex and the Apostolic Lifestyle." *Scriptorium* (1985): 150–58.

McDonald, Lee M. *The New Testament: Its Authority and Canonicity*. Vol. 2 of *The Formation of the Biblical Canon*. T&T Clark, 2017.

———. *The Old Testament: Its Authority and Canonicity*. Vol. 1 of *The Formation of the Biblical Canon*. Bloomsbury, 2017.

———. "Hellenism and the Biblical Canons: Is There a Connection?" Pages 13–49 in *Christian Origins and Greco-Roman Culture: Social and Literary Contexts for the New Testament*. Edited by Stanley E. Porter and Andrew W. Pitts. TENTS 9. Brill, 2013.

———. "Wherein Lies Authority: A Discussion of Books, Texts, and Translations." Pages 203–39 in *Exploring the Origins of the Bible: Canon Formation in Historical, Literary, and Theological Perspective*. Edited by Craig A. Evans and Emanuel Tov. ASBT 6. Baker Academic, 2008.

McGann, Jerome J. *A Critique of Modern Textual Criticism*. University of Virginia Press, 1992.

McKenzie, Donald. *Bibliography and the Sociology of Texts*. Cambridge University Press, 1999.

Mertens-Pack³. *Catalogue des papyrus littéraires grecs et latins*. http://www.cedopalmp3.uliege.be/.

Metzger, Bruce M. *The Early Versions of the New Testament: Their Origin, Transmission and Limitations*. Clarendon, 1977.

———. *A Textual Commentary of the Greek New Testament*. United Bible Societies, 1971.

Metzger, Bruce M., and Bart D. Ehrman. *The Text of the New Testament: Its Transmission, Corruption and Restoration*. Oxford University Press, 2011.

Millard, Alan R. *Reading and Writing at the Time of Jesus*. Sheffield University Press, 2000.

Mink, Gerd. "The Coherence Based Genealogical Method. What Is It About?" Institut für Neutestamentliche Textforschung. https://tinyurl.com/SBL7016f.

Mitchell, Margaret M. "The Emergence of the Written Record." Pages 177–94 in *Origins to Constantine*. Edited by Mitchell and Frances M. Young. CHC 1. Cambridge University Press, 2006.

Mitchell, Timothy N. Review of Matthew D. C. Larsen. *Gospels before the Book*. *JETS* 62 (2019): 641–45.

Moss, Candida. "The Secretary: Enslaved Workers, Stenography, and the Production of Early Christian Literature." *JTS* 74 (2023): 20–56.

Mugridge, Alan. *Copying Early Christian Texts: A Study of Scribal Practice*. WUNT 362. Mohr Siebeck, 2016.

———. "What Is a Scriptorium?" Pages 781–92 in *Proceedings of the Twenty-Fourth Congress of Papyrology, Helsinki, 1–7 August, 2004*. Edited by Jaakko Frösén, Tiina Purola, and Erja Salmenkivi. Societas Scientiarum Fennica, 2007.

———. "Writing and Writers in Antiquity: Two 'Spectra' in Greek Handwriting." Pages 573–80 in *Proceedings of the Twenty Fifth International Congress of Papyrology, Ann Arbor*. Edited by Traianos Gagos. American Studies in Papyrology, 2007.

Mullen, Roderic L., with Simon Crisp and David C. Parker for the United Bible Societies, eds. *The Gospel according to John in the Byzantine Tradition*. Deutsche Bibelgesellschaft, 2007.

Mussies, Gerard. "Reflections on the Apocryphal Gospels as Supplements." Pages 597–611 in *Reflections in Empssychoi Logoi—Religious Innovations in Antiquity: Studies in Honour of Pieter Willem van der Horst*. Brill, 2008.

Nässelqvist, Dan. "Reader's Aids for Whom? The Use of Lectional Signs in Early Christian Manuscripts." Pages 93–104 in *The Scriptural Universe of Late Antiquity*. Edited by Emmanouela Grypeou. AAG 3. Editorial Sindéresis, 2021.

Nicholls, Matthew. "Parchment Codices in a New Text of Galen." *GR* 57 (2010): 378–86.

Nichols, Stephen G. "Introduction: Philology in a Manuscript Culture." *Speculum* 65 (1990): 1–10.

Nieto, E. Martín. *Introducción general a la Sagrada Escritura*. Casa de la Biblia, 1966.

Nongbri, Brent. "The Construction and Contents of the Beatty-Michigan Pauline Epistles Codex (P^{46})." *NovT* 64 (2022): 388–407.

———. "The Construction of P.Bodmer VIII." *NovT* 58 (2016): 394–410.

———. *God's Library: The Archeology of the Earliest Christian Manuscripts*. Yale University Press, 2018.

———. "The Limits of Palaeographic Dating of Literary Papyri: Some Observations on the Date and Provenance of P.Bodmer II (P66)." *MH* 71 (2014): 1–35.

———. "Losing a Curious Christian Scroll but Gaining a Curious Christian Codex: An Oxyrhynchus Papyrus of Exodus and Revelation." *NovT* 55 (2013): 77–88.

———. "P.Bodmer XX+IX and the Bodmer Composite Codex." *Variant Readings* (blog), 31 March 2018. https://tinyurl.com/SBL7016c.

———. "Recent Progress in Understanding the Construction of the Bodmer 'Miscellaneous' or 'Composite' Codex.'" *Adamantius* 21 (2015): 171–72.

———. "Reconsidering the Place of P.Bodmer XIV–XV (P75) in the Textual Criticism of the New Testament." *JBL* 135 (2016): 405–37.

———. Review of *Kodex und Kanon: Das Buch im frühen Christentum*, by Martin Wallraff. *JECS* 22 (2014): 480–81.

———. "The Use and Abuse of P52: Papyrological Pitfalls in the Dating of the Fourth Gospel." *HTR* 98 (2005): 23–48.

O'Callaghan, José. *Nomina sacra in papyris Graecis saeculi III neotestamentariis*. Biblical Institute Press, 1970.

Orsini, Pasquale. "I papiri Bodmer: scritture e libri." *Adamantius* 21 (2015): 60–78.

Orsini, Pasquale, and Willy Clarysse. "Early New Testament Manuscripts and Their Dates: A Critique of Theological Palaeography." *ETL* 88 (2012): 443–74.

Otranto, Rosa. *Antiche liste di libri su papiro*. Edizioni di Storia e Letteratura, 2000.

Paap, Anton H. R. E. *Nomina Sacra in the Greek Papyri of the First Five Centuries*. Brill, 1959.

Pardee, Cambry G. *Scribal Harmonization in the Synoptic Gospels*. NTTSD 60. Brill, 2019.

Parker, David C. *Codex Bezae: An Early Christian Manuscript and Its Text*. Cambridge University Press, 1992.

———. "Et incarnatus est." Pages 311–22 in *Manuscripts, Texts, Theology: Collected Papers 1977–2007*. De Gruyter, 2009.

———. *An Introduction to the New Testament Manuscripts and Their Texts*. Cambridge University Press, 2008.

———. "Jesus in Textual Criticism." Pages 836–41 in vol. 2 of *Jesus in History, Thought and Culture: An Encyclopedia*. 2 vols. Edited by J. Leslie Houlden. Oxford University Press, 2003.

———. *The Living Text of the Gospels*. Cambridge University Press, 1997.

———. *Manuscripts, Texts, Theology: Collected Papers 1977–2007*. De Gruyter, 2009.

———. Review of *The Orthodox Corruption of Scripture: The Effect of Early Christological Controversies on the Text of the New Testament*, by Bart D. Ehrman. *JTS* 45 (1994): 704–8.

———. "Review: *The First Edition of the New Testament*." *JTS* 53 (2002): 299–305.

———. "Scripture Is Tradition." *Theology* 94 (1991): 11–17.

———. "Textual Criticism and Theology." *ExpTim* 118 (2007): 583–89.

———. *Textual Scholarship and the Making of the New Testament*. Oxford University Press, 2012.

———. "Through a Screen Darkly: Digital Texts and the New Testament." *JSNT* 25 (2003): 395–411.
Parsons, Mikeal C. "A Christological Tendency in P75." *JBL* 105 (1986): 463–79.
———. *The Departure of Jesus in Luke-Acts*. Sheffield Academic, 1987.
Parsons, Peter J. *The City of the Sharp-Nosed Fish: Greek Lives in Roman Egypt*. Weidenfeld & Nicolson, 2007.
———. "A People of the Book?" Pages 47–57 in *I papiri letterari cristiani. Atti del convegno internazionale di studi in memoria di Mario Naldini, Firenze, 10-11 giugno 2010*. Edited by Guido Bastianini and Angelo Casanova. STP NS 13. Istituto Papirologico "G. Vitelli," 2011.
Pattie, Thomas S. "The Creation of the Great Codices." Pages 61–72 in *The Bible as Book: The Manuscript Tradition*. Edited by John L. Sharpe and Kimberly van Kampen. British Library and Oak Knoll, 1998.
Paul VI. *Dei Verbum*. 18 November 1965. https://tinyurl.com/SBL7016l.
Paulson, Gregory S. "Die Geschichte des Novum Testamentum Graece/Nestle-Aland." Pages 85–99 in *Biblica Monasteriensia*. Edited by Holger Strutwolf and Jan Graefe. LIT, 2024.
———. "Improving the CBGM: Recent Interactions." Pages 295–307 in *The New Testament in Antiquity and Byzantium: Traditional and Digital Approaches to Its Texts and Editing; A Festschrift for Klaus Wachtel*. Edited by Hugh A. G. Houghton, David C. Parker, and Holger Strutwolf. ANTF 52. De Gruyter, 2019.
———. "To All Things an Appointed Time: Editing a Critical Edition of the Greek New Testament Lectionary with the Aid of Digital Tools." In *Reading the Gospel in Liturgy: Rites and Rituals, Sources and Systems*. Edited by Marie-Ève Geiger, Elena Velkovska, and Harald Buchinger. MB. De Gruyter, forthcoming.
Pelikan, Jaroslav. *The Christian Tradition: A History of the Development of Doctrine*. Vol. 1, *The Emergence of the Catholic Tradition (100–600)*. University of Chicago Press, 1971.
Penn, Michael. "Monks, Manuscripts, and Muslims: Syriac Textual Changes in Reaction to the Rise of Islam." *Hugoye* 12 (2009): 235–57.
Pereira Delgado, Alvaro. "Uno de cuatro, cuatro y no uno: El Diatésaron de Taciano y el Evangelio cuadriforme." *ScrTh* 52 (2020): 285–312.
Perrella, Gaetano M. *Introducción general a la Sagrada Escritura*. Translated by Juan Prado. Perpetuo Socorro, 1954.
Perșa, Razvan. "Autenticitatea textului scripturistic in 7,1 în comentariul hrisostomic la evanghelia după Ioan, (The Authenticity of John 7,1

in the Chrysostomic Commentary to the Gospel according to John)." *StTe* 2 (2014): 153–78.

Petersen, William L. "From Justin to Pepys: The History of the Harmonized Gospel Tradition." StPatr 30 (1997): 71–96.

———. "The Genesis of the Gospels." Pages 33–65 in *New Testament Textual Criticism and Exegesis: Festschrift J. Delobel*. Edited by Adelbert Denaux. Leuven University Press and Peeters, 2002.

———. "ΟΥΔΕ ΕΓΩ ΣΕ [ΚΑΤΑ]ΚΡΙΝΩ. John 8:11." Pages 191–221 in *The Protevangelium Jacobi and the History of the Pericope Adulterae, Sayings of Jesus: Canonical and Non-canonical; Essays in Honour of Tjitze Baarda*. Edited by Petersen, Johan S. Vos, and Henk J. de Jonge. NovTSup 89. Brill, 1997.

———. "What Text Can New Testament Textual Criticism Ultimately Reach?" Pages 136–52 in *New Testament Textual Criticism, Exegesis and Church History: A Discussion of Methods*. Edited by Barbara Aland and Joel Delobel. Pharos, 1994.

Petrucci, Armando. "Del libro unitario al libro misceláneo." Pages 249–76 in *Libros, escrituras y bibliotecas*. Ediciones Universidad de Salamanca, 2011.

Petzer, Jacobus. "The Latin Version of the New Testament," Pages 113–30 in *The Text of the New Testament in Contemporary Research: Essays on the Status Quaestionis*. Edited by Bart D. Ehrman and Michael W. Holmes. SD 46. Eerdmans, 1995.

Pfeiffer, Rudolf. *History of Classical Scholarship: From the Beginnings to the End of the Hellenistic Age*. Clarendon, 1968.

Piras, Antonio. "Gv 8,25 e la versione gotica della bibbia." Pages 149–72 in *Studi in onore di Vittoria Dolcetti Corazza*. Edited by Carla Falluomini and Roberto Rosselli Del Turco. Edizioni dell'Orso, 2015.

Pius XII. *Divino afflante Spiritu*. https://tinyurl.com/SBL7016k.

Poirier, John C. "Living Text or Exquisite Corpse?" *ET* 119 (2008): 437–39.

———. "The Roll, the Codex, the Wax Tablet and the Synoptic Problem." *JSNT* 35 (2012): 3–30.

Porter, Stanley E. "Recent Efforts to Reconstruct Early Christianity." Pages 71–84 in *Christian Origins and Greco-Roman Culture: Social and Literary Contexts for the New Testament*. Edited by Stanley E. Porter and Andrew W. Pitts. TENTS 9. Brill, 2013.

———. "What Do We Know and How Do We Know It? Reconstructing Early Christianity from Its Manuscripts." Pages 41–70 in *Christian Origins and Greco-Roman Culture: Social and Literary Contexts for the New Testament*. Edited by Stanley E. Porter and Andrew W. Pitts. TENTS 9. Brill, 2013.

Porter, Stanley E., David I. Yoon, and Chris Stevens, eds. *Studies on the Paratextual Features of Early New Testament Manuscripts*. Brill, 2023.

Rapp, Claudia. "Holy Texts, Holy Men and Holy Scribes." Pages 194–222 in *The Early Christian Book*. Edited by William E. Klingshirn and Linda Safran. Catholic University of America Press, 2007.

Ratzinger, Joseph. "Discurso en la Investidura de Doctor 'Honoris Causa' del Cardenal Joseph Ratzinger en la Universidad de Navarra." *ScrTh* 30 (1998): 387–93.

———. *Jesus of Nazareth: From the Entrance into Jerusalem to the Resurrection*. Ignatius, 2011.

Rico, Christophe. "Jn 8:25 au risque de la philologie: histoire d'une expression grecque." *RB* 112 (2005): 596–627.

———. *Le traducteur de Bethléem: Le génie interprétatif de saint Jérôme à l'aune de la linguistique*. Cerf, 2016.

Riesner, Rainer. "Joh 7,1: fehlender Wille oder fehlende Vollmacht Jesu?" *ZNW* 96 (2005): 259–62.

Rius-Camps, Josep, and Jenny Read-Heimerdinger. *The Message of Acts in Codex Bezae: A Comparison with the Alexandrian Tradition*. 4 vols. T&T Clark, 2004–2009.

Roberts, Colin H. "The Codex." *Proceedings of the British Academy* 40 (1954): 169–204.

———. "John 20:30–31 and 21:24–25." *JTS* 38 (1987): 409–10.

———. *Manuscript, Society and Belief in Early Christian Egypt*. British Academy and Oxford University Press, 1979.

Roberts, Colin H., and Theodore C. Skeat. *The Birth of the Codex*. British Academy and Oxford University Press, 1983.

Robinson, Maurice A., and William G. Pierpont. *The New Testament in the Original Greek: Byzantine Textform*. Chilton, 2005.

Rodriguez, Rafael. *Structuring Early Christian Memory: Jesus in Tradition, Performance and Text*. T&T Clark, 2010.

Rosenstein, Roy. "Mouvance." Pages 1538–47 in vol. 1 of *Handbook of Medieval Studies: Terms—Methods—Trends*. Edited by Albrecht Classen. 3 vols. De Gruyter, 2010.

Roth, Dieter T. *The Text of Marcion's Gospel*. NTTSD 49. Brill, 2015.

Rothschild, Clare K., and Trevor W. Thompson. "Galen: Περὶ ἀλυπησίας ('On the Avoidance of Grief')." *EC* 2 (2011): 110–29.

Royse, James R. *Scribal Habits in Early Greek New Testament Papyri.* NTTSD 36. Brill, 2008.

———. "Scribal Tendencies in the Transmission of the Text of the New Testament." Pages 461–78 in *The Text of the New Testament in Contemporary Research.* 2nd rev. ed. Edited by Bart D. Ehrman and Michael W. Holmes. NTTSD 42. Brill, 2013.

Ruhnken, David. *Historia critica oratorum Graecorum.* 1768.

Ryan, Stephen D. "The Word of God and the Textual Pluriformity of the Old Testament." Pages 123–50 in *Verbum Domini and the Complementarity of Exegesis and Faith: Catholic Theological Formation.* Edited by Scott Carl. Eerdmans, 2014.

Sanders, James A. "Scripture as Canon for Post-modern Times." *BTB* 25 (1995): 56–63.

Schenker, Adrian. "L'Écriture sainte subsiste en plusieurs formes canoniques simultanées." Pages 178–86 in *L'interpretazione della Bibbia nella Chiesa: Atti del Simposio promosso dalla Congregazione per la Dottrina della Fede.* Libreria Editrice Vaticana, 2001.

Schmid, Ulrich. *Marcion und sein Apostolos: Rekonstruktion und historische Einordnung der marcionitischen Paulusbriefausgabe.* ANTF 25. De Gruyter, 1995.

———. "Scribes and Variants: Sociology and Typology." Pages 1–23 in *Textual Variation: Theological and Social Tendencies?* Edited by Hugh A. G. Houghton and David C. Parker. Gorgias, 2008.

Schmid, Ulrich B., William J. Elliott, and David C. Parker, eds. *The Majuscules.* Vol. 2 of *The New Testament in Greek IV: The Gospel according to St. John.* NTTSD 37. Brill, 2006.

Schmidt, Daryl D. "The Greek New Testament as a Codex." Pages 469–84 in *The Canon Debate.* Edited by Lee M. McDonald and James A. Sanders. Hendrickson, 2002.

Schnackenburg, Rudolf. *The Gospel according to St John.* Vol. 2. Crossroad, 1968.

Schrader, Elizabeth. "Was Martha of Bethany Added to the Fourth Gospel in the Second Century?" *HTR* 110 (2017): 360–92, 473–74.

Schrader, Elizabeth, and Brandon Simonson. "'Rabbouni,' Which Means Lord: Narrative Variants in John 20:16." *TC* 26 (2021): 133–54.

Seeliger, Hans R. "Buchrolle, Codex, Kanon: Sachhistorische und ikonographische Aspekte und Zusammenhéinge." Pages 547–76 in *Kanon in Konstruktion und Dekonstruktion: Kanonisierungsprozesse religiöser*

Texte von der Antike bis zur Gegenwart, Ein Handbuch. Edited by Eve-Marie Becker and Stefan Scholz. De Gruyter, 2012.

Shepherd, Thomas R. "Narrative Analysis as a Text Critical Tool: Mark 16 in Codex W as a Test Case." *JSNT* 32 (2009): 77–98.

Shillingsburg, Peter L. *Scholarly Editing in the Computer Age: Theory and Practice*. University of Michigan Press, 1996.

Silva, Moisés. "Modern Critical Editions and Apparatuses." Pages 283–96 in *The Text of the New Testament in Contemporary Research: Essays on the Status Quaestionis*. Edited by Bart D. Ehrman and Michael W. Holmes. Eerdmans, 1995.

———. Review of *The Living Text*, by David C. Parker. *WTJ* 62 (2000): 295–302.

Simon, Richard. *Critical History of the Text of the New Testament, Wherein Is Established the Truth of the Acts on Which the Christian Religion Is Based*. Translated by Andrew Hunwick. NTTSD 43. Brill, 2013.

———. *Histoire critique du Texte du Nouveau Testament*. Leers, 1689.

Simonetti, Manlio. *Testi gnostici in lingua latina e greca*. Fondazione Lorenzo Valla, 1993.

Skeat, Theodore C. "Early Christian Book-Production: Papyri and Manuscripts." Pages 33–59 in *The Collected Biblical Writings of T. C. Skeat*. Edited by J. Keith Elliott. NovTSup. Brill, 2004.

———. "Especially the Parchments: A Note on 2 Timothy IV.13." *JTS* 30 (1979): 173–77.

———. "The Origin of the Christian Codex." *ZPE* 102 (1994): 263–68.

Smarius, Alexander. "Another God in the Gospel of John? A Linguistic Analysis of John 1:1 and 1:18." *HBT* 44 (2022): 141–71.

St. Bernard's Sermons for the Seasons and Principal Festivals of the Year. Edited by a Priest of Mount Melleray. Carroll, 1950.

Stanton, Graham N. *Jesus and the Gospel*. Cambridge University Press, 2004.

Steinmueller, John E. *Introducción general a la Sagrada Escritura*. Translated by José Alfredo Jolly. Desclée de Brouwer, 1947.

Stock, Brian. *The Implications of Literacy: Written Language and Models of Interpretation in the Eleventh and Twelfth Centuries*. Princeton University Press, 1983.

Stroumsa, Guy G. "Early Christianity: A Religion of the Book?" Pages 153–73 in *Homer, the Bible, and Beyond: Literary and Religious Canons in the Ancient World*. Edited by Margalit Finkelberg and Guy G. Stroumsa. JSRC 2. Brill, 2003.

———. *The End of Sacrifice: Religious Transformations in Late Antiquity*. Translated by Susan Emanuel. University of Chicago Press, 2009.

———. "On the Status of Books in Early Christianity." Pages 57–73 in *Being Christian in Late Antiquity: A Festschrift for Gillian Clark*. Edited by Carol Harrison, Caroline Humfress, and Isabella Sandwell. Oxford University Press, 2014.

———. "Reading Practices in Early Christianity and the Individualization Process." Pages 175–92 in *Reflections on Religious Individuality: Greco-Roman and Judeo-Christian Texts and Practices*. Edited by Jörg Rüpke and Wolfgang Spickermann. De Gruyter, 2012.

Sutcliffe, Edmund F. "The Council of Trent on the 'Authentia' of the Vulgate?" *JTS* 49 (1948): 35–42.

Swanson, Reuben J., ed. *New Testament Greek Manuscripts: Variant Readings Arranged in Horizontal Lines against Codex Vaticanus: Romans*. 9 vols. Tyndale House and William Carey International University Press, 1995–2005.

Tábet, Miguel. *Introducción general a la Biblia*. Palabra, 2004.

"Textual Changes in NA28." Institut für Neutestamentliche Textforschung. https://tinyurl.com/SBL7016g.

Tollinton, Richard B. *Clement of Alexandria*. Vol. 2. Williams & Norgate, 1914.

Torres Guerra, José B. "Literatura Griega: las bases del canon." *RFC* (2012): 21–48.

Tov, Emanuel. "The Nature and Background of Harmonization in Biblical Manuscripts." *JSOT* 31 (1985): 3–29.

———. *Scribal Practices and Approaches Reflected in the Texts Found in the Judean Desert*. STDJ 54. Brill, 2004.

Tov, Emanuel, Robert A. Kraft, and Peter J. Parsons. *The Greek Minor Prophets Scroll from Naḥal Ḥever (8ḤevXIIgr)*. DJD 8. Clarendon, 1990.

Traube, Ludwig. *Nomina Sacra: Versuch einer Geschichte der christlichen Kürzung*. Beck, 1907.

Trobisch, David. *The First Edition of the New Testament*. Oxford University Press, 2000.

———. *On the Origin of Christian Scripture: The Evolution of the New Testament Canon in the Second Century*. Fortress, 2023.

Tuckett, Christopher M. "'Nomina Sacra': Yes and No?" Pages 431–58 in *The Biblical Canons*. Edited by Jean-Marie Auwers and Henk J. de Jonge. Peeters, 2003.

Turner, Eric G. *Greek Manuscripts of the Ancient World.* 2nd rev. ed. Rev. and enl. Peter J. Parsons. BICSSup 46. University of London Press, 1987.

———. *The Typology of the Early Codex.* University of Pennsylvania Press, 1977.

Ulrich, Eugene. "The Notion and Definition of Canon." Pages 21–35 in *The Canon Debate.* Edited by Lee M. McDonald and James A. Sanders. Hendrickson, 2002.

Vanni, Ugo. *Apocalisse. Una assemblea liturgica interpreta la storia.* 12th ed. Queriniana, 2003.

———. "Liturgical Dialogue as a Literary Form in the Book of Revelation." *NTS* 37 (1991): 348–72.

Varvaro, Alberto. "The 'New Philology' from an Italian Perspective." *Text* 12 (1999): 49–58.

Vosté, Jacques M. "The Vulgate and the Council of Trent." *CBQ* 9 (1947): 9–25.

Wachtel, Klaus. "Notes on the Text of Mark." Pages 1–7 in *The Synoptic Gospels, Part 2: The Gospel of Mark.* Vol. 1 of *Novum Testamentum Graecum: Editio Critica Maior.* Edited by Holger Strutwolf, Georg Gäbel, Annette Hüffmeier, Marie-Luise Lakmann, Gregory S. Paulson, and Klaus Wachtel. German Bible Society, 2021.

Wachtel, Klaus, and David C. Parker. "The Joint IGNTP/INTF Editio Critica Maior of the Gospel of John." Paper presented at the Meeting of the Society for New Testament Studies meeting. Halle, 15 August 2005. https://tinyurl.com/SBL7016e.

Wachtel, Klaus, and Michael W. Holmes, eds. *The Textual History of the Greek New Testament: Changing Views in Contemporary Research.* Society of Biblical Literature, 2011.

Wallraff, Martin. "The Canon Tables of the Psalms: An Unknown Work of Eusebius of Caesarea." *DOP* 67 (2013): 1–14.

———. *Kodex und Kanon: Das Buch im frühen Christentum.* De Gruyter, 2013.

Walton, Briani. *Biblia Polyglotta prolegomena.* Weygandianis, 1777.

Wasserman, Tommy. "Beyond Palaeography: Text, Paratext and Dating of Early Christian Papyri." Pages 143–54 in *The Chester Beatty Biblical Papyri at Ninety.* Edited by Garrick V. Allen, Kelsie Gayle Rodenbiker, Anthony Philip Royle, Jill Unkel, and Usama Ali Mohamed Gad. De Gruyter, 2023.

———. "A Comparative Textual Analysis of P4 and P64+67." *TC* 15 (2010): 1–27.

———. "The Early Text of Matthew." Pages 83–107 in *The Early Text of the New Testament*. Edited by Charles E. Hill and Michael J. Kruger. Oxford University Press, 2012.

———. "Misquoting Manuscripts? The Orthodox Corruption of the Scripture Revisited." Pages 325–50 in *The Making of Christian Conflicts, Contacts, and Constructions: Essays in Honor of Bengt Holmberg*. Edited by Magnus Zetterholm and Samuel Byrskog. Eisenbrauns, 2012.

———. "Papyrus 72 and the Bodmer Miscellaneous Codex." *NTS* 51 (2006): 137–54.

———. "The 'Son of God' Was in the Beginning (Mark 1:1)." *JTS* 62 (2011): 20–50.

Wasserman, Tommy, and Peter J. Gurry. *A New Approach to Textual Criticism: An Introduction to the Coherence-Based Genealogical Method*. Edited by Michael W. Holmes. RBS 80. SBL Press, 2017.

Watson, Francis. *Gospel Writing: A Canonical Perspective*. Eerdmans, 2013.

Widow, Juan C. Ossandón. *Introduzione generale alla Sacra Scrittura*. EDUSC, 2018.

Williams, Michael A. *Rethinking "Gnosticism": An Argument for Dismantling a Dubious Category*. Princeton University Press, 1996.

Williams, Peter J. "An Examination of Ehrman's Case for ὀργισθείς in Mark 1:41." *NovT* 54 (2012): 1–12.

———. Review of *Manuscripts, Texts, Theology*, by David C. Parker. *TC* (2013). https://tinyurl.com/SBL7016h.

Willker, Wieland. *John*. Vol. 4 of *A Textual Commentary on the Greek Gospels*. 12th ed. Bremen, 2015. https://tinyurl.com/SBL7016i.

Yager, Susan. "New Philology." Pages 999–1006 in vol. 2 of *Handbook of Medieval Studies: Terms—Methods—Trends*. Edited by Albrecht Classen. 3 vols. De Gruyter, 2010.

Young, Frances M. *Biblical Exegesis and the Formation of Christian Culture*. Cambridge University Press, 1997.

Zahn, Molly M. *Genres of Rewriting in Second Temple Judaism: Scribal Composition and Transmission*. Cambridge University Press, 2020.

Zumstein, Jean. "Quand l'exégète rencontre le manuscrit: Le P66." Pages 221–39 in *Reading New Testament Papyri in Context*. Edited by Claire Clivaz and Jean Zumstein. Peeters, 2011.

Zumthor, Paul. *Essai de poétique médiévale*. Seuil, 2000.

Zuntz, Günther. *The Text of the Epistles; A Disquisition upon the Corpus Paulinum*. British Academy, 1953.

Zwiep, Arie W. "The Text of the Ascension Narratives (Luke 24:50–53; Acts 1:1–2, 9–11)." *NTS* 42 (1996): 219–44.

Biblical References Index

Hebrew Bible/Old Testament

Exodus
8	137
40	138

Numbers
5–8	138
13	138
25–36	138

Deuteronomy
1–7	138
9–12	138
18	138
19	138
27–33	138
29	137

Psalms
16	13
33:2–34	13

Proverbs
5–9	138
19–20	138

Jeremiah
31:31–34	2

Jonah
4:6–10	179

Deuterocanonical Books

Wisdom
11–12	138

Sirach
45	138

New Testament

Matthew
3:11	68
3:16	56–57
4:2	57
6:26	55
6:33	56
7:9	55
9:17	57
10:13	57
10:14	55, 57
11:27	57
12:48	56
13:56	57
14:15	56
14:33	64
17:3	55
17:19	55
15:39	55
20:31a	55
23:38	57
26:31	57
26:39	68
26:42	68
27:38	118
27:54	64

Matthew (*continued*)		
28:9	127	

Mark		
1:1	61–62	
1:11	61	
1:13	57	
1:20	57	
1:41	61, 207	
6:3	57	
6:36	56	
8:10	55	
8:12a	55	
9:4	55	
9:28b	55	
10:48	55	
14:27	57	
15:17	56	
15:27	118	
15:34	62	
15:39	64	
16	100	
16:9–20	47	

Luke		
1:1–3	2	
1:3	119	
1:76	68	
2:27	120	
2:33	119–20	
2:41	120	
2:43	62	
2:48	119–20	
3–5	13	
3:22	56–57, 68	
3:23–28	45	
5:5	53	
5:37	57	
6:4	47, 107	
8:21	56	
9:5	55, 57	
9:30	55	
10:4	127	
10:6	57	
10:7	127	
10:11a	55	
10:22	57	
11:12	55	
11:29	55	
12:24	55	
12:31	56	
13:34–35	57	
18:39	55	
21:38	48	
22:43–44	47, 50–52	
23:4	56	
23:32	118–19	
23:34	47, 52	
24:3	63	
24:39	127	
24:50–53	52, 220	
24:51	52, 63	

John		
1–12	13	
1:1	62, 216	
1:3	63	
1:18	62, 216	
1:49	64, 68	
2:16	129	
3:16	122	
4:29	66	
4:44	122	
5:4	47	
5:17	64	
5:43	64	
6:5	56	
6:32	64	
6:42	64	
6:43	129	
6:44	64	
7	48–49	
7:1	122–23, 212	
7:37–52	49	
7:46	65–66	
7:52	48–49, 67	
7:53–8:11	47	
8	48–49	
8:1–11	47	
8:11	48, 213	

8:12	49	15:28	119
8:12–20	49	15:29	107
8:25	124–25, 130, 194, 200		
8:42	67	Romans	
8:45a	125, 200	10:9	104
9:33	64		
9:41	122	1 Corinthians	
10:18	122	1:22	55
10:33	64, 67		
10:36	68	2 Corinthians	
11:4	67	10:9–10	1
11:34	67		
11:39	67	Ephesians	
11:47	66	4:5	11
11:50	66		
12:11	67	Colossians	
13:10	120	4:16	1
15–17	50		
15:25	67	1 Thessalonians	
17:21	7	1:2	11
18	15	5:27	1
18:14	66		
18:29	66	2 Timothy	
18:38c	56	4:13	1
19:2	56		
19:5	59, 64, 66–67	Hebrews	
19:10	122	9:14	140
19:14	59		
19:15	59	1 Peter	
19:28	65–67	4:16	79
20:16	128, 192, 215		
20:17	126, 129	2 Peter	
20:30–31	2, 214	2:11	79
20:31	53	3:10	79
21	49, 148, 192		
21:6	53–54	Revelation	
21:24–25	2	1	138
21:25	2	1:3	2
		1:8	62
Acts		22:7	2
1:1–2	52, 220		
1:9–11	52, 220		
15:1–19	148		
15:20	107		
15:23–29	107		

Manuscripts Index

Papyri

P1	40–42, 154
P4	11, 13, 16, 18, 37, 40–42, 57, 68, 136, 154, 196, 201–2, 218
P5	40–42, 154
P6	13, 42
P7	40–42, 154
P8	40–42, 154
P9	16, 41–42, 155
P10	40–42, 155
P11	11
P12	22, 40–42, 155, 196
P13	24, 40–42, 133, 137, 155
P14	11
P15	11, 16, 40–43, 136, 155
P16	11, 16, 40–43, 136, 155
P17	40–41, 43, 155
P18	16, 24, 41–42, 133, 138, 155, 208
P20	40–42, 155
P22	16, 24, 40–42, 133, 154, 205
P23	16, 40–42, 155
P24	16, 41–43, 155
P25	16, 42
P27	40–42, 155
P28	16, 40–42, 154
P29	40–42, 154
P30	16, 40–42, 137, 154
P32	40–42, 155
P33	11
P35	16, 41–42
P37	40–42, 56, 154
P38	14, 40–42, 154
P39	16, 40–42, 154
P40	40–42, 155
P45	3, 11–12, 33, 40–42, 55, 67–68, 137, 142, 154, 191, 196, 201
P46	12, 31, 33, 40–42, 104, 137, 142, 154–55, 210
P47	12, 41–42, 101, 155, 208
P48	16, 40–42, 154
P49	11, 40–42, 155
P50	40–41, 43, 154
P51	42
P52	14, 16–17, 40–42, 154, 211
P53	16, 40–43, 68, 137, 154
P54	137
P57	42
P58	11
P62	40–41, 43, 154
P64	11, 16, 18, 37, 40–42, 57, 136, 154, 196, 202, 218
P65	11, 40–42, 155
P66	1, 13, 16–17, 33, 40–42, 47, 49, 53–54, 56, 59–60, 62–68, 124, 154, 196, 203, 210, 219
P67	11, 18, 42, 196, 202
P69	40–42, 51, 154
P70	13, 16, 40–42, 57, 154
P71	40–43, 154
P72	13, 40–42, 58, 137, 154
P74	142
P75	17, 22, 33, 40–42, 47, 49, 51–52, 56, 62–63, 124, 137, 154, 196, 210, 212
P77	11, 16, 18, 40–42, 57, 154
P78	11, 41
P80	16, 42
P81	40–41, 43, 155
P82	40–41, 43, 155
P85	42

P86	40–41, 43, 154	P139	40–41, 43, 155
P87	40–42, 155	P141	40–42, 154
P88	40–43, 154		
P89	40–41, 43, 155		Majuscules
P90	14, 16, 40–42, 154		
P91	40–42, 154	01/א (Codex Sinaiticus)	12, 31, 39, 47, 51–53, 56, 62, 101, 119, 124, 128, 139–41, 147, 155, 203, 205
P92	40–42, 137, 154		
P95	40–42, 154		
P98	14, 16, 24, 41–42, 133, 155	02/A (Codex Alexandrinus)	12, 51, 56, 62, 139–40, 147, 156, 203
P99	11		
P100	40–42, 155	03/B (Codex Vaticanus)	12, 17, 47, 51, 60, 62, 80, 86, 119, 139–42, 147, 155, 217
P101	40–42, 57, 68, 154		
P102	40–41, 43, 154		
P103	11, 16, 18, 40–42, 57, 154	04/C (Codex Ephraemi Rescriptus)	62, 156
P104	14, 16, 40–42, 154		
P105	11	05/D (Codex Bezae)	12, 48, 52, 61–63, 102–7, 119, 125, 156, 182, 192, 197, 200, 202, 204, 211, 214
P106	40–42, 154		
P107	40–42, 154		
P108	40–42, 154	07 (Codex Basiliensis)	125
P109	40–42, 154	016	156
P110	40–41, 43, 57, 154	019	62, 119
P111	40–42, 154	022	51
P113	37, 40–42, 155	026	156
P114	40–42, 155	029	51, 156
P115	13, 41–42, 155	029	156
P116	16, 40–42, 155	032 (Codex Washingtonianus)	12, 33, 47, 51, 62, 119, 122–23, 155
P117	40–41, 43, 155		
P118	16, 40–42, 155	033	62
P119	40–42, 154	034	53
P120	40–41, 43, 154	037	62
P121	40–42, 154	038	62, 128
P123	40–41, 43, 155	042	54
P124	155	044 (Codex Athous Lavrensis)	47, 62, 128
P125	40–42, 155		
P126	22, 40–41, 43, 137, 155, 196	045	62
P127	13–14, 154	047	124
P129	12	048	156
P130	12	058	40–43
P131	12, 40–42, 155	063	62
P132	40–41, 43, 155	067	156
P133	155	088	156
P134	40–41, 43, 154	0106	40
P135	12	0141	62
P137	40–42, 154	0160	41–42
P138	40–42, 154	0162	40–41, 43

0166	156	**Vetus Latina**	
0169	41, 43		
0171	16, 40–42, 57, 155	2 (Codex Palatinus, e)	60, 120, 122
0185	137	3 (Codex Vercellensis, a)	60–61, 120, 122, 125
0188	16, 42		
0189	40–41, 43	4 (Codex Veronensis, b)	120, 122, 125
0201	137	5 (Codex Bezae Cantabrigiensis, d)	61, 122, 125
0206	40–43, 137		
0207	137	6 (Codex Colbertinus, c)	118–22, 125
0208	156	7 (Codex Sangermanensis I, g^1)	120–22
0212	16	8 (Codex Corbeiensis, ff^2)	60–61, 120, 122
0220	16, 40–43		
0228	40–43	10 (Codex Brixianus, f)	51
0232	42, 137	11 (Codex Rehdigeranus 1)	118
0240	156	11a (Würzburg Univ. 67)	120
0247	156	13 (Codex Monacensis, q)	122
0251	156	14 (Codex Usserianus primus, r^1)	60–61, 118
0274	137		
0289	156	16 (Codex Sangallensis, n)	122
0308	16, 41–42	24 (Fragmentum Milanense, ρ)	120
0312	42	26 (Codex Carinthianus, β)	120
		29 (Codex Sangermanensis II, g^2)	128
Minuscules		30 (Codex Gatianus, gat)	128
		35 (Codex Moliensis, ϰ)	128
f^1	62	48 (Codex Sangallensis 51)	128
f^{13}	51, 62, 128, 196		
1	119		
157	62		
196	122		
397	62		
460	42		
579	51, 62		
700	62, 119		
743	122		
1071	51, 62		
1241	119		
1424	62		

Lectionaries

l 844	51
l 2211	119

Modern Authors Index

Achtemeier, Paul J. 178, 191
Aland, Barbara 55, 63, 75, 83–84, 91–92, 105, 110, 112, 142, 178, 191, 198, 213
Aland, Kurt 65– 66, 74–75, 75, 91–92, 105, 110, 112, 142, 191
Alexander, Loveday 139, 191
Allen, Garrick V. 33, 218
Amphoux, Christian-Bernard 106–7, 204
Aranda, Gonzalo 168, 191
Arzt-Grabner, Peter 178, 191
Askeland, Christian 49, 192
Assmann, Jan 89
Auwers, Jean-Marie 29, 217
Baarda, Tjitze 61, 128, 192
Baert, Barbara 128, 193
Bagnall, Roger S. 16, 19, 22, 24–25, 27, 149, 192, 196, 205
Balaguer, Vicente 7, 114, 188, 192
Baker, John A. 134, 194
Barker, Don C. 15, 192
Barrett, Charles K. 103, 192
Barrett, David P. 16
Barthélemy, Dominique 165, 192
Barton, John Barton 3, 192
Bastianini, Guido 21, 212
Batovici, Dan 32, 35, 192
Bauckham, Richard 139
Beasley-Murray, George R. 59, 194
Becker, Eve-Marie 133, 216
Best, Ernest 104, 192
Bell, H. I. xiv
Benedict XVI 4, 59, 101, 174, 181, 187, 192
Berardino, Angelo di 172, 202

Berrouard, Marie-François 121, 129, 193
Beutler, Johannes 50, 193
Bieringer, Reimund 128, 193
Birdsall, J. Neville 110
Black, David A. 47, 86, 193, 204
Black, Matthew 75
Blanchard, Alain 22, 193
Blumell, Lincoln H. 19, 72, 193
Blunda, Jorge 85–86, 202
Boismard, Marie-Émile 50, 193
Bokedal, Tomas 133, 193
Bonati, Pietro 157, 164, 208
Bond, Helen K. 199
Bori, Pier C. 131, 193
Botha, Phil J. 177, 193
Bover, José María 74
Bowman, Alan K. 18, 178, 193
Brakke, David 89
Breed, Brennan W. 101, 171, 193
Brown, Raymond E. 50, 125, 158, 194
Bryant, John 96–97, 194
Buchinger, Harald 81, 212
Bultmann, Rudolf 59, 186, 194
Burridge, Richard A. 136, 202
Burton, Philip 121, 123, 194,
Byrskog, Samuel 103, 178, 194, 219
Capes, David B. 13, 198
Carl, Scott 165, 215
Caballero, Juan Luis 172, 195
Campenhausen, Hans von 134, 194
Caragounis, Chrys 124–25, 194
Carbajosa, Ignacio 7, 158, 167, 169–70, 194
Cavallo, Guglielmo 35, 195
Casanova, Angelo 21, 212

Cerone, Jacob N. 47, 193
Cerquiglini, Bernard 95–96, 132, 195
Chapa, Juan vii–viii, 20, 24, 29, 35, 55–56, 82, 90, 101, 116, 134, 136, 163, 172–73, 188, 195
Charlesworth, Scott D. 11, 28, 32–35, 195
Chartier, Roger 35, 195
Childers, Jeff W. 31, 205
Clarysse, Willy 16–18, 41–42, 211
Classen, Albrecht 95–96, 214, 219
Clivaz, Claire 22, 34, 49, 51–52, 93, 100, 163, 196, 201, 208, 219
Coles, Revel A. 193
Colwell, Ernest C 11, 110, 196
Comfort, Philip Wesley 16
Congar, Yves M. J. 173, 196
Coogan, Jeremiah 23, 36, 60, 66, 143, 196
Cosaert, Carl P. 58, 196
Cox, Claude 165, 192
Crawford, Matthew R. 143, 145, 153, 196
Crawford, Sidnie White 39, 196
Cribiore, Raffaella 15, 149, 196
Crisci, Edoardo 146, 197
Crisp, Simon 75, 78, 197, 210
Cromwell, Jennifer 15, 197
DeConick, April D. 199
Daniel, Robert W. 15, 197
Deiana, Giovanni 157, 197
Dela Cruz, Roli 182, 197
Delobel, Joel 63, 84, 198, 213
Demasure, Karlijn 128, 193
Denaux, Adelbert 84, 213
Derrida, Jacques 95
Desjardins, Michel 30, 205
Dormandy, Michael 137, 146, 155, 197
Duncker, Peter G. 166, 198
Echegaray, Joaquín González 158, 170, 194
Ehrman, Bart D. 10–11, 45, 48, 51–52, 60–69, 72–74, 77, 80, 91, 100–106, 114, 118–20, 159, 163, 182, 194, 197–99, 202–4, 209, 211, 213, 215–16, 219

Elliott, J. Keith 27, 66, 115, 134–35, 139–42, 191, 198, 216
Elliott, William J. 77, 198, 215
Emmel, Stephen 23, 198
England, Emma 101, 114, 194
Epp, Eldon J. 10, 13–14, 18–19, 23, 36, 52, 71, 86, 88, 91, 99–104, 106, 108, 110–12, 134, 136–38, 140, 142, 142, 159, 170, 185, 198–200
Estrada, Bernardo 101, 195
Evans, Craig A. 34, 149, 196, 209
Eve, Eric 178, 200
Eynde, Damien van den 173, 193
Eynde, Sabine van den 128, 193, 200
Falloumini, Carla 124, 213
Fabris, Rindaldo 159, 200
Farstadt, Arthur L. 78, 200
Fee, Gordon D. 52, 72, 91, 197, 199–200
Fernández Marcos, Natalio 168, 200
Finkelberg, Margalit 16, 181, 208, 216
Fitzmyer, Joseph A. 10, 158, 179, 194, 199–200
Förster, Hans 125, 200
Foster, Paul 24, 45, 205
Foucault, Michel 95
Frösén, Jaakko 72, 209
Gäbel, Georg 218
Gad, Usama Ali Mohamed 218
Gagos, Traianos 20, 210
Gamble, Harry W. 2–3, 19, 22, 26, 36, 38–39, 101–2, 134, 139–40, 178–80, 184, 199–200
García-Moreno, Antonio 123, 166, 201
Gathercole, Simon 11, 41, 201
Geiger, Marie-Ève 81, 212
Gilbert, Maurice 171
Gonis, Nick 193
Goodman, Martin 3, 201
Goody, Jack 178, 201
Graefe, Jan 74, 212
Grafton, Anthony 138–39, 143–44, 201
Grant, Robert M. 149–51, 201
Gravend-Tirole, Xavier 163, 201
Grech, Prosper 172–73, 201

Grenfell, Bernard P. xv
Grobel, Kendrick 59, 194
Grossi, Vittorino 172–73, 202
Grypeou, Emmanouela 32, 210
Guijarro, Santiago 6, 85–86, 202
Gurry, Peter 14, 79, 204, 219
Gurtner, Daniel M. 24, 136, 202, 205
Habermann, Abraham M. 38, 202
Haines-Eitzen, Kim 20–21, 29, 38, 56, 58, 61, 101–2, 178, 184, 202
Hanson, Richard P. C. 103, 172, 202
Harrison, Carol 23, 217
Harvey, Susan Ashbrook 147, 204
Harl, Marguerite 169, 202
Harrauer, Hermann 141, 202
Harris, Rendel 102, 119, 202
Harris, William 178, 202
Hartman, Louis F. 171
Head, Peter 11, 57, 64–68, 136, 202
Heath, Jane 89, 203
Heilmann, Jan 32, 203
Hendel, Ronald 40, 203
Hernández, Juan ix, 6, 24, 31, 39, 51–52, 56–57, 63, 68, 74, 77–80, 86–87, 92–93, 101, 203, 205
Hill, Charles E. 11, 22, 35, 41, 51, 55, 57–58, 84, 91, 101–2, 136, 183–84, 195–96, 201–7, 219
Hill, Edmund 129, 192
Hixson, Elijah viii, 14, 54, 101, 204
Hodges, Zane C. 78, 200
Holmberg, Bengt 103, 219
Holmes, Michael W. 11, 24, 72, 74, 77, 79–80, 82–88, 90–92, 99–100, 102, 105, 118, 147, 151–52, 163, 170, 172, 194, 197–200, 202–5, 213, 215–16, 218–19
Houghton, H. A. G. 64, 81, 103, 120–22, 125, 129, 192, 203–4, 212, 215
Houlden, J. Leslie 30, 211
Horgan, Maurya P. 10, 199
Horsely, Gregory H. R. xiv, 26, 204
Hort, Fenton J. A. 74, 79, 80, 86, 110
Horton, Charles 55, 191
Houston, George W. 141, 204

Howard, George 29–30, 204
Hüffmeier, Annette 218
Hughes, Kyle R. 50, 204
Humfress, Caroline 23, 217
Humphrey, John H. 178, 204
Hunter, David G. 147, 204
Hunwick, Andrew 114, 216
Hurtado, Larry W. 1, 13, 22, 24, 26–33, 36–38, 40, 101–2, 198, 205
Izquierdo, César 173, 205
Jaroš, Karl 16
Johnson, Johanna viii
Johnson, William 22, 24, 35, 37, 39, 89, 205
Jolly, José Alfredo 157, 216
Jones, Alexander 23, 145, 205
Jones, Brice 39, 145, 205
Jonge, Henk J. de 29, 48, 213, 217
Jongkind, Dirk 101, 205
Judge, Edwin A. 138, 206
Kampen, Kimberly van 23, 141, 198, 212
Kannaday, Wayne C. 58, 102, 104–5, 206
Karavidopoulos, Johannes 75
Kearns, Conleth 171
Keith, Chris 2–3, 39, 47, 89, 102, 171, 178, 181, 206
Kelhoffer, James A. 109, 206
Kenyon, F. G. xiv
Klauck, Hans-Josef A. 177, 206
Klingshirn, William E. 141, 153, 186, 206, 208, 214
Kloppenborg, John S. 89, 139, 178, 191, 206
Knust, Jennifer 48, 110, 171, 206
Kobelski, Paul J. 10, 199
Koester, Helmut 19, 84, 90, 182, 199, 206
Kotsifou, Chrysi 141, 206
Kraft, Robert E. 33, 135, 206, 217
Krasovec, Jože 172, 201
Krauß, Anna 32, 203
Kreinecker, Christina M. 178, 191
Kroehnert, Otto 151, 206

Kruger, Michael J. 22, 34, 37, 41, 51, 55, 57–58, 84, 91, 102, 133, 136, 184, 195–96, 201–6, 219
Lake, Kirsopp 102, 207
Lakmann, Marie-Luise 218
Lampe, Geoffrey W. H. 72, 207
Lanier, Gregory R. 101, 207
Larsen, Matthew D. C. 26, 87, 89, 110, 207, 209
Larson, Jason T. 146, 148, 207
Law, Timothy M. 168, 207
Leggett, Katie 11, 71, 207
Leipziger, Jonas 32, 203
Lied, Liv I. 97–98, 207
Lieu, Judith 89
Lim, Timothy H. 4, 207
Llewelyn, Stephen R. xiv, 22, 185, 207
Lorenz, John 61, 207
Lowden, John 186, 208
Luijendijk, AnneMarie 19–21, 31, 34–35, 38, 186, 208
Lundhaug, Hugo 97–98, 207
Lyons, William J. 101, 194
Maas, Paul 99, 208
Maehler, Herwig 141, 208
Malherbe, Abraham 177, 208
Malik, Peter viii, 101, 138, 208
Manicardi, Ermengildo 101, 195
Manucci, Valerio 158, 208
Markschies, Christoph 16, 141, 151, 208
Marte, Joanní 142, 202
Martini, Carlo 75, 157, 164, 170, 208
McCormick, Michael 26, 208
McDonald, Lee M. 4, 133–35, 149, 151, 199, 201, 206, 208, 215, 218
McGann, Jerome J. 97, 209
McKendrick, Scot 31, 91, 198, 203
McKenzie, Donald 89, 209
Merk, Augustine 74
Mertens-Pack3 149, 209
Metzger, Bruce M. 45, 52, 73–75, 104, 119–20, 123–24, 199–200, 209
Metzinger, Adalberti 166, 198
Milán, Fernando 83, 195

Millard, Alan R. 178, 209
Miller, Troy 199
Mink, Gerd 78–79, 209
Mitchell, Margaret M. 2–3, 209
Mitchell, Timothy 89, 209
Morrill, Bruce 77
Moss, Candida 30, 209
Mugridge, Alan 20, 32, 72, 138–39, 209
Mullen, Roderic L. 78, 210
Murphy, Roland E. 158, 194
Mussies, Gerard 119, 210
Myrshall, Amy 203
Naldini, Mario 21, 212
Nässelqvist, Dan 32, 210
Nestle, Eberhard 74
Nestle, Erwin 74
Nicholls, Matthew 23, 210
Nichols, Stephen G. 95, 210
Nicklas, Tobias 100, 134, 195, 198
Nieto, E. Martín 157, 210
Nongri, Brent 10, 12–19, 21, 23–25, 41, 137–38, 210
Obbink, Dirk 193
O'Callaghan, José 28, 74, 211
O'Hogan, Cillian 203
Olbricht, Thomas H. 177, 193
O'Sullivan, Orlaith A. 91, 198
Orsini, Pasquale 13, 16–18, 41–42, 211
Otranto, Rosa 141, 211
Paap, Anton H. R. E. 28, 211
Pardee, Cambry G. 54, 211
Parker, David C. 30–31, 49–50, 54, 61–62, 64, 71, 77–78, 81, 84–85, 88, 90, 93, 100–103, 106–15, 117–18, 130, 140–41, 146, 160–62, 170, 183, 186–87, 192, 198, 203–5, 210–12, 215–16, 218–19
Parsons, Mikeal C. 63, 212
Parsons, Peter J. 15, 18–19, 21, 27, 30, 33, 63, 84, 149, 184–85, 193, 212, 217–18
Pattie, Thomas S. 141, 212
Paul VI 187, 212
Paulson, Gregory S. vii, 11, 71, 74, 80–81, 207, 212, 218

Modern Authors Index

Pearson, Birger A. 19, 199
Pecere, Oronzo 146, 197
Pelikan, Jaroslav 173, 212
Penn, Michael 98, 212
Pereira Delgado, Alvaro 54, 57, 212
Perrella, Gaetano M. 157, 164, 166, 212
Perşa, Razvan 123, 212
Petersen, William L. 10, 18, 48, 54, 57, 84–85, 88, 90–91, 110, 121, 199–200, 206, 213
Petrucci, Armando 146, 213
Petzer, Jacobus 118, 213
Pfeiffer, Rudolf 72, 150, 150, 213
Phillips, Maya viii
Pickering, Stuart R. 138, 206
Pietersma, Albert 165, 192
Piras, Antonio 124–26, 131, 213
Pisano, Stephen 170
Pitts, Andrew W. 15, 23, 37, 151, 207, 209, 213–14
Pius XII 164–65, 213
Poirier, John C. 23, 112, 213
Porter, Stanley E. 15, 23, 37, 71, 101, 151, 177, 194, 200, 207, 209, 213–14
Prado, Juan 157, 212
Purola, Tiina 72, 209
Pusey, Philip E. 127, 197
Rapp, Claudia 153, 214
Ratzinger, Joseph 59, 101, 188–89, 195, 214
Read-Heimerdinger, Jenny 102, 214
Reid, J. Nicholas 101, 207
Rhodes, Erroll F. 92, 105, 191
Richardson, Peter 30, 205
Riches, John 99, 199
Rico, Christophe 124–27, 214
Riesner, Rainer 123, 214
Rius-Camps, Josep 102, 214
Roberts, Colin H. 2, 20–21, 26–29, 32, 36, 134–35, 214
Robinson, Maurice 78, 214
Rodenbiker, Kelsie Gayle 218
Rodriguez, Rafael 178, 214
Rosenstein, Roy 96, 214
Rosselli, Roberto Del Turco 124, 213

Roth, Dieter T. 61, 214
Rothschild, Clare K. 23, 214
Royle, Anthony Philip 218
Royse, James R. 11–12, 31, 38–39, 55–56, 60–61, 63–68, 101, 104, 110, 215
Ruhnken, David 150–51, 215
Rüpke, Jörg 3, 217
Ryan, Stephen D. 165, 169, 171, 215
Safran, Linda 141, 153, 186, 206, 208, 214
Salmenkivi, Erja 72, 209
Salvesen, Alison 168, 207
Sanders, James A. 134–35, 149, 152, 199, 201, 206, 215, 218
Sandwell, Isabella 23, 217
Schenker, Adrian 169, 171, 173, 215
Schick, Maria 75, 197
Schmid, Ulrich 61, 77, 103–6, 215
Scholz, Stefan 133, 216
Schmidt, Daryl D. 133, 140, 152, 215
Schnackenburg, Rudolf 49, 63, 215
Schrader, Elizabeth viii, 67, 128, 215
Schröter, Jens 134, 195
Schubert, Paul 15, 197
Schücking-Jungblut, Friederike 32, 203
Segal, Alan F. 13, 198
Seeliger, Hans R. 133, 215
Sharpe, John L. 23, 141, 198, 212
Shepherd, Thomas R. 100, 216
Shillingsburg, Peter L. 160, 216
Silva, Moisés 74, 77, 112, 216
Simon, Richard 73, 114–15, 165, 216
Simonetti, Manlio 52, 216
Simonson, Brandon 128, 215
Skarsaune, Oskar 11, 204
Skeat, Theodore C. xiv, 1, 11, 21, 27, 36, 134–35, 196, 202, 214, 216
Smarius, Alexander 62, 216
Soden, Hermann von 74
Souter, Alexander 74
Spickermann, Wolfgang 3, 217
Stanton, Graham N. 1, 23, 36, 136, 202, 216
Steinmueller, John E. 157, 216
Stevens, Chris 101, 214

Stevenson, Paul 167, 194
Stewart, Robert B. 90, 204
Stock, Brian 89, 203, 216
Stroumsa, Guy G. 3, 16, 23, 89, 181–82, 208, 216
Strutwolf, Holger 10, 49, 74, 77, 81, 84, 192, 212, 218
Sutcliffe, Edmund E. 165, 217
Swanson, Ruben J. 86, 217
Tábet, Miguel 157, 168, 173, 191, 201, 217
Tàrrech, Armand Puig i 101, 195
Thatcher, Tom 89
Thiede, Carsten Peter 16
Thompson, Trevor W. 61, 214
Tilly, Michael 100, 198
Tischendorf, Constantin von 73–74
Tollinton, Richard B. 58, 217
Torres Guerra, José B. 150–51, 217
Tov, Emanuel 33, 54, 149, 209, 217
Traube, Ludwig 28, 30, 217
Trobisch, David 86, 90, 146–48, 207, 217
Tsiknakis, Kostas 75, 197
Tuckett, Christopher M. 29, 217
Turner, Eric G. 15, 19, 21, 32, 36–37, 138–39, 146, 184, 217
Ulrich, Eugene 149, 218
Unkel, Jill 218
Vanni, Ugo 2, 218
Varo, Francisco 158, 170, 194
Varvaro, Alberto 95, 218
Velkovska, Elena 81, 212
Vogels, Heinrich Joseph 74
Vööbus, Arthur 75
Vos, Johan S. 48, 213
Vosté, Jacques M. 164, 218
Wachtel, Klaus 10, 49, 77, 80–81, 99, 192, 200, 212, 218
Wallraff, Martin 25, 133, 137, 140, 143–45, 152–53, 186, 211, 218
Walton, Briani 165, 218
Wasserman, Tommy 11, 33, 40–41, 48, 57, 62, 68, 79, 84, 103, 110, 137, 171, 206, 218–19

Watson, Francis 153, 219
Wayment, Thomas A. 19, 193
Weiss, Bernard 74
Westcott, Brooke F. 74, 79–80, 86
Widow, Juan C. 166, 219
Wikgren, Allen 75
Williams, Megan 138–39, 143–44, 201
Williams, Michael 66, 219
Williams, Peter J. 61, 112, 219
Willits, Joel 136, 202
Willker, Wieland 123, 125, 219
Wilson, Robert Mcl. 103, 192
Wilson, Stephen G. 30, 205
Woolf, Greg 178, 193
Yager, Susan 95, 219
Yoon, David I. 101, 214
Young, Francis M. 2, 143, 209, 219
Zacharias, Daniel 34, 196
Zahn, Molly M. 39, 219
Zetterholm, Magnus 103, 219
Zumstein, Jean 34, 49, 163, 196, 201, 208, 219
Zumthor, Paul 95–96, 219
Zuntz, Günther 72, 219
Zwiep, Ariel W. 52, 220

www.ingramcontent.com/pod-product-compliance
Lightning Source LLC
Chambersburg PA
CBHW021352300426
44114CB00012B/1190